PRAISE FOR

The Practical Seductress

"Sue's story left me laughing and wincing with recognition at memories of the 1970s sexual revolution. Coming of age during that era, we were naive and hopeful that the gender double standard could be overcome by our passionate pursuit of equality. Young women today would be wise to learn from this book that our rights as women cannot be taken for granted."

—LAURIE MORIN, author of *Shero's Journey*

"A quick read packed with emotional candor and wit and all about sexual desire? Yes, please! *The Practical Seductress* inhabits a space between hilarity and heartbreak, and weaves between pain and sharp humor, while staying grounded and focused on desire."

—AMY L. FREEMAN, essayist for *The Washington Post*, *HuffPost*, and Parents.com

"A story fueled by intricate and entertaining storytelling; Sue bravely puts herself out there—sharing raw, honest tales of a girl's quest to overcome the sexual double standard. While she unravels and re-ravels her coming of age in a captivating, quick read, her journey toward womanhood and becoming a resilient, empowered feminist will leave a lasting impression. Her witty writing confronts difficult topics head-on and evokes the whole spectrum—from shock and outrage to hilarity and tears of joy."

—CYN MEYER, founder of Second Wind Movement

The
Practical Seductress

The
Practical
Seductress

How I Learned to
Take My Hat and Run

Sue Camaione

SHE WRITES PRESS

Published 2024
Printed in the United States of America
Print ISBN: 978-1-64742-624-8
E-ISBN: 978-1-64742-625-5
Library of Congress Control Number: 2023909113

For information, address:
She Writes Press
1569 Solano Ave #546
Berkeley, CA 94707

Interior design by Stacey Aaronson

She Writes Press is a division of SparkPoint Studio, LLC.

Note to the Reader

The Practical Seductress is based on my life experiences. I have at times employed creative nonfiction and literary techniques to include scene, dialogue, description, and voice. In the end, I believe that it reflects my memories, however flawed and however slanted. I have attempted to look neither better nor smarter nor more sympathetic. However, as every writer in the genre of memoir knows, this is an attempt at best and a flaw of character at worst that includes the very human traits of failure, mistakes, and good old-fashioned hubris. May this memoir act as a guide on life's foibles, vulnerabilities, and comical moments with a goodly dose of resilience to help offset the trauma that so many women survive.

In memory of Edna Hill Adsit—
mentor, teacher, suffragette, grandmother.

Yet censure strikes hard at women, while men, the true agents of trouble,
hear no reproach.
Euripides, *Electra*

Contents

PART THREE
Reinvention

The
Practical Seductress

Introduction

My grandmother once said, "Every mistress wants to be a wife and every wife a mistress." She was the lone divorced woman in our 1960s neighborhood. She had been a stalwart suffragette, a 1920s flapper defying the norms. She spoke truth to women, and they listened. She seemed to hold intimate knowledge on how to balance the opposing roles—mistress and wife—assigned by a world enmeshed in sexual double standards. Men chased adventures, she would say, while women fought shame. What a girl needed was a practical guide on seeking adventure, sensuality, and desire with a how-to section on surviving brutal deceptions, lies, and abandoned trust. All for the sake of love.

PART ONE

Escape

1

Emergence

I enjoyed living the duality of wife and mistress. It captured in my soul an expression of sexual delight and freedom that had now gone awry. While in the throes of labor, at Boston's Brigham and Women's Hospital, I began dissolving into a boneless heap of sweat and blood-soaked shame. I began shaking uncontrollably, screaming, and crying my way through the most natural of life processes.

Married for almost a decade, I missed my wildness, the secret joy of breaking rules. I missed the feral ferocity I once possessed to run amok, an untamed spirit. I glanced down at the medicine-ball-sized belly of my impending motherhood. Now more than three weeks past the due date for delivering my first child, I questioned every word of the "I am woman, hear me roar" chants that I'd once believed. *Grow up*, I told myself, *you're thirty-one years old, not a naive teenager*.

In the fog of exhaustion, the driving agony behind natural childbirth seemed to hold an ancient biblical feel to it. Something an agnostic like me should have dismissed, but such is the power of childhood religious training. *What better way*, I wondered, *could a male-God entity find for punishing female sins?*

Okay, Sue, bury desire forever. Collapse any future lust. Vow to do this right here and now.

"Shit!" I felt a violent loss of control as my body began to push without any effort on my part. Buried in my heart, I knew I deserved this pain. I knew I needed to mold myself into good old-fashioned saintly selfless motherhood without delay.

A rather brusque British nurse charged into the delivery room and upon hearing me utter the expletive said, "My, young miss, such language." I tried to ignore the blood stains on her sleeves near her wrists. She glanced down to where I stared.

"Occupational hazard." She flicked some of the dry blood off her uniform. "You must calm down and control yourself. You may be here a long time."

One hour melted into another and another. Almost eleven hours later, with contractions less than a few minutes apart, the no-nonsense nurse returned. She shook her head as she raised the paper trail from the monitor.

"Something's wrong." She reached for a syringe on the silver metal tray. Without further discussion, she stuck me hard with a large needle filled with Pitocin while I was in the middle of a contraction. She turned her wrist over, palm up, and glanced at her Timex watch. "Well, now that should speed things along proper." She glanced at my husband, Andy, who seemed to have left the conversation entirely. Instead, he was engaged in examining the instrument panel on the machine's monitor.

I had no information about the drug Pitocin. I did not remember reading about it in any of the academic journal articles I had read. Seconds after the nurse administered the drug, the contractions intensified. Pain far worse than I ever could have imagined swept through my abdomen. Within seconds, my entire body went into involuntary convulsions.

No matter how hard I tried, I had no way to stop seizures caused by the drug, induced at the wrong moment. I started to faint between contractions. My body was no longer my own. Natural childbirth dissolved into half-conscious fainting and pain—emissions expelled from every orifice of my body.

Andy suddenly turned and pulled off the paper trail on the monitor. "Look here." He pointed to the flat line on the graph. "It's not registering." He tugged at his scrappy beard, a sign that he was thinking, focused, hypothesizing.

"What?" was all I could get out as my body began convulsing again.

He turned back to me, looking confused, as if he couldn't fathom for a moment the reason he was in the room. "In my estimation," he began, the scientist in him taking over, "you didn't need the drug. She misread the results. Common error."

Although he was a marine geochemist and not a doctor, I realized he was probably right. I immediately felt guilty and wondered if this "common error" was simply punishment. How dare we bring an innocent child into our not-so-secretive quasi-open marriage? I ignored Andy's amorous adventures. Instead, I began to enumerate all my ill-thought-out moments of lost sexual control—stupidly squandering my virginity to a married man, unwittingly inviting a rapist into my suite, marrying in haste, and finally, mounting my lover sans birth control in the office loft the same night I made love to my husband. I had no doubt my selfishness had caused this pain.

The seizures slowly abated, though, and the Lamaze training kicked in. The hoo-ing and haa-ing gave me the illusion of control—only my version was more of a violent horror movie scream that shook the corridors of the baby factory floor. The stiff-upper-lip, control-yourself Anglo in me crumbled, and my

Sicilian, relentless-emoting side dominated. A piercing shriek emitted from my throat as the pain increased. I would collapse unconscious for a moment only to be awakened again by another violent contraction.

The delivery nurse returned. An orderly popped his head in the door. "Is she okay? Is everything all right in there?"

"Yes," the nurse answered. "No need for alarm. She's scream-ing in perfect rhythm."

Between contractions, my husband swayed back and forth in place, unable to figure out his role. He tugged uncontrollably on his beard. Strands of black hair fell to the floor. "I can't stay here, Sue. I've got to go check on my work deadline, repark the car. Go to the bathroom." He paused as he tried to pry my fingers off his shoulders. "Talk to Kendall."

Upon hearing his lover's name, I screamed, "Eff you. You're never leaving me again. Deal with it."

The nurse shook her head. "She's an emotional one, she is." My husband, massaging his shoulders where my fingers had snapped onto him like a bear trap, did not disagree.

Freaking shut up, Sue, I told myself. *His lover. Your lover. Right now. Here in the hospital. It doesn't matter. Play the part so many women have played before. Stop the self-pitying fear that this is punish-ment for wrong choices, for having taken a lover to bed, for the confusion of birth rights that this choice might render.* How could I ever be a good mother? How could I guide my not-yet-born daughter to maneuver around a world that insists men embark on seductive adventures while women are punished for doing the same? What could I possibly convey to this tiny human about how to survive as a female?

And yet, despite the pain, the guilt, the fear, I knew my reluctance to let go of my lover, only moments before giving birth, would be my undoing. I stared unblinking at the hospital's fluorescent bulbs overhead, wondering how I had found myself in this tangled web, and praying that my soon-to-be-born daughter might someday forgive me.

2

Exposed

The "incident," as my mom referred to it, occurred when I was six years old in 1960 living in the inner city of Syracuse, New York. On that day, I had been told that my mom was sick with pneumonia. I couldn't pronounce the word but knew that it was serious since she'd been bedridden for many weeks with no sign of improvement.

That night, I was sitting outside my parents' bedroom door listening to my mom gulping air, attempting to breathe. The city's streetlights flickered in the twilight, shedding a spasm of orange into the hallway where I stood waiting for Dad. I could hear her violent, fitful coughing from their bedroom. I peeped inside and saw the outline of Mom's petite body shaking as she spit out clumps of brown-red blood into her torn tissue.

"Get some sleep," I heard my dad say. Peeking through the door, I saw his hulking shoulders hunched over the bed. He gave my mom a quick kiss on the cheek, then rose, his weight releasing the creaky springs.

I didn't understand how my mom, normally kind of jumpy, couldn't get up off the bed. I saw her thin fingers shake as she reached out to my dad and touched his arm. The gesture startled me, as she rarely asked anyone for help.

He turned and saw me in the hallway. He put his index finger to his lips, then waved, gesturing me into the living room. "Sue, I don't have any choice. We need the money. I'm leaving you in charge tonight. Your grandmother will be here tomorrow to watch over you girls."

"Why do I have to?" I stuck out my lips in a pout. "It's not my fault she's sick."

"Sue, it's not anyone's fault." My big, strong daddy sighed. He stared at me for a moment through his black-rimmed glasses. A dark wave of uncombed hair flopped over his forehead. "I don't have time for your shenanigans today."

"But it's not fair." I stomped my bare foot. It slapped against the cold linoleum floor. I wanted to sound sure of myself, not whiny. My mom hated whiners, but I couldn't help myself. "Why do I always have to be the one to take care of Sharon?" What I really wanted to do was read my Aesop's fables book, draw pictures of animals, and pretend I was an only child for one night. Then I could turn on the radio to drown out my mom's coughing without dealing with my little sister.

"Well, for one thing, young lady, you're two years older. You're in first grade, for heaven's sake. You're a big girl now." He closed his eyes and rubbed the bridge of his nose. He pushed his glasses back in place and stared at me for a moment. "I don't want to hear another word. Let your mother rest."

More complaining on my part would only be met with my father's bare hand, or worse, his belt, slapped hard against my backside, but I didn't want to give up without a fight. "I hate this," I muttered to myself and folded my arms across my moth-eaten sweater.

He stood up to leave for his night shift as a printer at the newspaper. As he grabbed his brown paper bag with the dry baloney sandwich, he said, "Take care of your sister. I'm already late. I'll be home before morning."

He hugged Sharon, then turned to kiss me goodbye. A stray wetness hit my cheek. It seemed like he was crying, which kind of scared me, but Dad was an emotional guy. One moment, he'd get super angry. Then a few minutes later, he'd break down and hug you so tight you couldn't squirm away from his big embracing arms. He turned back and waved once more. We both sat on our shared bed staring at the door. His leather shoes pounded down on the warped wooden steps of the hallway stairs.

I opened a can of Beefaroni and stirred it into the dented tin pot. While it heated up, I gave Sharon a big glass of milk to shut up her constant "I'm hungry" bellyaching.

Once we finished, I dressed her for bed. "You can at least help me out here. Stop wiggling, you little brat." I tried to imitate my mother's best "behave yourself" tone, but she'd never call Sharon a brat. That was my word for her.

Sharon began giggling, jumping up and down on the bed. I bounced along the edge until she was plumb worn out. Then I crawled into bed beside her, my job done for the night. My dad worked overtime, but I fell asleep knowing he would be home to fix us breakfast.

The morning light barely peeped through the ever-present gray clouds of our apartment's thin curtains. In the semi-light, I woke up startled and cold. Sharon had wet the bed once again. In frustration, I turned to push her out of the way to pull the sheets off. I felt nothing. Her spot on the bed was empty. Maybe she had gone to use the potty chair. I removed my pee-soaked pajamas, grabbed the bed covers, and walked across the hall to the bathroom. I placed the rolled-up sheets in the bathroom hamper, stamping down the mess and shutting the top.

After I washed my hands, I suddenly realized how quiet it was. My sister wasn't in the bathroom. I tiptoed quietly so as not to wake up my mom. At the front door, I saw that it was open. I'd forgotten to lock it last night.

My dad would be angry. How many times had he told me to lock up? "It's not a safe neighborhood," he would say to remind me not to trust anyone to enter in his absence.

In a flash of panic, I realized my baby sister had fled, her wet handprint still on the door.

I felt like somebody had kicked me in the gut. I couldn't breathe. I couldn't talk.

I nodded my head to wake up. *Could this be a bad dream?* Then I smelled her stinky, wet pajamas flung to the floor next to the steps. *Dad's going to kill me.* I ran to look out the bay window. Under the streetlight I caught a glimpse of Sharon as she skipped down the street, naked, happily dancing, and free as a jaybird, as my grandma liked to say.

She ran as fast as her chubby legs could carry her in a wobbly side-to-side stride. Her glee filled the quiet, dark alleyway. I knew I wouldn't be able to stop her or scold her from my perch on the windowsill. I also knew my mom was in no shape to run into the street to coax her to come home. My dad had not yet returned, so the thought of him punishing us wouldn't faze Sharon, although it crossed my mind.

"Oh no," I shouted, then put my hand over my own big mouth to keep from waking up my mom. I had to get my sister back home without anyone noticing, but she was now beyond my sight.

I checked the big Mickey Mouse clock on the kitchen wall. Mickey's long arm reached the bottom. Almost five thirty. Dad would be home soon. "Sue," he had told me, "If something goes wrong, I'm blaming you. You're in charge. Don't make me hurt you." The thought of his leather belt against my butt, the welts burning for days, forced me into action.

I shot out the door and leaped down the stairs two at a time, grabbing the oak rail for balance. When I landed on the cold cement porch, I suddenly realized that I, too, was as naked as a jaybird. But if I went back upstairs to get dressed, I'd lose her. I could run much faster than Sharon, and I knew it. I began running and tried to cover myself with my hands and dash down the sidewalk at the same time. I lost sight of her as she careened around the corner. Her laughter filled the semi-dark alleyway.

Electric lights snapped on as neighbors heard me shouting, "Sharon, stop! Wait!" Her joy-filled giggles carried down the pre-dawn street of rental apartments and dilapidated duplexes.

"Geez, Sharon, stop, please," I begged her. What if something went wrong? What if a car hit her? Even worse, what if one of the early morning drunks grabbed her? I hurried. Gulps of air kept me on her trail. She dodged me, though, with her chaotic twists and turns. My mother's words returned to haunt me: "Sue, take care of your little sister. I'm depending on you to keep her safe until I get better."

I watched my sister's waddling naked butt turn from Fage Avenue to Oneida Street. It pained me to realize my mother would be far more than disappointed if the milkman or a nosy neighbor witnessed the two of us running naked down the street and reported it back to her.

When Sharon slowed down, checking left and right, wondering where to turn next, I caught up to her, grabbed her hand, and placed it firmly in mine. Relieved and happy to have captured my escapee sister, I realized that the crisp morning air kind of felt good on our overheated bodies.

The smoky lingering smell of burned maple leaves mingled with a fresh autumn breeze. I glanced around. No one stood in the street. Too tired to run anymore, happy my sister was safe, I casually walked back down the street with her, and we rounded the corner hand in hand.

"What you girls doing out here showing off your bare-assed selves?"

I stopped. A sudden chill hit me. I turned.

"Miss Trudy?" I asked, unsure of what I was seeing. Miss Trudy wore her torn dress and ripped stockings like a queen walking home in the first morning light. Her curly blonde wig was slipping off her head, exposing black-and-gray hair underneath. She didn't seem to care.

"You trying to take over Trudy's job?" She laughed, but it came out more as a coughing cackle.

I had no idea what she meant and wanted to get home before my dad did. In one swift move, Trudy grabbed my face, pulling my chin toward her. She stared unblinking and calm as if observing a wild animal. Women shunned Trudy and moved to the other side of the street whenever she appeared. Men joked about her constant presence on the streets. My dad had told me to avoid her. I stood frozen in place. I grasped my little sister's hand tightly, fascinated by Trudy's intensity and yet repulsed by her smell.

"You're a little looker," she said as she studied my face. "You sure as hell are going to make the boys cry. You're a wild one, you are. Ain't no taming you."

"Let go of me." I yanked her arm away. She dropped her hand from my burning face. "We got to go home."

Her fingers curled into fists, then opened and fell to her sides. She began to laugh. With a flourish of a curtsy I only saw in movie musicals, she let us pass.

I grabbed my sister's hand so tight she yelled, "Ouch," but she shut right up, mostly because Miss Trudy scared the bejesus out of her too. We picked up our pace and headed for home.

Miss Trudy's raspy voice continued to fill the silent street. "Mark my words, kiddo, you are going to break some hearts. It's in your face, you little hussy. You ain't no different than Miss Trudy."

Her screeching laughter could be heard down the street. We moved closer to our walk-up apartment. The farther away we got, the safer I felt. When we were almost home, the door of the apartment building next to ours swung open, banging against the peeling paint on the bent metal railing.

My friend Scooter, in his Howdy Doody pajamas, emerged from the doorway. It wasn't unusual for him to be out and about while everyone else still slept. Scooter's dad had a reputation as a drunk and spent most mornings sleeping it off, while his mom left early for her nurse's aide shift at the local hospital. Scooter, like us, enjoyed a kind of freedom of movement that escaped our better-watched-over neighbors' kids.

"What you guys doing all naked?"

My mom told me to be careful around "poor Scooter," as she called him. "He's a bit smitten with you."

"What does that mean?" I had asked.

"Well, for one thing, Scooter obeys your every whim. I've seen you test him out regularly." I didn't want to ask her what "whim" meant. She'd only send me to the big, dog-eared copy of *Webster's Dictionary* in the corner of her room. I figured she was referring to my bossiness. "Scooter, get my shoes," I'd demand, or "Scooter, give me some of your ice cream," which I found romantic since we could not afford Mister Softee's treats, and Scooter happily shared. Even though I considered him the love of my life, I took advantage of him at every opportunity and licked most of his luscious ice cream before he could stop me. He never complained, but Scooter's mother wasn't happy with her son's weak behavior around me. One time, pointing at me, she shouted to all who could hear, "That girl is a bossy one, she is."

A few weeks ago, while my grandma took care of us, she overheard this snippy remark.

She simply shook her head and grinned. "My granddaughter is *not* bossy. She's a leader." She waved vaguely in Scooter's direction. "He's simply her follower." She placed her hand on my shoulder. "As he should be," she added to put an end to the matter. She had been blinded by glaucoma, and that day on the sidewalk, she turned me away from the offending gossip and felt her way back down the sidewalk. Her hand fell lightly against my arm while, with her other hand, she waved her curved pinewood cane left and right to sweep away any annoying rumormongers.

Now, as I saw Scooter, it occurred to me that there might be a certain safety in numbers. More nakedness on the street meant more blame all around and less punishment directed at me.

"Come on, Scooter," I said and waved my hand to him. "Take off your clothes. It feels super good." He hesitated, which surprised me, so I changed tactics. "Are you too scaredy-cat to do it? Double dare you." Since he was an older man at the age of seven, and somewhat hesitant but anxious to prove his emerging masculinity, I instinctively knew when to increase my threats. "Do it, or I won't let you play with us ever again." My last demand may have been the notorious bossiness the neighbors had reported, but it did the trick.

Scooter shrugged his shoulders once, then slowly took off his clothes as if mesmerized by the entire encounter. I knew he had been focused on not wanting to lose my friendship. I watched him slowly undress. My little sister began jumping up and down in glee now that we had a third party to our escapade. I realized that by simply smiling at him, not averting my eyes, and taunting him with dares, I was able to exert power over him.

In one gallant gesture of freedom, Scooter threw his pajama pants and top over the fence and raised both his hands in a big V of triumph.

I couldn't help but notice what was between his legs. "What's that?" I pointed. "A worm got you or something?"

He immediately threw his hands over his boy parts.

His father came out of the house, spooking us all. His clothes were rumpled, his shirt half out of his pants, the leather belt unhooked, his feet bare. "What the hell is going on here?" He staggered into the street.

A siren screeched in echoing patterns, piercing the morning air. The police car woke up everyone in the surrounding apartment buildings. People began to filter onto the sidewalks in robes and slippers half on their feet. They began to laugh. My sister was too little to know what the neighbors found so darn funny. A few pointed at us, shaking their heads. One lady in pink curlers gave us the shame-shame gesture of one index finger sliding across the other. Her pursed lips wrinkled tight over her dangling dead cigarette.

Scooter, I knew, without my aid, led a sheltered life with his strict mom. Nobody would suspect him as the instigator. "Ah, that Suzy," I heard one guy say. "She's a corker, and she just about uncorked that Calabria boy." I glanced around at the pointing fingers and red faces. The sounds of raucous laughter increased. It seemed obvious to all that I was the culprit of this unladylike display.

I barely remember the police throwing blankets over us,

sweeping us up, and taking us home. "Nothing to see here. Go back home," they told the neighbors.

I remember that day running into my parents' bedroom to beg my mother to "please, please, pretty please with a cherry on top" forgive me as she wearily pulled herself out of bed, a worn quilt loosening from her frail shoulders, coughing wildly without stop as the cops waited.

"Sue, I trusted you," she said after they left. The disappointment in her voice fell harder than any slap would have. "You were supposed to be watching your little sister. And to pull Scooter into your rebelliousness. Why would you seduce that poor innocent little boy?"

I had no answer. My parents and the entire neighborhood agreed about me using my feminine wiles, a term I didn't even understand, to drag Scooter into our so-called spectacle.

When my father arrived home, he duly punished me. I felt the heat of his leather belt stinging my backside for days. But the belt left fewer scars than my mother's painful sadness at no longer trusting her oldest daughter.

I gingerly dressed for school that same morning, my head filled with words thrown at me from the street. Hussy. Shameless. Bossy. Corker. Heartbreaker. Though my mother recovered, my reputation as the naked girl who had led a poor sweet boy and her baby sister down the wrong path cemented in my young mind. I did not know what most of the words and jokes hurled at me that morning meant.

Although the memory of the incident faded with time, I would not learn until much later how much power those words I had heard in the streets affected me. Or how my choice of future partners and the exploratory nature of sexual encounters would possess me for life.

3

Under the Willow Tree

Just before President Kennedy's assassination, we had moved to the quiet New York village of Chittenango, far from the news of the day. It was a community of people who'd lived in the same town and the same houses for generations. As the new girl from the big city moving to the countryside where everyone knew each other, and no one knew me, I could begin my life anew, pretending to be a sweet and compliant girl, the kind everyone adored.

The village's humble claims to fame included a spectacular waterfall and being the hometown of L. Frank Baum, the author of the Oz book series. To commemorate Mr. Baum's birthplace, a few residents on a bet had painted a fake yellow brick road down Main Street. A dingy bar called The Oz sat at the edge of town, where anyone from age fourteen and up could get exceedingly drunk for pennies. Although the waterfall had more out-of-town visitors, The Oz was by far the more popular hangout for our neighbors.

It seemed like an almost perfect 1960s sitcom suburb of working-class life, complete with ramblers that housed families with five or more kids in cramped spaces. By the time I turned eleven, I had two siblings to babysit. Most days, I ignored their constant fighting. I concentrated, instead, on doing my homework at the kitchen table.

"It's my doll," Sharon hissed in a fierce whisper. She shook her head back and forth, her wavy brown hair covering her hazel eyes. "I'm almost nine. You're just a kindergarten baby. You've got to do what I say."

"I'm not a baby," my little brother, Mark, retorted in a high-pitched voice that only a four-year-old could muster. He grabbed the doll in defiance. "I want it."

"Shush, you two." I put my finger to my lips like a teacher trying to quiet a class of unruly children. "Stop fighting. Shut up or Dad will wake up."

My mother's recovery from pneumonia five years earlier had been complicated by another pregnancy. Mark fell into our world, noisy and rambunctious. Once he grew past babyhood, he needed private space away from the girls, which my parents found in the pantry closet. They set up a rickety cot and a small dresser that banged up against the wall as he tossed in his sleep or jumped on the lumpy mattress. A bamboo-stick screen served as his bedroom door. He spent hours placing bent metal toy soldiers neatly in rows on his cot. Then he'd throw them into the air in a grand explosive burst and repeat the process of aligning them again, only to kill them off, explosion after explosion.

Just as Sharon had felt like a pest to me, Mark seemed to pose a constant annoyance to Sharon, challenging her place in the family. Each day became a struggle for dominance.

"Yeah, Mark." Sharon stuck out her tongue. "You know how mad Dad gets when you wake him up."

I was in charge during the day while my mother commuted by bus to the plastics factory on the edge of Syracuse. My father worked the night shift at various jobs. He was forever trying to get in a few hours of sleep before rising late in the day to begin the long trek into the city.

Whenever necessary, I shot my siblings what Sharon called "Sue's freaky face stare." It usually stopped them. All three of us had firsthand experience with what happened when we accidentally woke up Dad. He carried the burden of supporting his growing family at the age of thirty-one. In his sleep-deprived state, he sometimes seemed eager to take out his anger and disappointments on his own flesh and blood.

That morning I struggled to stay focused on my homework as Mark grabbed the three-foot-tall bride doll they had been fighting over and flung it past the kitchen table where I sat. The doll struck the kitchen door full force, its golden fake locks bursting from its plastic body. He ran to grab the doll's decapitated head before Sharon could stop him.

I placed my pencil in the English textbook to mark my place, hoping to regain order and finish my homework, but feared it might be a futile effort.

Mom had left for work well before the sun rose to catch the bus off NYS 5, the lone highway that led into the city. It sometimes took her over an hour to reach the factory district. She spent her day walking back and forth along a conveyor belt, standing for eight hours or more, with her petite frame yanking on heavy metal levers to slam down steel plates that molded plastic boots in 120-degree heat. Accidents with burned arms and lost fingers haunted me. I wanted her to quit. Until then, I knew she needed me, her oldest, to raise my siblings, because if I didn't, she'd warned me of dire consequences.

Her gray-blue eyes, the color of morning fog, had stared at me without flinching. "I know this is a lot of responsibility for you, but I need you to listen carefully and take it seriously. If I lose my job, we'll be homeless. We will *all* go hungry."

On top of that, a few months earlier, my dad had been blacklisted as an instigator for trying to unionize a non-union shop on his employer's dime. Every week he had moved to a different job, working long hours and any nightshift he could get. I never understood what had happened to pull the rug out from under him. "I'm one of life's losers," he told me one night in his darkest hour, his disappointment evident. I stayed silent, not knowing how to respond or what he even meant.

His resentments for having so much on his young shoulders, combined with self-hatred, left him in a state of constant agitation. "I love you guys so much," he would emote one moment to remind himself why he continued playing the role of patriarch when he could barely pay his bills. In the next moment, he'd shout, "I'm going to teach you kids a lesson," as we scurried from his sight.

We never knew which dad would show up. His lack of sleep every night, not knowing if he'd have a job the next day and being startled awake, sometimes created what we thought of as Monster Dad bursting from the bedroom. In those moments, he aimed his rage at us.

"You broke my doll." Sharon's whisper increased in volume with her outrage.

I feared our father would wake up but felt powerless to stop their fighting.

Mark started dancing a sideways jig along the peeling linoleum. "It's a rocket now." He demonstrated by shooting the doll skyward. The bride's gown opened like a parachute as it crashed to the floor.

Sharon fell on the floor and tightened her grip on the doll's legs. Mark grabbed the plastic arms with his little fists. A tussle for possession ensued, and their voices rose to a screech.

The door to my father's bedroom opened. My chest felt a surge of fear, cutting off air. *Don't freak out*, I told myself. *Just get them under control.*

A low groan built into an angry bear growl, and the heavy *plop-plop* of my father's naked feet slapped against the cold linoleum. We all froze in place.

Panicked, I grabbed my brother and threw him into my sister's bedroom closet hidden behind the thin cotton curtain. He seemed startled and shaken. We instinctively knew to stay still, like deer observing a hungry predator.

"What in the hell are you kids arguing about? You woke me up." The opening of his green plaid flannel robe twisted around his waistband as he pulled it around his hips. He held his worn brown leather belt in one hand, the buckle end dragging behind him, clicking along the tiles in time with each step.

As he came closer, I pushed Sharon under the bed and motioned with my index finger to shush. I figured maybe if she shut up and stayed there, she would be safe from his reach. I was faster than both of my siblings. I dodged my dad with a few quick leaps. I knew if I wanted to get his attention off Sharon and Mark that I could make my dad run in circles around the house. It could take a long time before he tired of the chase if he was angry though.

Ten minutes of running later, I would reemerge within his eyesight. Often, by that time, he was too tired to care and would simply walk back to his bedroom. To keep him happy, I would apologize in the most subservient way I could muster. He once told me, "Sue, I'm tired of you using your feminine wiles on me." By smiling in a sideways tilt, lowering my head, and staring up at him through long lashes, I could make his anger soften. My siblings knew the routine well enough and used the distraction to hide from his view. It was a tried-and-true sibling survival tool that in the past had never failed.

But not that day.

That day my feminine wiles seemed wanting. Suddenly, I realized I'd lost my advantage by taking the time to hide my siblings in two different directions in the same bedroom. It drove my tactics out of kilter. No amount of subservient smiling and batting of eyelashes could stop our attacker. He held the leather belt in his hand, as though he could see through the distraction guise. He went right past me, directly to the bed where my sister was hiding.

She screamed and began pulling herself into the farthest reaches under the bed to escape the long arm flailing to grab her. My father dropped down to his knees. She was trapped.

I stood in shock for a moment. He had walked right past me. He ignored my brother in the closet too. Divide and conquer and make each kid scream as the others watched frozen. That was his technique. "Putting the fear of God in those kids," he called it—with him as God, was our interpretation. Who could fight God? Who could defend themselves against his rage? Who could outrun a dad God?

Something in me jolted awake. I was determined that no God, father or not, would be allowed to harm Sharon and Mark that day. I had to think fast. I turned in his direction and stepped in front of him. I began babbling.

"We're sorry, Dad, really, really, really sorry. We'll be super quiet from now on. Promise." He stood up and pushed me away. Hard. My body slammed into the door inches from my brother's terrified face.

"Sharon." His voice shook the small house. His strong six-foot, 220-pound frame towered over the bed. "COME HERE NOW!" His robe tangled in twists and turns at his waist as he held tight to the belt. "You woke me up. I've had it with you kids."

My sister screeched hysterically. My brother cowered in the closet. He knew he was next.

My father's long arm reached under the bed to pull out my sister. She started fighting hard, kicking, and sliding up and down the underbelly of the bed. In frustration, he yelled, "You're all going to pay for this!"

We knew that he meant what he said. Sharon started to cry in gulping shakes of her entire body. Mark whimpered uncontrollably.

My mind fleetingly traveled to action shows we watched after school. Ridiculous Batman punches. Ka-pow fistfights to save Gotham. Karate chops over evil villains' heads. Wonder Woman twirling like a dervish into a bathing-suited crime fighter while her lasso whipped over her head ready to take out the bad guys. Life slowed to an infinitesimal moment of clarity of choice.

I knew what to do.

I pulled myself into the bedroom closet and grabbed my brother's hand. The two of us might be able to escape, but what about my sister? Without hesitation, I threw my brother's thin body out into the hallway. Then I pushed deeper into the closet. I needed a running start. Sharon's hysterical crying distracted my father. His back was to me.

I stared at his hunched-over figure. He complained daily about the pain from old football injuries to his lower back. Without a thought about the consequences, I had a target. I threw myself out of the closet like a racehorse at the starting gate. On the count of one, two, three, I took a flying leap.

Into the air my skinny legs flew. My feet landed—*thwack*—digging hard into my father's lower back. I instinctively had directed a blow to his kidneys. I dropped back from the force onto the floor.

He jolted up and then fell back, grabbing his hips, his face contorted in pain. Before I could think, I rolled over and slipped under the bed, then grabbed my sister's hand, wet from rubbing away tears. I yanked her from under the bed and stood her up quickly. I pushed her toward the door. All three of us charged down the narrow hall. My father's screams filled the house. I could hear him swearing and calling me all sorts of names, some of which, like "cock-sucking something," I had never heard before.

Sharon to my right and Mark to my left, I screamed, "Run!"

My father's shouts could be heard from the bedroom window. "Wait until I get my hands on you kids. Running away will only make it worse."

We glanced at each other as we ran out the front door. No way could it be worse to escape down the street than to stay and deal with Dad. We had experience with his rage. Lots and lots of experience. Once he was spent, he'd calm down and might even forget about us completely. Maybe we'd get a slap or a quick punch to the arm as we walked by, but the belt would be forgotten.

So, we ran. As fast as we could to gain distance. I doubted this was what my mother meant by "full responsibility." If our dad was hurt, he couldn't work, and we'd lose our house. We'd go hungry. Wouldn't it then be "all my fault" because we ran?

I urged my siblings to "run, run fast, don't stop" and led them down to a small swampy area at the bottom of the dead-end street we called the gully. This was our sanctuary from home.

We slipped into the grove of thick, deep green weeping willow trees to catch our breath, to cry, to hold each other tight, to recover. Despite the cold, dark soil and lack of light in the hole, we held tight to each other in relief. It was all we knew to do with nowhere else to go. We had no way to determine the length of time necessary to calm down a man in rage, dissatisfied with what life had given him. A man who felt shamed by choices he had made that caused him to be blacklisted, to lose his job, and to lose his ability to support his family.

Mark wiped his tears on my now dirty dress. Sharon hid her head in my lap. Our collective breathing began to slow.

"You know what, Sharon?" Mark said. His eyes glistened. He seemed suddenly upbeat and excited.

"What, Mark?" Sharon asked, calmer now that she was out of harm's way, the decapitated doll forgotten.

"Sue flies like Superman! Like on TV." He lifted his hands upward.

My sister shook her head at our little brother's excitement. "She's not Superman. She's not even a boy. She's just a girl who can jump really high."

My brother begged to differ and began flapping his arms up and down as if to fly away, an imaginary cape trailing him. He fell into both of us. All three of us began to roll over the muddy tree roots exposed from years of our escaping harm. We began laughing and threw our heads back in glee. A joyous, warm giggle of childhood relief unleashed from us as we held on to each other.

My sister doubled over in hysteria. Tears began to fall from her face, replacing the laughter. My brother continued to flap his arms, flying like Superman. The sway of teardrop leaves from the weeping willow held us safe within its green, flowing sanctuary.

Mark stopped moving and grabbed my hand. I saw a stream of tears run down his thin face. "I like our hiding place. It's safe here."

I squeezed his tiny hand and smiled; a tear of my own slipped down my cheek. I looked at each of my siblings, knowing that we could survive only if we stuck together. We hugged, rocking our bodies in sibling unison. From this safe place nestled in the embrace of the weeping willows' hallowed ground, we believed we could wait out the storm of any avenging God.

4

Daughter Love

In the summer of 1965, we were living in dairy-farming country. My mom joked that "the town had two thousand inhabitants, if you counted the cows." Large families shared long winters with dark secrets that emerged after months of cabin fever. On days with snowdrifts high enough to cover front doors, children would leap out bedroom windows to get to school on time.

During the short summers, houses became empty entities, not used for anything other than places to eat and sleep. Stay-at-home mothers tossed kids out the door. The exhausted moms soothed their shattered nerves with whiskey-laden coffee in the morning, beer in the afternoon on their front lawns or tiny kitchens, and wine tossed down with "mother's little helpers" (Valium) to tolerate the screams of multiple kids.

My blind grandmother lived with us for most of the year. My mom, her youngest daughter, had spent her youth taking care of my grandmother when her eyes were surgically removed due to glaucoma. Glass eyes inserted into her eye sockets did not derail my grandmother, a former schoolteacher, from being an avid reader. Braille and talking books became her companions. She had pen pals from all over the world. At the age of eleven, I became her letter reader. Unlike other grandmothers with home-cooked meals and cozy hugs, we were exposed to her synopsis of whatever she was reading at the time, with an expectant detailed discussion beyond our comprehension. My siblings zoned out. I listened intently.

My mother, a closeted liberal, was more circumspect. She felt out of her element in the working-class neighborhood. Having forgone college, marrying at eighteen and becoming pregnant with me only a few weeks after her informal wedding ceremony, she struggled to find time for herself. Before reaching the age of twenty-six, my mother had pushed three of us into the world. Desperate for knowledge away from this tiny enclave, she became as voracious a reader as her own mother, desperately trying to ignore the noisy clan she had produced.

Every spare moment my mom had, she could be seen holding a beer can in one hand and a library book in the other. Reading was her escape. Her dreamland. It was the only way to satisfy her desire to travel, to live a far more adventurous life than the one she had. Delving into the realms of psychoanalysis gave her grounding on why she had made such lowly choices that led to her giving birth to me, her oldest child, a month after she turned nineteen.

She was wry-witted. When we asked, "Mom, where are my shoes?" her answer was "I don't know. I don't have your feet." We learned early not to ask about dinner since her response became: "I don't know. What are you cooking?" Neither begging nor whining worked. "Mom, make me a sandwich." Without lifting her eyes from her multiple readings of Jung's *Psychology of the Unconscious*, one hand clutching her Genesee Cream Ale, the other waving in the air, she would say, "Poof. You're a sandwich." And on and on it went, every day a new quip with nary a sandwich.

The deal was clinched to move to Chittenango when Mom found out that the local elementary school had been named after Simón Bolívar, the "liberator" of Latin America. She had been reading history books with titles such as *Masters and Slaves, The Pan-American Experience*. Her revolutionary beliefs took root from the various rebellions of the Americas.

"We need to stop aping European models," she declared one day, slamming a thick leatherbound library book shut. The Che Guevara of housewives often made sudden statements to her kids as if we were college students in an auditorium awaiting the professor's words of wisdom.

From this determined expression of militant readings of history, all four kids eventually found themselves wandering the halls of the school named after revolutionary hero Simón Bolívar. The school's name was enough to satisfy the progressive views of my mom, a daughter of a suffragette. It also explained why she had married my father, a man of emotional extremes, a true believer in equality, the local union organizer, and, as he called himself, "a social democrat only because the word 'socialist' scares people."

Together they journeyed the 1960s as two dedicated book-reading rebels from their teenage wedding day through the births of their four children within a conformist enclave of domesticity. All before they reached the age of thirty.

Unfortunately for me, she believed we had a duty to help the less fortunate. I thought this odd since everyone on the block, including us, was living on the edge and barely able to make mortgage or rent payments.

My Italian father, raised by parents unable to speak anything but a few words of broken English, had seemed exotic to my mother, while my father held her family's British ancestry—which had arrived on the shores of Mystic, Connecticut, in 1633—in awe.

Mom and Dad met at the movie theater. She worked in a glass booth as a ticket taker. My father, attempting to sneak in to see his beloved musicals, spotted the blue-eyed beauty and changed tactics. His flirtatious Latin mannerisms dismayed her at first, but soon his entreaties worked. Within months, my father became the first non-Anglo to join her family, and she became the first non–Italian Catholic to join his. Despite a few voices on both sides declaring this mixed marriage would result in mongrel children, they married mere days after Thanksgiving—less than six months after that fateful evening at the movie house.

My mother's parents lost their farm during the Great Depression. Poverty fell hard over their lives. They never recovered. The result of this childhood experience, even though my mother lived in the exact same economic situation as our paycheck-to-paycheck neighbors, was that she never lost sight of noblesse oblige.

So, while she refused to cater to her own kids' needs for a sandwich and expected self-sufficiency, she had a weak spot in her heart for helping others. "You need to be nice to Frank Merry. He needs a friend," she insisted. Frank was my age. He spent his days on the street and in school staring unblinking at passersby from under a shelf of greasy hair. I knew what my mother was referring to but didn't want to deal with the sullen kid next door. I also didn't want to deal with the neighborhood bully, Eddie, who beat on Frank daily.

I had my own run-in with Eddie. He would tease Sharon, calling her "piggy," and she would run behind me as I mouthed off at him to "leave my sister alone, you stupid shithead." At that, he'd grab my arm and twist it behind my back until my knees sank into the gravel, scraping my skin clear off.

My father's advice: "If you're going to fight, fight dirty." Knowing Eddie had it in for me for not bowing to his demands, I had carefully selected and placed a concrete chunk inside my metal Cinderella lunchbox. Sure enough, one day as I turned the corner, the school bus out of sight, Eddie grabbed me. I gave him a warning. "Leave me and my sister alone, or else you're gonna get it."

He laughed, then lunged at me. Remembering my dad's words, I quickly slammed my lunch pail upside Eddie's head with all my might. He fell, *clunk*, dead weight to the ground. I picked up my dented lunch pail, threw away the cement chunk evidence, and skipped home.

Days went by. Eddie did not bother my sister or me. On the third day, my mother marched into the house. "Why didn't you tell me that you'd knocked our neighbor's kid unconscious?"

I played coy. "How do you know I did it? Could've been anybody."

She sighed. "For one thing, your shattered glass thermos is how I know it was you. I am so ashamed. I defended you only to find out you were violent to this child."

In the corner, my dad was trying to stifle a laugh. He couldn't keep it in any longer. "Good job, kid."

A fight ensued. Dad finally gave in to Mom and told me I had to apologize to Eddie, which I half-heartedly did. My dad began to brag to the other fathers: "My daughter knocked that kid out cold. She's a tough one. He better not mess with her again." With his backing, I learned an important lesson in self-defense. Fight dirty—and remember to remove the thermos.

Unfortunately for Frank, I didn't defend him against Eddie. I figured that was his problem. The kickball games that started at sunset on the dead-end street included everyone except Frank.

Eddie had successfully kept Frank from playing with us, knowing Frank's dad could not and would not defend himself against Eddie's mean drunk dad.

One day, Eddie stopped my sister and me from joining the street game. "Girls can't play. Get lost, skinny legs and fatso."

We were the only girls on the block and far more athletic than any of those stupid boys. I started to charge him only to be pulled back by Eddie's father.

"It's time you girls went to play inside. Street games are for boys." He pushed me to the gutter. I fell, rolling over and spitting out gravel. I glared at him.

Ignoring my crying sister, I ran to get my dad. In a rush I told him what had occurred. In mere moments, he put his shoes on, grabbed a baseball bat and mitt, and bounded out of the door. The two of us trailed behind.

"Nobody," he bellowed, "ever tells my girls they can't play." He glared at Eddie's father. "What's up, Edward? You afraid my little girl will beat the shit out of your boy again?" The two men stood close, but my dad's fierceness made him back down.

"Fine, the boys will play with me," Eddie's dad said. He began to walk down the street.

My dad, not to be outdone, said in his big booming voice, "Who wants to play a real ball game? Who wants ice cream after?"

The entire neighborhood shouted with glee and followed my father. My sister and I ran up the street with my dad and the other boys to start the new game.

He waved over to let Frank join us. My mother, from the doorway, nodded ever so slightly, and for a moment, my pride in my father's heroism soared. I wouldn't say my father was a feminist, but he did hate inequality and unfairness in any guise. It was seeing him as the heroic savior of the weak that made the following days that much harder for me to comprehend, much less forgive.

Our victory was short-lived. Eddie spent the next week torturing everyone who'd played on our team. He particularly targeted Frank, who had a weak stomach and was constantly slouched over. Eddie knew this weakness and would grab him around the waist, squeezing him hard until he bent over in pain.

I did not want to play with either of them, but my mother demanded that I "play with little Frank, because he needs a friend right now." I didn't particularly like Frank, but he was better than Eddie. I just hated that I was forced to play with him because of his weakness. *Get your own damn chunk of cement*, I thought.

One day, Frank had had enough. He took his father's tire iron and waited for Eddie. As Eddie approached, he jumped up and hit him hard enough to send a bloody tooth flying. This shocked me, and I felt a little guilty since the cement incident had made me notoriously worshipped on the block. This was fighting dirty at its best.

Unfortunately for Frank, Eddie's father witnessed the incident and grabbed him. Eddie's dad began kicking Frank down the street, humiliating him, knowing Frank's own father, a small man with no means to defend himself, would be cowering inside, afraid to approach the big man beating up his son. Without a second thought, I charged inside to tell my father what was happening.

He looked outside and shook his head. "Nothing we can do." He went back to reading his newspaper.

Would no one defend this boy who had become a whipping post? I was turning into my mother, worrying about those less fortunate, and I hated it. I counted on my father. My hero. He was strong, bigger than life. Despite the black-and-blue marks that he left on our bodies, I thought of him as a just man. He knew, and I knew, that if he went out there, the other father would back off. My dad could minimize the humiliation. Yet he refused to leave the sofa. He refused to help the "less fortunate kid," as my mom would say. My anger grew with each turn of the newspaper pages as they crinkled in my father's hands.

"Well, if you're not going to do anything," I finally said, "then I will." With that, I picked up the baseball bat and rushed outside, screaming to Eddie's father, "You let that boy go or I'm going to let you have it upside the head like I did your stupid kid."

Eddie's father, the man who raised the bully, his own abusive anger evident, his manhood challenged by a girl, stopped in shock for a moment. Instead of confronting me after he regained his sense of pride, he shouted to my father, "Get your girl out of here before she gets hurt."

My father rushed to my side and threw me over his shoulder, the bat falling to the dirt. We hurried inside and shut the door. I wiggled free and ran to my bedroom window to watch.

For the rest of the humiliating march to Frank's house, Eddie's father kicked him, punched him, and slapped him repeatedly in front of the entire neighborhood. I opened the window and could see Frank's parents peering out the window, shuddering in fear, leaving their son alone to fight this man. When Frank saw them, pure shame and self-hatred filled him. I could tell by his cowering in the dirt and giving up. I wondered if this was what my mother meant by "being less fortunate." Not having a father to come to your aid, like I did. Not having a father to run outside and play ball with you and stop the bullying.

My mother was at work, so I couldn't ask her. Would she have made a difference though? I doubted it. When it came to my father's decisions, my mother always buckled for the sake of keeping the peace.

I, too, was ashamed, not for Frank but for myself, for my own father's unwillingness to rescue Frank.

He saw me glaring at him. "Don't get involved in other people's business." He returned to his newspaper.

I resolved never again to give in to my father's mood swings, especially those that abused my siblings and me. He was not the strong hero I thought. He was a hypocrite. Instead of standing up for those less strong, as he declared in his union speeches, he allowed another man to bully a boy. I watched as Frank crumpled to the ground, stood up, and fell by the force of yet another blow. In that moment, I knew I'd never again forgive my father for his inaction nor dismiss his cruelty toward us.

A few days later, I was eager to get to Marty's Mart. In the back of the store, a pinewood apple crate was filled with old comic books. Returning aluminum cans and glass bottles earned us a dime. If you collected trash, you could cash in on a bunch of comics by week's end. I had enough in refunds to purchase three Classic Comics, my favorite series. These comics were easy to read and made book reports far more efficient.

My mother heard about the incident in the street and forced me to play with Frank even more. So, to get her off my back, I asked Frank if he wanted to go with me to the store.

He stood in the doorway, his head down like a beaten dog. I was hoping he'd say no, but he nodded yes. He didn't move forward. "Frank, do you want to go to the store or not?" Finally, he sauntered out in slow steps.

The Classic Comics went quickly because of homework assignments. I had to get there fast. I wanted to refund my paper bag of bottles for *The Tell-Tale Heart*. I heard it was gory, and I was dying to read the comic, but Frank was dragging me back and keeping me from buying and holding that prized possession in my hands. I didn't want another kid in my class to beat me to the punch, so I started getting really pissed off.

"Frank, can ya hustle? Crate's going to be empty by the time we get there."

I don't know what set him off—my tone, my nagging, or my pace—but suddenly he reached out and yanked the bag from my hands. The cans went flying. One Coke bottle was flung across the road, and the jelly jar dropped to the curb, cut in half, shards stuck in the gutter.

"What the heck you doing, dummy?"

"Shut up," he said, his tone strange and calm. He stared straight at me, ignoring the mess at my feet. His fists grew tight, his face red. I'd never seen him angry. He'd always acted kind of cowardly. After his beating in the street, he had withdrawn. Now, a new Frank emerged. "Don't never call me dumb again." His eyes glowered, and I stepped back, trained to dodge anger.

"Sheesh, okay, okay." I stooped to pick up the shards of glass. The bag was ripped. I knew I'd have to get a new one. This was all my mom's fault for forcing me to play with this stupid kid no one liked anyway. "I'm going home," I said. "Don't ever come with me again." I stomped off. He stood there and continued to stare at me.

Finally, he slumped to the ground. "Don't blame ya. I'm a piece of shit."

Instead of telling him that no he wasn't, I turned away. "Yeah, Frank, you're a shit."

That night I told my mother that I refused to play with

Frank. "I don't care how poor they are." My mother shook her head, sighed, and went back into the kitchen to grab her evening beer and novel while I sulked on the sofa.

That she didn't fight me was a relief. No more weird-ass Frank to have to play with. Good riddance to bad trash, as my grandma would say. I went to sleep ticked off that I didn't have the Edgar Allan Poe Classic Comic to read and now I'd have to read the entire freaking story and write a real book report. Soon enough, I got involved in the story, though, and was kind of scared too. I stayed up late to finish it.

The comic book with colorful pictures would have seemed less real. I stuck my head under the covers, hoping to make the sound of the tell-tale heart and its constant beating go away. After much tossing and turning, I fell asleep only to be awakened by the sounds of sirens, the smell of acrid smoke, and people running in the street.

I opened the window curtain to see what was going on. I didn't want to wake up my sister, so I quietly left the room. The front door was wide open. I could see neighbors in pajamas and robes running barefoot down the street, shouting to each other in front of the house two doors down. It was the Merry house. Frank's house.

I started to run too. I wanted to see what all the commotion was about. Suddenly, my mother came up from behind me and grabbed me by the waist so hard that she knocked the wind out of me. I couldn't breathe for a second. My mother, unlike my father, never hit us or was physically violent in any way.

"What the hell, Mom." I yanked away from her and turned in time to see the bodies, shrouded in blankets and faces hidden, laid down one next to the other on the front lawn. Frank's mother was screaming wildly and lunging from one body to the next.

She lifted a gray blanket, and I could see it was Frank despite half his face charred and missing an ear as if it had melted away.

"Come here now!" my mother screamed. It made me turn back in shock. My mother rarely raised her voice and never in public. She pulled me hard and yanked on my arm. I thought maybe I was having a weird dream like the tell-tale heart story. But the pain my mother was inflicting on my twisted arm and her unusual determination told me otherwise.

She threw me into the house. "Go to bed and do not look out the window. Do you hear me? Do you understand?"

I nodded.

She ran back into the street. I started to cry. I went to my room and pulled the covers over my head. After a bit, I peeked out the window to see men in an ambulance lifting Frank's lifeless body onto a stretcher and into the ambulance.

I never saw Frank again. It made me sad. But it also made me mad. There wasn't even a funeral. My mom said something about it being too upsetting to view children's bodies, but that didn't make any sense to me. I couldn't even say goodbye. When I heard kids gossip about Frank in the street, I simply turned and walked away. I returned to my schoolwork and tried to forget that night.

I had been sick on and off again, missing school. I became friends with Carol, who was even sicker than me. We spent afternoons in a closet room with a resource teacher trying to catch up on the classwork. After a few months, I felt better and had far more energy. I was relieved when school ended for summer. Once again, I was doing cartwheels, hanging upside down from trees, and throwing slimy earthworms on the heads of unsuspecting boys. The summer passed, and I returned to school.

The first day of school, I searched for my friend. She was nowhere to be found. I asked my mother, "Did Carol move? She's not at school."

My mother paused and took a deep drag on her cigarette before saying, "Carol had leukemia. I'm sorry, Sue. While you were recovering in the hospital, your friend died." She waited for a reaction. I stared at her, my mouth open, unmoving. "The teachers advised me not to tell you until your health improved and you were strong enough to take the news. I should have told you earlier . . ." She let her voice fade.

My mind reeled. I couldn't even speak. They thought that by lying to me it would be a-okay? "I could've gone to the funeral at least."

"That funeral was no place for a girl." My mother pursed her lips and clutched her hands into a joined fist.

I realized then that not only had she lied to me, but she'd also hidden the fact that she'd attended the funeral. How had she hidden her feelings so well? How could I ever trust her again? I felt guilty too, as if I had no right to feel happy and alive while my only friend died.

At the kitchen table I could see the neighborhood mothers. They were quietly talking, shaking their heads. I overheard one say, "The poor Merry family," and another, "That boy was not right in the head. Who would think he could set his own house on fire, killing his sisters? Whatever made him do that?" Upon seeing me enter, one woman lifted her hand to hush the neighbors.

I turned back to my mother. She was not going to hide another child's death from me. I'd seen the bodies. I'd smelled the charred flesh. I could take it. I was tough.

"Why did he do what?" I asked, determined to get an answer.

"Never mind," our next-door neighbor said. She clutched

her cigarette in shaking hands. Her eyes misted. "You don't need to worry about that."

My mother waved her hand for me to go to my room, without answering the question. I left, knowing I would never again trust an adult to tell me the truth. For weeks, I dreamed of Carol in a coffin I'd never seen. I would wake up with Frank at my bedroom window—a boy ghost staring at me like a lost dog, like he was that last day when he made me lose my chance at a Classic Comic book.

Frank Merry was dead. Carol Darling was dead. I lived. Why? Were they loved less? Would they be missed by anyone? Why hadn't I been a better friend? Nothing made sense, and I had no one to ask since I no longer trusted my parents. From that day on, no matter what was thrown my way, I would never again rely on the honesty of adults. If I wanted the truth, I'd have to seek it out myself.

5

The Immaculate Deception

When my mother was pregnant with baby number four, she handed me a textbook. "Read this," she said. "If you have any questions, ask me. You're almost twelve. In some societies, that's old enough to learn the facts of life."

She shifted her eight-months-pregnant body off the end of the sofa where she had perched with the guidebook. She pulled herself up and duck-walked her tiny frame back to the kitchen.

Guide to Human Reproduction, read the title. The cover photo was of a woman half reclining, pregnant belly exposed, thin blanket covering her nether parts. Legs split wide open, her feet in metal stirrups, while uniformed female nurses huddled around a seemingly expert male doctor. The woman grimaced in pain. The model nurses were posed demurely next to a stone-faced doctor. I felt both fascinated and anxious. I had to read it.

I pulled up my knees and propped the hardcover book on my girl-thin thighs as I sat lengthwise on the sofa. My sister and brother were engaged in some tug-of-war on the floor over a deflated football each had declared they owned. In some ways, with my mother in the kitchen and my siblings distracted, I was alone with information about the most important mystery of life.

The opening pages displayed detailed photos of giving birth with all its attendant blood, guts, and gore. The first section was subtitled: "Birth." The segment on sex came at the end of the photographic horrors on giving birth. I figured maybe my mom's purpose in sharing the medical book was more to scare the crap out of me than to educate me.

The whole biological process, laid out in grainy black-and-white photos, dampened my enthusiasm for the act that led up to the miracle of birth. My mind shifted from awe to sheer terror.

I skimmed the scary photos, feeling uneasy, and went directly to the chapter I had decided to focus on that would lead to more practical information—"The Sexual Response."

I knew other girls' mothers never spoke of biological processes. One girl even told me her mom rarely touched, much less kissed, her dad. My parents were younger, more open-minded, and physically demonstrative. While the girls and boys around me were left to the confusion and mystery of love and kisses and warm embraces or the possible joys of sex, my mother cut to the chase and gave it to me raw.

She was expecting to give birth any day now. My curiosity about how it had all happened, and my endless questions, led her to give me the medical tome. It baffled me how this "miracle of birth" had even happened between my parents. My father worked the night shift. My mother worked days. On the few occasions when they were together, the bedroom door would be shut and locked, and anyone knocking on it during these sacred unions was met with a slap upside the head. We stayed away from that locked door to preserve our lives.

Nonetheless, that did not keep us from entering our own

adjacent bedroom closet to listen in on our parents behind closed doors. Thin walls in a cheaply made fabricated house gave us entry into the mysteries and secrets of the bedroom activities my parents engaged in during these precious moments. They were young, healthy, eager, and in love. We would take empty glasses, since we had seen this on a TV detective show, and hold the open end against the wall, placing our ears on the bottom end of the glass to magnify sound. From there we could hear my father's deep voice murmuring, my mother's higher-pitched retort, followed by both parents' laughter, with an ensuing silence that confused my sister and me. Soon after, we would hear rather loud sighing and groaning that seemed to build to a threshold of maternal moaning.

"What is Dad doing to Mom?" my sister once asked.

"How do I know?" I shifted the glass to listen. "I think she's safe."

We were both curious about this weekly scheduled activity. My brother never bothered. He was too busy racing his metal cars.

"Curiosity killed the cat," my father had remarked one day when he emerged from the bedroom and saw the two of us at the closet, ears close to the drinking glasses.

"Is Mom okay?" I asked.

He laughed, pulled his robe tighter, and walked back into the bedroom.

Mom had become a sort of self-made intellectual by then, reading Freud, Jung, Adler, and the entire Kinsey report. Her avid academic readings had led her to believe it was time for her tutored version of sex education to explain her pregnancy. Her own academic curiosity had been stymied by the era in which she came of age. Being a smart girl in the 1950s was equated with being a spinster, shunned by men and forever lonely. "Smart girls," she'd been told, "scared off boys."

My curiosity soared. I struggled to pronounce the anatomical words about the sex act as if it were an illicit stage play. This approach only increased my confusion. I read and reread the chapter numerous times. I knew if I confronted my mother with questions, given her sharp manner, I had better be prepared.

The day arrived. My siblings were out with my father playing football. My mother and I were peeling potatoes for the evening dinner. I took a deep breath, trying to steady my voice. "Can I ask you questions about the book?"

She stopped peeling. "What book?" She stared at me, then nodded her head. "Oh, that book," as if she had forgotten. "Certainly. What's your question?"

"Well, I just want to make sure I got this right," I said, my words coming out in slowly enunciated cadences. "The man puts his piii-nest into the woman's valgornia, and that is sex."

My mother, in all her self-discipline, did not laugh at my mispronunciations. She simply corrected them.

I tried again. "The man puts his penis into the woman's vagina, and that is sex," I declared, this time satisfied and proud of myself.

"No," my mother stated flatly. She picked up another potato.

What? What did I miss? I shook my head to clear the thoughts and put my own potato back down into the pan with a loud plunk to get her attention.

She looked up and sighed. "The act of penetration is not sex. That is reproduction." She went back to peeling potatoes and handed a big gnarled one to me to settle the matter.

The book had a section on reproduction, but it was filled with out-of-focus photos of a woman with her head thrown back. Nothing more. The model in the photo seemed to be in obvious pain, and it showed in the bulging veins on her neck. The section on the "sex act" did seem to imply some sort of ecstasy. Each time I read that chapter, though, I felt more confused. I was not to be dismissed. I tried again.

"Okay, Mom, then what is sex?"

My mother paused and sighed loudly as if irritated. "Sex," she reported in an academically strong voice, "is much more."

"More what?"

She gave up on the potato and dropped it *ker-plop* into the tin pan, irritated with this inquisitive burgeoning young lady she had created and now was attempting to educate on a subject matter many considered inappropriate.

"Sex," she stated clearly, "involves rubbing." She stared at me. "Lots and lots of rubbing. That helps the lady. Not so much the man. But that is sex."

This response was not helping my comprehension one iota. "Rubbing what? Why does the lady need more rubbing?"

"Oh, for heaven's sake, Sue." She threw both hands into the air. Her tone seemed exasperated, and I knew that was the end of my lesson. "Let's concentrate on making dinner. It's best for you to find out for yourself in a few years. For now, you know more than enough—I dare say, more than most." That ended the discussion, and I was never brave enough to investigate this "rubbing" syndrome any further while under her roof.

That night I mulled over the conversation and the photos as I walked to attend my Holy Communion catechism class with four other bored kids and the local priest at the Episcopal church. Being the avid reader I was, I had dutifully read all the religious texts and biblical verses assigned. The other kids attended with the promise of a bicycle or roller skates. I asked my parents what I would receive as a communion gift, and my father replied, "A cheap gold cross, if you're lucky." This response did not dampen my enthusiasm to learn since I anticipated such an answer. It gave me the freedom to dive into the subject of Christ's life and death with abandon while the other kids fidgeted and wished I would just shut up.

Tonight's lesson segued nicely with my medical reading and my questioning about sex, armed with the proper pronunciation of body parts. Our church-assigned godmother, Sister Cecilia, a rather stout and unmoving elderly Italian grandmother of our village, called us all to order. We sat in a semicircle at one end of a big sofa with the priest on the opposite side in a hard-backed chair.

A rather young progressive priest, Father Marcus had introduced folk music and guitars to the Sunday services, much to the chagrin of Sister Cecilia and others of her generation. Nonetheless, he was the only one available to us, so we had to make do.

"Tonight, children," Sister Cecilia said, "we will be discussing the Immaculate Conception and the Virgin Mary's miraculous birth of the baby Jesus."

I leaned in. I had reviewed the glossary definition of "virgin" in my mother's medical guidebook. Heady from the discussion of sex and rubbing, armed with a smattering of physiological knowledge, I was ready to engage. I waited excitedly to discuss Mary's story.

"Our fair Mary, mother of Christ, was graced by God by being free of original sin."

So far, I thought, *so good*. I knew that. I didn't understand what it meant, but I knew the term from our studies.

"Mary gave birth to Jesus due to this miracle. She was

without original sin. She became pregnant without the aid of any man except by the virtue of God. How do you think she knew that happened, children?"

I was confused. What about the husband, Joseph? Didn't he have a part in this play?

"When Mary was with child," Sister Cecilia continued, "God sent the angel Gabriel to Nazareth, a town in Galilee. He went to Mary to tell her that she was the favored virgin pledged in marriage to Joseph."

Okay, I thought. *She was a virgin. She got married to Joseph. She got pregnant*—and this was the part where my mother's medical education kicked in—*and she had a baby.* Why was this "blessed," and what in the heck did it mean that she was "favored"? I remained silent, thinking I had missed some small detail that would make this story comprehensible. I waited dutifully to hear what that might be.

"This is why Mary remained a virgin." An ecstasy seemed to rise in Sister Cecilia. Her eyes glazed. The fluorescent lights flickered. She looked at each of us, bowed her head, and placed her hands in her ample lap, the folds of her cotton dress crumpling with the weight.

I looked up and blinked at the unnatural lighting, trying desperately to see what Sister Cecilia had seen up there in the ceiling. I attempted to wrap my mind around the virgin story. I mulled it over and was stymied. Nothing in the biblical story matched the information in the medical textbook my mother had given me.

"There are no questions about how our Lord came into this world." She folded her chunky ankles into the corner of her chair and smiled.

The other kids sat in the semicircle picking their noses,

scratching their mosquito bites, looking down with half-sleepy eyelids, shifting in the uncomfortable hard plastic chairs.

My arm shot up. "I have a question."

"Yes, please ask anything," Father Marcus said encouragingly, rapturous that anyone was engaged in this conversation.

"I don't understand how a virgin can give birth."

He smiled. "Mary was favored by God."

"I read in a medical book that a virgin is a girl who's never had sex with a man."

"Yes," Father Marcus agreed.

"Then how could Mary give birth?"

"This child is too much." Sister Cecilia shifted her massive weight.

"No, no, it's okay. I think an inquisitive child is a child of God."

I looked around at the other kids, who had already started gathering their books and papers to go home. They were glaring at me.

"Joseph got Mary pregnant," I said.

"Well, no," said the priest, "let me explain. Mary was blessed by God. She was, in that way, the chosen one, the bride of God."

This was more than my biologically minded brain could handle. "So, she had sex with God?"

"No, she had no sex." Sister Cecilia pulled herself off the chair. The skin under her chin doubled over in layers, shaking. "She was a virgin. Married to God to give birth to Jesus. You are so impertinent."

"I'm sorry, Sister Cecilia, but I'm trying to understand. Really, I am. How is that even possible? Wouldn't God have to have a penis? And wouldn't that penis be way too big for Mary, since he's God?" I was proud that I had pronounced every word, including "penis," correctly, thanks to my mother's tutelage.

Every kid started to giggle. One dropped her bag so fast that she hit Eddie, my neighborhood nemesis. He yelped in pain. "Geez, you're such a stupid show-off."

The priest raised his arms, waving his hands to keep the peace. "Please settle down now."

"How blasphemous!" Sister Cecilia said. "She is an evil child." She pointed her thick index finger at my nose.

"Why?" I was vehement. "I just want to know how Mary got pregnant without Joseph. If she's the mother of God's son, wouldn't that make her God's wife?"

"I am calling your parents, young lady," Sister Cecilia said.

From the look of fury in her eyes, I knew that she would've "slapped me into tomorrow," as she liked to say, if Father Marcus hadn't grabbed her hand.

"I will deal with it," he said. "Everyone else, please leave."

Once alone with the priest and watching Sister Cecilia huff off, I felt terror about what my punishment might be.

I knew my behavior would exasperate my mother, who was forever telling me "not to have such a big head simply because you read a lot." My father, raised a devout Catholic altar boy, had rebelled in his teen years and become vehemently anti-religious, so I wasn't too worried about him. My grandmother who lived with us, and who was decidedly liberal yet believed in spiritual authority, would most likely be amused. That left Father Marcus to punish me.

He sighed. "Sue, you are the only student who does the reading, who knows biblical passages by heart, who can reel off all Ten Commandments. Why, oh why, would you want to destroy your soul with such blasphemous thoughts? I have half a mind to ensure you don't celebrate Holy Communion with your class."

Great, I thought, *no fake gold cross*. Just a dress that had cost my family too much never to be worn, and I would be exposed to my mother's anger at being a "show-off" and not respecting adults. Not to mention the possibility of going to hell in the bargain and still not knowing how Mary got pregnant.

Instead, Father Marcus, of the Joan Baez singing and anti-war songs, laughed. "You will graduate," he said, "but please no more discussing anatomical body parts with Sister Cecilia, or you will cause her apoplexy."

He stood up and picked up my book bag and handed it to me. "It is said that curiosity killed the cat, but satisfaction brought him back. I hope one day you will reflect on your curiosity and know the satisfaction of understanding faith is not logic. Faith is humanity rising to try to be better, to believe in the comforting kindness of a pure Mother who loves them as God loved her. That is the story, and I hope someday you may find the need to believe the story and restore your faith. In the meantime, please attend your communion on Sunday and try to not tick off Sister Cecilia."

I smiled with great relief. The following Sunday I kneeled at the altar decked out in my too-expensive fluffy white dress with the other kids all in a row. The priest placed the wafer on my eager tongue, looked down, and winked at me, our secret safe between us for all eternity.

As I fingered my fake gold cross, I thought about Mary. Did she have one heck of a night with God to get us all to the point of worldwide celebration of her only begotten son? Or had she simply been a girl like me, confused and curious about her role in life?

6

John's Return

Labor Day weekend at my aunt's beach cottage, overlooking the bay of Henderson Harbor on the eastern edge of Lake Ontario, was the summer's highlight. That year, 1969, we gathered to celebrate my cousin John's rather sudden nuptials.

From a distance I spied John, barely nineteen years old, standing tall and lanky at the end of the dock. His blond sun-tinged hair flip-flopped in the wind. He personified the strong-but-silent type so many movies of my generation touted as pure masculinity. He had tensile strength on boats, hauling in catches and lifting large motors onto dry dock. Once, we were caught out on the lake with an incoming storm. Lightning flashed around the boat. Thunderous applause made us scurry to shore. Our mistake in timing was evident by our lack of ability to row the boat fast enough. John, without a thought to his own safety, had jumped on the Jet Ski and sped along the choppy waves. The Jet Ski leaped into midair only to crash onto the next whitecap.

As I watched him rush toward us with no fear of his own drowning or lightning strike death, my heart soared. What a man. What a hunk. What a cousin. I was in love. My love formed an unshakable path that day on the stormy waters as he threw each of us over his seat and sped back to land.

At fourteen, my body was barely beginning to show signs of development. Every day felt like an agitation of sexual confusion. Was I a tomboy or a femme fatale? I didn't know which way my body would turn.

Bored by adults singing Sinatra songs while topping off shots of cheap brandy and feeling too old for the childhood water tag games by the dock, I turned to my violin. I stood downwind of the boat shed to escape the lakeshore breeze carrying the smell of rotting fish. No one wanted to be around me while I screeched out bad renditions of Vivaldi. Even the cat would run and lunge at the screen door to escape the cacophony arising from my violent bowing across out-of-tune strings.

Freedom from the relatives' ears led me to set up the music score of "Flight of the Bumblebee" in the crux of a dying oak tree. Reading the multiple notes in rapid succession seemed a bit ambitious. Instead, I closed my eyes and let my fingers fly over the E string, wildly playing offbeat. I finished and curtsied to the tree, envisioning a virtuosa performance at Carnegie Hall.

The sound of hands clapping made me turn. John wore a sly, sexy smirk. He winked at me. My skin burned hot.

"Keep going, Suzy Q." He sat down on the stoop.

That wink uplifted me. My ego exploded. I had made John happy, if only for a moment. Truth be told, I loved John. Truly and wholly in the way that only a teenager can. He motioned me to continue.

I finished with a flourish, then looked to the doorway for John's approval.

He stood up to open the outdoor fridge, picked out a Budweiser, wiped the sweat from the silver metal, and in a few long-legged strides, disappeared back inside the screen door.

My spirit fell from ecstasy to self-disdain in the time it took that backdoor screen to open and slam shut—my audience of one gone. My orchestra teacher had told me, "You may never be a musician, but you sure play with the intensity of one: wild, un-tamed, and passionate." Disappointed by John's departure, I hoped he could feel and hear my passion too.

I packed my violin back into its torn blue velveteen-lined case, slammed it shut, and tucked my music book under the leather sling. I decided to meet my friend Richie before sunset.

It was one of those rare afternoons along the shores of Henderson Harbor where the sun shone full and bright. Clouds drifted high in wispy layers.

Richie sat up and waved me over to the top of the hill. I rushed into the lush grass. We both fell, backs to the ground, and looked at the sun, making circles using index fingers and thumbs, focusing wide-eyed upon the gold circle.

"Squint your eyes," Richie said. "Can you see sparkles?"

I tried to get my mind off John's sexy smile. I shook my head to clear the vision and looked directly at the lazy summer sun. I squished my eyes into slits. "Oh yeah, there. I see it. A whole lot of sparkly lights."

"Turn your head really fast. It's like streaked lightning. Crazy."

"Ahhhhhhh, crazy is right. It's goofy."

I looked down the hill filled with clover, rocks, sticks of various sizes. A lush cattail grove of white fluff covering the large brown sticks waved in the breeze over the swamp below.

"Let's roll to the bottom," I said, knowing we were probably too old for these games yet missing the sheer joy of somersault-ing down the hill. "Let's see if we can make it to the base before falling into the swamp." I positioned my body in a log roll, ready to push off.

"Race you," he said. "One, two . . ." And he was off.

"Cheater!" I yelled.

I threw myself down and began to tumble. The best way to roll was to extend arms and legs. Once you got going, gravity did the rest. Rocks hit my ribs. A warm, dewy wet rug of green softened the blows. The smell of newly blossoming clover swept over me like drugstore perfume. It was as if the clover sprang forth to cover the swamp's sulfuric odors.

We speed-rolled to the bottom. If you were expert at the movement, you could go full tilt until you hit the perch just before it landed you into the soggy bog. Only the hard sticks of the cattails could stop you then.

"I'm winning," Richie yelled.

"No way." I doubled my efforts not to be outdone.

"Winner gets a kisssssss . . . ," he hissed. His body rolled down the hill, but he missed the mark and landed smack against a tree and turned, flop, into the swamp.

I got up on my knees to stop myself from following him. I saw no use in getting all soggy dirty. Plus, I'd be in trouble with my mom for ruining my clothes, much less not "acting like a lady." I heard her voice from the night before when she caught me in the mud chasing bullfrogs.

"Sue, you should take more care. No guy wants to date a tomboy."

I had scowled at her. "Mom, no guy wants to date a girl with no tits. I doubt they care about a few croaking frogs."

"Well, think about it this way." She had wiggled her mouth so that her cigarette lifted, then fell into the left corner of her mouth while red-lit ashes hit the checkered linoleum floor. The linear track of the cigarette's glow shed the only light in the dark room. "Marilyn Monroe was a late bloomer. Elizabeth Taylor was a late bloomer." She had repeated this so many times that I think she realized she needed to add one more model. "Sophia Loren was a late bloomer too." She paused. "Actually, I'm not sure about that last one since Italian girls do develop pretty fast."

"Mom, you're not helping." I pointed to my chest. "So much for your theories. I'm Italian, and nothing's happening. I'm the only braless girl in my class."

"You're only half Italian," she reminded me. "Voluptuousness doesn't come from my side of the family, so don't get your hopes up too much."

Thanks for the reminder, Mom, I thought. The whole conversation rang in my ears as I watched Richie roll about in the mud at the bottom of the hill.

I remembered the time a boy's T-shirt had been hung from the door of my English class with my name written on it. My classmates giggled. Those black bold letters—SUE—announced to the whole class that I was the lone flat-chested wonder, the only girl still in a T-shirt. Richie had stood in the middle of the classroom waving the black magic marker like a sword pointed straight at my ribcage. He was laughing harder than anyone else.

I'd burst into tears that day and run out the door, into the woods behind the school. I didn't return until I'd washed my face in the creek and the bell rang for the next class.

Richie, the perpetrator of that gag, had told me, "It's just a joke. Thought you'd laugh. You're like one of the guys. Why'd you run off and cry like a girl?" That rebuttal had made me want to cry all over again. Instead, I punched him in the shoulder and slammed my locker shut.

"I won. Fair and square." He was now standing up at the

bottom of the hill as he brushed mud from his pants, his face covered in the brown fluff of cattail pollen.

I resented him for not having to stay clean, for never having to be told to *be a lady*. "You cheated. Like always."

"I still get a kiss." He swiped the pollen from his lips.

With the T-shirt incident still fresh in mind, I answered him. "You want a freaking kiss? Yeah, right. Go kiss a toad." I knew it made no sense, but I wanted him to forget about that kiss. I'd never been kissed, and I wasn't about to practice on this nitwit.

I picked myself up to leave and pulled strands of grass and sticks from my forever-tangled hair. My mother had cut it super short in a "boy" style since, as she said, "you're always upside down," referring to my gymnastic tumbles with headstands, handstands, flips, and knees over branches hanging upside down from trees most days. I once heard her tell a neighbor, "I have no idea what Sue's face looks like. She's always upside down. I can tell you what her butt looks like though." They had both thought that was very funny as they glanced over at me hanging upside down from the swing with my feet looped around the top of the rope.

But now, I could see Richie running up the hill toward me. Before I had time to turn, he was on me. I felt my back against the moist grass as his hands grasped both my arms. Stunned, it wasn't until a moment later that I realized how much bigger he had grown over the summer.

"Knock it off. Get your freaking hands off me, Richie."

"Not until I get that kiss. You owe me."

His face lowered over mine. I'd never seen this look before. It frightened me. "Get off me, you jerkwad." He refused and held my wrists tighter over my head.

I pulled up my torso and kicked to get him off. He was unmovable and determined. The sun suddenly shifted behind a billowing cloud, threatening a rainstorm. I shivered with the drop in temperature even as Richie's warm body sat on my stomach.

His eyes glistened wildly. What was going on? I had known Richie since third grade. He wasn't a boyfriend. He was just the guy down the street who played kickball and made up science-fiction stories of monsters from cloud formations. He never looked at me. Never glanced my way when other girls were around. But now. Now he was totally focused, his eyes drilling into mine. I didn't like this look.

"Please," I said and hated myself for sounding so mealy-mouthed.

Richie took that as assent for the kiss and came in fast over my lips, locking down hard, grinding until my teeth felt like they would rip open my tender skin. For a moment, only a moment, I felt a tingling warmth, but it disappeared as I attempted to regain my independence. I kicked again.

He released me. "Got what I wanted. You got what you had coming to you. You lost. I won. Tough titties."

"Tough what?" I twisted and jumped up, pure rage giving me power. "Get away from me, you pervert."

Richie laughed. "See you later, alligator." He waited for my retort of "in a while, crocodile."

Instead, I said, "Go to hell, Richie."

I could tell I'd shocked him. He regained his power and grinned in triumph as he bounded up the hill, leaving me to ponder the confused sensations of tingly pleasure with the loss of free will.

I ran back to the cottage as fast as I could, both desirous and angry. Angry not at Richie so much as at myself for falling victim to his sneakiness. When I entered the covered porch, I heard the radio blasting from the dock where John and his soon-to-be wife, Joyce, sat.

My sister and I had become makeshift bridesmaids. Sharon pranced around in her fluffy dress. I was late. I ran inside and threw on the flowery pink dress I detested. Then I joined Sharon, who smiled widely, loving her blue puffy dress while holding a bouquet of wilted daisies ripped from the edge of the beach. As I stepped into line, I could have sworn my mom shot me that "be a lady" look.

After the brief ceremony, I stood on the beach watching Joyce as she swayed and laughed in loud hysterical shrieks. Her body lunged one direction, then the next, too close to the water. John had lifted his chin, glanced at her, and shook his head. After the ceremony, Kenny, John's little brother who was my age, decided we should have a sandcastle competition. "Bet you mine will be bigger," he said. I ignored him at first. "Betcha a buck I win."

That caught my attention; a buck could buy me a root beer float, a cinnamon hardball candy, and a comic book at the local store. "You're on!"

My dress kept getting caught on the rocks and the flotsam and jetsam I was attempting to use as building materials, but I didn't care. Within a few minutes, it was clear I might be out a whole dollar bill for my troubles. The memory of my morning's loss to Richie still burned on my damaged lips. I didn't want to grow up. I didn't want a boy's attention. I didn't want to leave sandcastle building behind. I only cared for John.

I looked around for more materials. A long shadow billowed over me. I looked up to see my heart's beloved.

"Hey, Suzy Q, it looks like you could use some help in the castle-making business." With that, John, on his own wedding day, fell to his knees and proceeded to work magic.

"That's cheating," Kenny whined.

"You said you were the best." John shook sand from his hands. "What do you care? I think we need an objective judge." He called over his newly wedded wife. I was appalled. How could John bring her over to judge me? She wasn't good enough for him, I thought.

Joyce good-naturedly arrived and started giggling for no apparent reason.

"Honey, you might want to let up on the booze," John whispered.

"Hell, no," she responded and almost fell over. "I'm celebrating my wedding day." She began to sob. "Don't go, Johnny, please. Canada is so close. Let's pack today. Head north."

I glanced from Joyce to John. I looked at Kenny, who simply shook his head. Joyce ran to the dock, slipped, and fell in. John walked slowly to the edge of the dock, sat down and opened a pack of cigarettes, lit one, and waited for her to get up the ladder.

"What's with her?" I asked Kenny.

"Ah, she's just mad that he got drafted. Going to 'Nam next week. She's preggo too and batshit crazy."

Crazy about him, I thought as I watched him gently place a towel around her shoulders and pull her close to him.

I had seen a few guys go off to war. None returned, or if they did, they no longer lived near us and did not visit their families. The war I protested in my safe enclave of high school halls, never really knowing much more of Vietnam beyond the shocking photos in the first edition newspaper, suddenly seemed real.

This was John. My John. My hero. He had to come back. He just had to, and that was that.

The following summer of my junior year became problematic on so many levels. I was finally beginning to develop, and hormones were driving every mood and decision. Where once I had encompassed the soul and heart of a free spirit, I was now trapped in a dissociative body that emerged into unwanted shape-shifting. I desired passionate full-on love. Simple teenage lust held no magic for me.

School continued. John's postcards were forgotten, sealed up in an empty cigar box. Joyce had given birth to a baby boy. Everyone rejoiced. I heard more than once variations on the theme "It's good she got knocked up just in case John doesn't return."

But John did return, late the following summer, altered beyond my previous year's memory of him.

Silently, he would walk to the pier alone every evening, his body slumped sideways, his head tilted toward his left hand. He sipped on a beer and slowly inhaled from the half-lit cigarette. The evening ritual allowed him to ignore his family, the lake, his past, and the very normalcy of life in the country that now seemed surreal to him. He refused to talk about what he'd witnessed. His silence spoke his trauma like so many other draftees returning from Vietnam.

I liked to wake up early to watch the fish jump out of the water trying to catch the skimmers for breakfast. One morning, I had curled up on the porch swing rereading for the third time my favorite book—*A Tale of Two Cities*.

John pushed open the torn screen door, saw me, and sauntered over to the porch swing. He sat down and looked at me for a moment, staring at who knew what, then spontaneously hugged me. The warmth and strength of his embrace overwhelmed me. That hug reminded me of why I had fallen in love with him. He was my first love. A few tears escaped my eyes that I brushed aside. I had missed him so much. *Will my old John return to me?* I wondered.

He pulled back to sit by my side and lit his morning cigarette while throwing down a huge mug of thick black coffee. His wife and the baby were still asleep upstairs. My uncle soon emerged. His morning ritual was to prepare the boat for the first of the morning's fishing expeditions. He glanced over at both of us and nodded, taking a seat nearby. All three of us watched the rising sun glitter along the eastern edge of the lake's surface. Seagulls flew overhead, diving at leaping trout. It seemed an all-too-familiar yet now strangely disconnected scene from former childhood summers.

My uncle cleared his throat. "So, what did they teach you in 'Nam?"

John stared out at the glistening waves. He took one drag from his cigarette and, with slow, measured exhalation, watched the smoke float away from his lips before speaking.

"They taught us how to kill."

I was shocked. My naivete about what John had experienced hit me like a cement truck, smashing my beliefs of home, of John, of family, of my own country.

"Funny," my uncle said, "that's the same thing they taught us in World War Two."

For most of that morning, the three of us sat staring in silence as the seagulls flew in ever-widening circles over the bay's peaceful waters. The sun rose higher and higher in the late summer sky as my childhood floated away on the waves of John's trails of smoke.

7

Huntress

By 1971, the war in Vietnam had begun to wind down, an omen of America's resounding defeat. Confusion and quietude had become our constant companions. No celebrations. Only a sad remorse and an underlying bitterness. My cousin John and so many others wanted to obliterate the experience once they had moved back home, staying hidden in the years ahead, barely speaking.

Summer's carefree fantasies faded that year, lost to childhood's end. My body, as if in revenge, grew and completely reshaped itself into an alien form. My wild-child tomboy form disappeared, replaced by male gazes that haunted my every move. My mother held a low opinion of anyone who valued appearance above character. Confusion on physicality was unworthy of discussion, so with her, I remained mute.

My father took a different approach. He seemed highly relieved in the early years of high school that I remained in boyish form. He would turn on his record player and carefully place the needle onto the vinyl. The crooning smooth voice of Ben King singing "Stand by Me" soared over the sounds of the record's skips and scratches that filled the tiny living room.

"Suzy." He bowed. "Shall I have this dance?"

With that, I would step onto his shoes as he lifted me into a swing dance. My father's love of dancing and musicals never ceased to amaze me. He watched every movie musical ever produced, could sing every note in a beautiful tenor, and danced each move with the precision of a Broadway showman. I inherited his love of dance. I could never sit still. Dance was our emotional expression in those days. I could easily leap around furniture, tossing my legs over unsuspecting siblings in the living room.

Pure joy of motion filled me. My body leaped from chair to sofa and back again. He would switch the record to Chubby Checker's sing-shouting to "The Twist." Within seconds of hearing those first few calls to dance, we would be off again, waving our knees back and forth, going in low for the quiet notes and jumping up high for the crescendo. My mother would simply shake her head. She had no rhythm. Dancing was a painful counting of steps she could never quite master, and she thought my dad and I were "just showing off," her most critical response to our shared physicality.

Then, suddenly, it changed the year I turned sixteen. My body. My dad. My life. In the summer between sophomore and junior year, my body exploded. My joints were in constant pain. Muscle and skin stretched taut. Bones ached. Breasts grew wildly out of proportion. I left my sophomore year in June wearing an undershirt and returned in my junior year three inches taller, sporting an hourglass figure with an overfilled, brand-new C-cup bra.

My younger sister Sharon came into the room one day as I was analyzing these somewhat frightening end-of-summer results, and laughed. Sharon had been wearing a bra for over two years.

"You kind of look like an upside-down L." She pointed to the mirror.

I turned sidewise. "Crap," I said, "you're right." She laughed because I looked so ill at ease and rather goofy in my new body.

When I complained to my mother, she just sighed.

"What if you had been wrong? What if the lessons of Marilyn and Sophia Loren had been a big fat lie? What if it had never happened? Then what?" I was a little pissed at her dismissiveness.

"Are you quite finished with the self-pity?" She got up off the bed. Whining fell on the far-end scale of her patience level.

She had a point. What was I complaining about and why? "I just want to know how in the heck you knew this would happen?"

"I didn't know for sure." She picked up her library book, a sure sign that the conversation had concluded. Without looking up, she added, "Your breasts are not too large. Your body is simply too small."

The first day of school that year I walked home as the garbage truck came up behind me. A man grabbed my ass. The others whistled and shouted encouragement. "Hey, girl, you got some juicy-fruit big ones. Makes me want to eat you up."

In one swift move, I turned around, fists clenched, ready for battle. I was alarmed and momentarily confused as I stared at Gino, our local garbage man, who'd known me since I was nine. He leered at me as if he'd never seen me in his life. I teetered between being freaked out and angry.

"Mr. Gino," I shouted, "go eff yourself." He laughed and so did the other men, not recognizing the girl they used to wave to every Thursday.

Disdain for the boys every time I made an entrance grew, but what I hated most was the fathers' changed behavior. *What is wrong with these horny old creeps?* If my dad knew about this, he would have smashed all their faces in.

Sarcasm became my new weapon. "Let's discuss your assessment of my body parts with your wife, Mr. G." He backed off, finally recognizing the girl in the barely burgeoning woman.

My father's denial at my new shapeliness resulted in him no longer touching, hugging, or dancing with me. I was heartbroken. Any joy we once shared disappeared. He didn't want me going out with boys. He didn't want any boy calling me. He commanded that I could not shave my legs, and believe you me, Italian girls are plenty hairy. "Shaving is a sign to boys that you want them. Maybe when you're older." My mother said to ignore him and handed me her Lady Gillette razor.

Boys would call. My mother would report the name of the boy as she held her hand over the phone.

"To hell with that guy, Mom. I'm not talking to him. Hang up." She sighed and returned to the call to let the boy of the moment know "Sue is indisposed," 1970s-speak for "get lost."

My father's mood lightened each time he heard me reject yet another suitor.

One day a friend, James—the school valedictorian, chubby, and a very shy guy—came over to study chemistry. As we reviewed the periodic chart, my father marched out of the bedroom and grabbed James by the shirt, lifting him clear off the floor, his glasses askew, his face filled with terror. Dad threw James out the door in one shove. James landed in grass, rose quickly, and raced down the street.

"Dad, James's a nice guy. Why'd you do that?" I paced around the sofa trying not to lose my cool. "This is freaking embarrassing. How will I ever live this down? How can I show my face at school? What the hell is wrong with you?"

Half expecting him to slap me, I ducked, only to find my father slumping into his overstuffed fake-leather chair. He waited a moment and then told me about walking into his childhood cold-water flat to find his drunk uncle raping his little sister, who was only five. Barely nine years old at the time, he wasn't even sure what was happening. His sister cried out in pain, begging him to make the uncle stop.

"I really tried to stop him." My father's eyes glazed over. His gulping sobs surfaced from deep within a once buried memory. "I yelled at him. I hit him. He just threw me away like a piece of trash. It's all my fault." His crying scared me more than all the years of his rages.

"I didn't protect my sister. That was my job. She never recovered. I'd do anything to make sure that never happens to any of my girls." His hazel eyes and long lashes glistened with tears. "I shouldn't have thrown out that boy. I overreacted. Not thinking. I just want to protect you."

He began to cry again as if this secret now exposed had become a torrential river of fear and self-loathing. I put my arms around him to still his violent shaking. All at once I realized why my newly developed figure frightened him so much. He knew he had no control over my sexual fate and the horrible things some men were capable of doing.

Despite his fears, I realized I'd still have to face my classmates' teasing and taunting about my father's violent reaction to a gentle teenage scholar. I could hear it now. "Don't date Sue. Her dad will literally kill you. He's a whacko nut job."

As I walked the school hallways over the next few weeks, the boys stayed away from me and the girls gathered in packs, whispering. I knew I had to find a way around my father's ever-growing set of rules. After all, I was not his five-year-old sister.

I decided to get a job and save my pennies to flee his home, his rules, and his childhood ghosts.

I found myself showing up half a dozen times to apply for a job at the local five-and-dime, W. T. Grants, one of the few employers in town. The only job advertised was in the pet and garden shop, which required lifting fifty-pound bags of gravel and twenty-gallon fish tanks, challenging tasks considering my ninety-pound petite size. On my fifth attempt, the HR lady shook her head, her perfectly shellacked hairdo staying firmly in place. She pursed her mouth into downward wrinkles.

"You're going to keep coming back until I give you a job?"

I nodded and waited. No response. "Just try me out," I said. "I'm stronger than I look." She waved forms at me to sign since it was the only way to make me go away.

Three days a week after school, I would walk two miles along the highway shoulder to get to the store. The furniture department was next to toys and pets. Any piece of furniture sold commanded a commission.

One day, a young couple came up to me. No salesman seemed to be present, so I filled out the forms for the sofa. I would get 10 percent, which came to a whole month's salary. A week went by. No commission appeared on my paystub. I confronted the floor manager.

"You can't get a commission. Only furniture salesmen are eligible," he said.

I was not to be deterred. That money was part of my dream of freedom. "I sold it. The commission is mine."

"No can do." He shook his head.

"Why not? I earned it. If I hadn't been there, the store would be out the sale."

It dawned on me that only men worked in that department.

Women worked in toys, pets, lingerie, and clothing. No commissions existed in any of those departments.

"Fine. I refuse to help ever again."

He laughed as I walked away, flipping him the bird.

The next evening as I hustled to complete my trigonometry homework before rushing to work, my father sat heavily at the kitchen chair next to me and glowered. I ignored him and kept working. I was immune to his violent mood swings by then. I had an escape plan firmly embedded in my teenage brain, and I didn't have much time to implement it.

My blind grandmother bent over the sink as she washed the few remaining lunch dishes to prepare for dinner. Her thin fingers carefully searched for every plate, fork, and cup in the sink in slow motion. My father ignored her.

My father usually ate his supper early before going to his night shift. That night, my mother had missed the bus after work, so no dinner had been cooked. Adhering to old-fashioned norms, he grew angrier with each passing minute that no woman, neither my grandmother nor me, was waiting on him.

Fresh from my encounter with the store manager, I was thinking, *No commission, no sale—no allowance, no service.*

"Make me a burger." He slapped both hands on the table on each side of my math book, making me jump. He stared at me. "I earn the money around here. You live under my roof. I don't care if you have a job or not. Your first job is to cook for the family when your mother's not here." He refused to blink, and the veins in his neck bulged. "Where's my burger?"

My old fears of being kicked or slapped or grabbed fell away. He no longer held the same power over my life. The clock was ticking. I needed to finish my trig. I picked up my pencil.

He grabbed my hand with such force that I dropped the

pencil to the floor, making my grandmother turn quickly. She couldn't see, but her hearing had grown more sensitive. Without a moment's hesitation, she twisted the wet towel in her hand and snapped it at him, slapping him square in the face. His face contorted into shocked anger.

"Leave Sue alone. She's trying to make something of herself." She returned to the sink and added in a firm voice, "Unlike you." My grandmother's disdain for my mother's marital choice was evident in her response, but there was nothing my father could do about it. My grandmother commanded respect.

He regained momentum to direct his hurt pride in my direction. "You think you're better than me? Irregardless of what you think you're doing, college is not happening for you, so don't even bother."

"You mean 'regardless,'" I corrected his grammar.

"No man will want you if you keep up this smart-ass shit. No man likes a fighting woman, much less a snob." With that, he got up, sans supper, and marched out the door.

I was grateful to my grandmother and her fearlessness. Dad could be plain crazy and illogical, but his own needs often conflicted with each other. First, he wanted no man in my life. Then, he wanted to create domestic Sue. How was I supposed to be both a tough girl fighting off boys and then a homemaker waiting to serve a man his burger? He was the one who taught me to be a fighter.

"He's just a blowhard letting off steam," my grandmother said. She continued to wash each individual dish with care and place one after another in the rack, first feeling for the safety of the rungs. "Go back to studying. You have an exam to ace, or you'll never get out of this provincial hellhole."

My grandmother, my ally, departed our house shortly after

that day to live in a cramped bedroom closet in her oldest daughter's home, her disability payments helping pay the rent. Although I missed her presence, her fortitude and audacity were permanently embedded in my soul.

Even in her absence, I felt inspired to stand up for myself whenever possible. My grandmother had shown me the way. Her quick surprise response had weakened my father's resolve. I formed the next step of my escape plan. Step one, I ascertained, was to find a compliant young man, someone strong, who would stand up to my father.

As fate would have it, that assessment of my romantic needs led to Brian, a six-foot-five-inch basketball player, a senior who had been watching me at cheerleading practices and who I had ignored as another drooling boy, another annoyance. But now I took another look at the handsome solution to all my problems. I watched as he deftly skirted around other players, dribbling the ball with finesse and leaping to victory—Score!

8

Natural Selection

After a few weeks of aching arms, in frustration, I dropped the books crushing my tits and did as my grandmother had suggested: "Stand up straight. Knockers out. Walk proud." That was the day my rage against boys and my battle with my body turned to tactical warfare. It was also the day that Brian walked by, smiled, and cast his gaze downward, not at my body but at my angry blue eyes.

"Hey, gutsy girl." He smiled, his front teeth slightly bucked.

"Gutsy?"

"Yeah, I heard you had a little run-in with the principal." The tip of his beaked nose fell over his unruly strands of newly grown blond mustache. He tilted his head sideways. "The whole school is talking about it. I heard they changed the policy because of you. You got some moxie, girl."

I was the topic of talk? This was a new complication. I had once asked a pack of girls gossiping in the hallway what they had heard about me. After a silent moment in what passed as deep adolescent thought, one answered, "Nothing." The others shook their heads in affirmation. "No one talks about you." She shrugged her shoulders and added, "Sorry."

Being talked about felt intriguing, but being targeted by one of the senior varsity basketball players felt downright tantalizing. Whatever reason he had to assess my character, this could be the start of a new persona. I could reemerge into the crowded halls of high school as the "girl with moxie," but I was a little vague as to why.

"You don't remember the confrontation?"

Brian stood up, and I realized he was almost six and a half feet tall, confident, older. Who better to take on my strict Sicilian father and allow me some freedom?

"You're referring to the snow pants incident?" I did my best impression of the other girls and batted my long black eyelashes. He blinked as if the lenses in his glasses needed to be adjusted. This technique did not seem to impress him. I was losing him. *Regain control*, I told myself, *or the entire plan is lost.*

I stepped away from him, testing my abilities to seduce. I couldn't help but notice that as I stepped in one direction, he followed.

Normally, I wore a skirt throughout the winter storms until my knees cracked and bled from the bitter cold. One day, the principal called my name over the loudspeaker. I had entered his office with some trepidation. He was a roly-poly short man, seemingly affable. His tie fell well below his belly, getting trapped in his legs as he sat down in his torn leather chair.

"I expected more from an honor student," he began. When I didn't answer, he waved at my attire. "You're not a rule breaker. You know that girls are not allowed to wear pants. We hold ourselves to a high standard. It's unbecoming of a lady."

"I want to understand," I reassured him. "Gentlemen dress to stay warm in winter. Ladies get frostbite on their knees?"

He shifted forward, his tie dragging against the seat. "You

are inside, young lady. There is no frostbite in your classroom. Go back to your locker right now and change immediately."

"I'm not changing." I stood. I was late for English class. We were discussing "Ain't I a Woman?" from Sojourner Truth, and I didn't want to miss it.

"If you don't put on a skirt and remove those pants before you leave today, I will be forced to expel you."

His demands set my teeth to grinding. "Do whatever you need to do. I'm attending class in pants." I picked up my books. "And I intend on wearing pants every day until graduation. So, if you don't want to see a girl in boys' clothes, you need to expel me. NOW!"

I don't know why I was so upset, why I felt the surge of rage to challenge an authority figure, or why I had even emphasized the word "now," but at the tone of my voice, he crumbled. I could almost feel the tide of history coming down upon him.

From the teachings of my suffragette grandmother to protests of the Vietnam War, the civil rights movement, and the rise of the women's liberation movement, this man knew he was losing his clutch on power.

He shook his head. "You're one of my top students."

For a moment, I felt sorry for him. "Thank you" was all I could think of to say. I knew that I had attacked his core values without giving him any way to save face, but I refused to back down.

I never heard another word about expulsion. I habitually began to wear pants. Snow pants, work pants, hip-hugging jeans. The staticky announcement came over the loudspeaker a few weeks later.

"Starting with the new school year, girls shall be allowed to wear pants on inclement weather days only."

I didn't think much of it since I was determined to wear

pants rain or shine, but some hailed it as progressive. For the moment, this tiny hamlet in Upstate New York seemed to have given up the ghost of its patriarchal past. Since I did feel sorry for the principal, I had not entirely connected my rebellion with the passage of the policy, which was why when Brian confronted me, it came as a surprise. In victory, I realized my obstinacy had led to Brian—my first official boyfriend.

Tactical pursuit of him became part of a strategic path toward freedom. For one thing, he owned a car, was an excellent student, and was college bound.

No one in my family had attended college. No one knew about how to apply for scholarships, grants, loans, and work-study. College was not in the plan. My parents had no money for spending on something so frivolous as an education for a girl. The financial restraints led me to intensify my studies, knowing high school might be my only chance for an education. While other teenagers partied, I studied, spending any extra moment I could in the solitary embrace of the school's library. I valued time with teachers. I loved learning. In this way, knowledge remained my true lover.

Brian and I spent hours together in the library, whispering behind the math books where few ventured. He wanted to be an engineer, so he was no stranger to this section. His parents were divorcing, something rare in the village of Chittenango, and his response was to find someone to attach to, someone loyal, someone who would be by his side forevermore.

We became an "item" kept secret from my father. I spent hours in the cemetery drawing charcoal and pencil renderings of Brian among the various hillside gravestones. The Anguish family tombstones particularly intrigued me. The engravings were from the 1700s. The combination of crumbling limestone over granite covered in ivy and moss fed my fascination with morbidity, combining art, death, and life. In this spot, Brian and I would roll in the dewy uncut grass of soft graves as he lavished wet, sloppy kisses all over my face.

In a moment of jealous spite, my sister Sharon ratted us out. She had seen us from the school bus as Brian leaped over the stone fence and lifted me up to hide from prying eyes.

I expected rage and more rules to pour down upon me; instead, my father seemed relieved to have someone else enlisted to watch over me. Brian's sheer body size and clear ambitions intimidated him a bit, although he would never admit it. My mother, on the other hand, seemed less than enthusiastic.

"He's pretentious," she stated, I think mostly due to the fact that his parents had more money. "At least he has a car," she added, ever the pragmatist, "and you can safely get back and forth to work at night."

Not wanting to take the chance on getting pregnant, and with no birth control clinics within a twenty-mile radius, we spent our stolen hours in frustrating embraces and liquid kisses with wandering hands. Brian intensified his desire to a fevered pitch. His daily demands that I say "I love you" were wearing me down. Instead of freedom from the constrictions of paternal angst, I'd fallen into a pit of male neediness and desperation. This was not the freedom I'd envisioned.

We walked the hallways, our fingers intertwined. I surreptitiously started to look around at other possibilities. In my desire for the ever-elusive teenage popularity, I would smile at everyone in the hallway and wave my hand in the air like some desperate ex–beauty queen hoping to draw admirers. Strangely, it seemed to work. Girls spontaneously hugged me. Boys nodded in deference to my towering boyfriend.

The only problem was the more I waved and smiled, the more my muscles ached, my stomach clenched, and my head pounded.

To fit in with the athletic crowd, I befriended Debbie, the girlfriend of Bobby, the lead basketball player. One day, Bobby, Debbie, and her little brother headed our way. Bobby, I could see, was concentrating on flicking his fingers at Debbie's brother's forehead. The boy had obviously come from the junior high side of the building to walk home with his sister that afternoon. Short and squat, with an acne-riddled face, he flinched every time Bobby hit him. He began to sweat, and the droplets made his thick black-rimmed glasses slip down his short nose.

Suddenly, Bobby smacked the boy behind the head, making him fall face-first to the cement. His glasses went flying. Others laughed as the boy's tears fell to the cold floor.

Rancor rose within my soul. If my little brother had been teased or physically harmed, I'd be ready to lash out at the bully. I knew the victorious Bobby held some charm with teachers and girls, his heroic status due to his being the team's top scorer.

At that moment, though, nothing could persuade me that Bobby was anything other than a clod of field manure.

"Leave him alone." I bent down to help the boy.

"What did you say to me?" Bobby towered, hovering, leaning in. Without his eyes leaving my face, he said, "Brian, handle your woman."

"Excuse me?" I moved closer. He was bigger. Sure. But I held the sharp corner of my Geometry workbook in both hands as a weapon. I glanced down to focus his attention, for him to see where I aimed the book. "I repeat," I said in slow, even tones, "leave that boy alone. You think being cruel makes you a big man?"

I put my arm around the boy and shot a sharp look at Debbie. She flinched, and a light went off in my head. I knew that flinch. It stemmed from years of a hand slapping down any infraction.

In that moment, I realized that as some of us grew bolder with each slap, prepared to fight back, others, like Debbie, diminished themselves to disappear, to stay safe. Fear became measured in slight degrees, a mathematical calculation of fight or flee, that added up in a matter of seconds.

The hallway filled with curious students. The looks of shock and bemusement and a few shouts of "Show her, man, give it to her" on one end and "You go, girl" on the other divided the genders.

Bobby shifted his stance and took a step back. Slowly, as if approaching a wild animal, Debbie put her fingers lightly on her boyfriend's shoulder.

He shook his shoulders, his gray eyes shifting to slits of dark anger. "Get off me. Jesus, you're a pain." She stepped back, her gaze downward like a dog demonstrating submission. Her capitulation seemed to release something within him. He checked out the faces of his classmates as if measuring which way to respond, then stopped and stared directly at Brian. "You and me. We got to have a little talk in the locker room, my man."

"What in the heck does that mean?" I asked Brian after Bobby had left and Debbie's brother had raced out the door.

"Sue, you got to understand. You made him look weak in front of everybody. You were like a freaking viper lashing out at him. He almost lost his shit. Now he'll make sure you don't confront him again."

"How is he going to do that?"

Brian's long nose pointed down, his glasses slipped, and his sharp blue eyes pierced me for a moment. "You don't get it. He won't punch you. He'll punch me."

"That makes zero sense."

"To a girl maybe it makes no sense."

"And what sense does it make to a guy?"

"That I can't control my girlfriend." His eyes shifted and softened. He came closer and placed a hand on my shoulders. "You know I don't think that way, right?"

"No, I don't know that." I swatted his hand away. "A girl is a guy's pet or something to control, like some mad dog you own?"

"Ah geez, don't start. I'm trying to explain. Listen to me. The guys on the team have a code. If your girlfriend pisses off another guy, then it's your fault because you can't control her. I'll be the one he punches."

"Well, if that happens, you can tell him to punch me instead."

"Forget about it. I'll take the punches." He threw his hands up in the air. "I love you, but you're impossible."

I refused to walk the halls with Brian thereafter. The team noticed. Whistles and catcalls of "Here comes the bitch" were uttered as I walked by.

I was no longer popular.

The knives to my gut disappeared. My head cleared of the pounding pain. I felt light and happy. I was me again.

In an odd reversal, my withdrawal from Brian only increased his desire. He begged to meet me in the cemetery "one last time."

I thought it was to say goodbye or maybe to beg for forgiveness. Instead, he proposed marriage.

"It's not a real ring," he apologized. "I'll get you one once I get a job." He placed the zirconium glass ring on my limp finger. "If you're worried about my going to Vietnam, I'll get a college deferment."

I jerked upright, thinking of my cousin John who had gone to war. My once ebullient, fun cousin. My first love. Damaged by war, returning worn out, moody, depressed. Brian's remark held merit. His parents could afford college. He would get a deferment, while my cousin and so many others had been mercilessly drafted for no purpose.

Since I could not be drafted, I felt guilty and gave in to Brian. I knew getting married might defer the draft through college and help him avoid John's fate. That was all that mattered.

For days, I attempted to drum up enthusiasm for marriage. To others it passed for a high school fairy-tale romance. When I told my mother I was engaged, she deadpanned, "Engaged in what?" She looked at me and then at the glass ring and shook her head in disappointment.

Brian's jealousy of other suitors escalated. His glowering stares and intimidating height frightened many. I missed talking to guys—especially my male musician and artist friends—but they stayed away now, deathly afraid of Brian's hallway rages. Especially after he slammed his fists into a locker so hard he bent the metal grill simply because a male friend smiled at me.

The only escape during that time resided in my role as first violinist and mistress of the orchestra. *Camelot*, a complicated musical based on the life of King Arthur as told to Merlin, with the discovery of Lancelot and Guinevere's illicit love affair in center play, seemed an ambitious choice, given the small population of willing thespians. I practiced daily for hours during spring break to prepare for opening night. My fingertips bled, then healed, leaving calloused pads to glide less painfully along the catgut strings. Playing feverishly off-key on my private altered beat, driving my musical director insane, had become a type of therapy, a fleeting form of freedom.

On the night of the play, I arrived early, nervously pacing the hall outside the music room. My mother walked up to me. My blind grandmother held her hand over my mother's forearm for balance. "Your father's not coming," she said. "He didn't give a reason."

Bile rose in my throat. "I don't care what he does or why. I'm not his emotional pawn anymore."

My grandmother stopped and said, "All right then. It doesn't matter what he does or thinks. It's your performance. Your choice. Your life. Not his. Remember that."

I entered the orchestra pit and lifted my bow to begin the opening overture. It required a strong, steady hand over the bow with fingers firmly placed in rapid succession. Instead of steady, though, I went wild. Fingers bounced along the neck of the violin. I slammed the bow against the E string.

The director's baton hitting my arm woke me up.

"Follow me," he whispered feverishly, as if the entire production would fail due to my crazy performance of the opening medley.

At intermission, Brian jumped into the pit. "What happened?"

"What happened is I'm done with this place."

The look on his face told me my careless rage, so like my father's bipolar moody responses, could destroy another human in a moment.

My anger grew out of proportion to the event. It was as if this moment defined my ability to escape. Brian, my protector, who would do whatever I asked, had become a barrier to my escape plan. I returned to my seat in the orchestra pit, more assured than I had been in a long time. The musical was a success, and the audience stood for an ovation.

In the last month of my senior year, my guidance counselor called me down to the office. He sat me down and said, "You seemed to have missed the deadline to apply to college."

"I'm not going to college. I have no money. Being broke is a family tradition," I said, attempting humor.

He didn't laugh. Instead, he started rummaging through drawers, pulling out legal pads of forms. "Time to break with family tradition." He rolled a pen in my direction. "You're one of my best students. You aced the SAT. You have great references. You're a Regents Scholar and National Honor Society member. Do you want to go to college or not?" I nodded a fervent yes, almost hurting my neck, which surprised me.

I had never experienced such vehement support for my education from anyone other than my grandmother. I had no idea if it was a rare event or the norm for a school counselor. Although at first, I felt concerned about how to finance it, that feeling eased when he promised to find a scholarship, somehow.

We spent hours researching and calling to see if any scholarships existed. One did, and we connected with Onondaga Community College in Syracuse. Somehow his determination gave me a courage that I did not know I possessed. He was right. I really wanted to go. I was desperate to leave. I thirsted for education the way some desire fame, fortune, and glory.

After I had completed the paperwork to establish my financial aid, I was accepted and given a Pell Grant, loan, and work-study. Just as I finally envisioned a new future, Brian arrived begging me to marry him. He knelt on the floor, his head in my lap, sobbing, his long arms grasping my waist, trapping me in the chair.

"Please, let me go." I began crying too.

He stopped and grasped my shoulder, making me wince in pain. "Never," he said.

A chill rushed through my body. I began to shiver.

At that moment, my mother walked in, looked at me, and asked, "Do you want him to stay? Do you really want to be trapped in marriage at such a young age?"

I shook my head, one vigorous no.

With that, my decidedly nonviolent, uninvolved mother stepped forward. She grabbed the back of Brian's collar and twisted it into a knot so tight that for a moment I wondered if she might strangle him. I think his surprise at the quick attack from this petite woman, a mother in defense of her daughter, kept him frozen in place. She dragged him to the door and half pushed, half kicked him onto the porch stoop.

He stood up quickly on the doorstep, recovering from the shock, changing tactics. "I'll commit suicide right here on your front lawn if you won't let me marry Sue."

"That's none of my business," my mother said with dead calm. Her eyes drilled a hatred into him I had never seen before. "Sue told you to leave. Now leave. If you even attempt to kill yourself on our lawn, I'll kick your sorry carcass to the curb for the crows to eat."

With that, she slammed the door on his face and locked it. She turned to me and said, "Go pack. You're leaving for college now."

I stared at her. "But classes don't start until fall."

"The dorm's open for summer classes. I checked. You're already registered. No need to stay here any longer. You're going."

Shaken and confused, yet relieved, I went into my room as my mother commanded. What little I had to pack took less than an hour. I was sitting on my bed next to my lone suitcase, my grandmother's manual typewriter, and my violin case as my mother walked in. She gestured to me to come into the living room. *Who's Afraid of Virginia Woolf?* was playing.

"Sit. Watch. Learn," she said.

Mesmerized by Liz Taylor's sarcastic booziness and Richard Burton's piercing glares, we talked about the premise of marriage until two in the morning.

"The bus should be here by eight," she said.

I was in a daze. This bus would be taking me toward an uncertain future guided by my mother's insistence that I move on with my life.

My brother, Mark, who was eleven, hugged me tight, then ran away. My baby sister, Julie, barely in kindergarten, began to cry hysterically and held tightly to my knees. Momentarily, I felt a surge of sweat pour down my back. The sadness at leaving my siblings overwhelmed me. Sharon, only a few years behind me in escaping, seemed more morose. She picked up my suitcase and handed it to me. "You know it's all going to hell now that you're leaving."

"Don't be ridiculous," Mom said as she loosened Julie's grip on my leg. "Sue will miss her bus if you don't stop this nonsense. It's time for her to go."

"I'm really sorry, Julie." I gulped. Sharon had her back to me. My brother Mark waved from the steps. I turned to my mother. "I feel so guilty about leaving them. What should I do?"

"I hate dramatic exits. You know I never went to college, so I don't have any advice for you. But I'll tell you this much, and please listen carefully." She pulled my arm toward her and glanced at my watch as if reassuring herself that the bus to the city and my escape needed to stay on schedule. "Sometimes the best thing you can do is to know when to take your hat and run."

My mother then handed me my cute store-bought blue beret and said, "Run."

PART TWO

Manhunt

9

Frustrated Virgin

In 1974, gender roles began to crumble. Some clung to Snow White's "my prince will come someday." I had another goal.

A few days before college reopened in my sophomore year, I sat staring into the big chocolate doe eyes of my college dorm-mate, Len, asking for her wisdom on a topic that consumed me. Her intimate knowledge about womanly affairs far exceeded mine. I raised my hands in prayer and bowed to her expertise.

"Len, I need help. I'm going to be nineteen. I've got to make it happen or it never will."

Len nodded, acknowledging the "it" as the cumbersome burden of my ongoing struggle to lose my virginity. Len possessed both a young compliant boyfriend and an older attentive married lover. She shrugged and lifted her long black eyelashes skyward. "It'll happen when you want it to happen."

"My mom was a teenager when I was born. Ergo, even my own mom was no longer a virgin at my age. How sad is it to be living in the era of 'free love' only to realize your own mom beat you to the sexual punch?" I threw myself histrionically onto the hard dorm bed. Pillows jumped in unison on either side of me. "This is making me grouchy."

"Of course you're grouchy." Len sat up. "You haven't been laid. Besides, who wants to screw a chick who says 'ergo'?" She returned to her *Cosmo* magazine.

What did it mean to be a virgin anyway? For a moment, I returned to the days of my Holy Communion when I had questioned the story of a teenage girl's pregnancy from the King James Bible. I knew nothing at age twelve. I wondered if my frustration might be due to a simple lack of carnal knowledge. How could I relieve myself of this burdensome virginity? I knew I needed guidance.

A month earlier, I had visited Planned Parenthood. I wanted to ensure no accidental pregnancies would ever occur if the process got underway. I popped little white pills in a circle tray of thirty days, despite a lack of suitors.

"My youth escapes daily," I said. "I can almost hear someone shouting, 'Get thee to a nunnery!'"

Len flipped the pages of her *Cosmo*.

"What am I doing wrong? Why can't I get a date?"

"You kind of stunk for an entire semester," she reminded me.

She was right. The smell of formaldehyde had permeated my every pore in freshman year. Biology classes, and the dead animals I dissected, had embedded the preservative in my hair, skin, fingernails. The *eau de biology* had put a crimp in my dating life. It never bothered me what the chemical's toxicity might do. I was enthralled by how mammalian anatomy worked layer by layer, skin to bone.

Len threw the *Cosmo* across the room, hitting the basket near the door. "You're not normal. You don't even pretend to be normal. I think your motor-mouth literary rantings, for one, are a big turnoff to guys."

She was right. A Shakespeare-quoting, smelly essence of

death did not exactly set the stage for a great bar hookup. But a semester later, and preservative-free, I thought the future held promise since I no longer smelled of dead fetal pig or a strung-out alley cat.

"No more pickled animals," I declared. "Do I not smell like a proverbial bed of roses?"

She smirked. "Try not to say words like 'proverbial' on a date either."

I couldn't tell whether she was sympathizing or mocking me. "What am I supposed to do?"

"How about setting your sights a little lower? You don't have to date only National Merit winners."

She was right. I liked brainiacs. I believed that if a guy had a certain degree of cranial capacity, he'd be a great teacher too. After all, I had a lot to learn. I needed a tutor in the sensual arts. "Got it." I marked an imaginary note on my palm. "Runner-up shall suffice."

"Not funny, if you want to get laid." She sat upright. "What's wrong with bedding dumb guys? Some of them are very sweet and will do anything for you. What about that orderly you work with in the nursing home?"

"Rick? He does seem to have a down-home-on-the-farm decency about him." I paused. "Only two problems. He's divorced and more than a decade older."

From earlier attempts at conversation with Rick, it seemed his life consisted of work, beer with a few friends at the local bar, and seeing his young son on weekends. When I asked him about his future education, he said, "I don't need schooling. Dealing with an ex-wife taught me plenty."

"What about your dreams?" I'd asked.

He shook his head, his sable-brown ponytail tossed back

and forth along his broad shoulders. "No dreams, no goals, no worries. Living is enough."

I'd stood before him in disbelief. I wanted desperately to study, gain an education, travel, make love, and talk for hours about politics, the women's movement, civil rights, ending the war, and, of course, the sexual revolution I was obviously missing. Maybe Len was right. I needed to lower expectations if I wanted to conquer my virginity.

"He's kind of cute. I just don't know."

Len ignored me.

"He rarely speaks. Maybe I could regard his silence as mysterious."

"He's perfect," she said. "Quiet, older, not wiser."

She pulled on her coat and waved as she walked out the door, leaving me to ponder my manhunt alone.

What if Len had a point? If I lost my virginity, I believed the world would open to unlimited adventures. But first, I needed to plan to be ravished. Surely, losing one's virginity couldn't be any more difficult than planning any other project. I'd use scientific methodology to gather information, hypothesize, set parameters in options from the immediate collegiate arena, and assess possible candidates to choose a virgin-busting male.

Or, as Len suggested, I could pursue Rick. He seemed an easy target. His eyes followed my every move. I had caught him dropping items from his medical cart as he stared, blushed, and grinned. *It's decided*, I thought. *Tonight begins my offensive attack.*

I showered, doused Len's Tabu on my hair and neck, then donned my nurse's aide uniform, as a matador would his cape. I pulled on separate layers of clothing to face the charging bull. A swipe of mascara to bring out my blue-green eyes behind my aviator-style Gloria Steinem glasses, a touch of gloss to enhance my narrow lips, and a blue barrette to pull back my out-of-control, wavy dishwater-blonde hair. I was outfitted to enter the arena in full gear, my body the red cape.

After I'd punched the timecard near the staff lounge, I glanced around. No Rick.

In the hallway, ninety-six-year-old John-John, who goosed the female aides with his cane as they walked by, grinned and attempted to shove his cane up the crack of my butt. I eluded him and wagged a finger.

Wild, raucous laughter filled the cafeteria when I walked inside the open doors. Mae, one of the livelier patients, crooked a finger, motioning to me. I walked over. She held up a fruit cocktail cup they served as an appetizer. "What am I going to do with this?" She pointed to the top of the cup. "No cherry."

"Oh, Mae, sorry, I'll get you a cherry."

"What am I going to do with a cherry at my age?" Mae made a circle with her left index finger and thumb. She placed her right index finger through the hole. The ladies erupted into high-pitched laughter, slapping the table. Mae turned her head upward and smiled. She'd forgotten her dentures again.

"Young lady, don't tell me you don't know where your cherry is? Didn't your mama teach you anything? It's your hymen, darling. If no man popped your cherry, you're still a virgin. Which is something I ain't been since I was a fifteen-year-old bride!"

Heat rose from my neck as red blotches of embarrassment spread. It seemed even the nursing home residents knew I was a frustrated virgin.

"Oh my, from that blushing I'm guessing you're a virgin. At your age?" Mae shouted, "Somebody get this girl a man pronto!"

I smiled and waved as if in on the joke. How could she know? Did everyone?

After cleaning up, I walked toward the whirlpool room. I heard angry shouting. I recognized Dr. Marie. Her voice rose to a screech. Her daughter rarely visited, but I remembered her telling me that her mother had been the first female mathematics professor at Cornell University in an era when few women even attended college.

Opening the door, I saw Marie's wet hair shaking like Medusa's snakes. I could hear her refusals to be washed. Whoever was bathing her needed help.

I ran inside, my heart racing. Near the tub I could see the target of my plan—Rick. He was struggling to drape a wet towel around Marie. I snapped up a clean towel from the shelves and threw it to him. He grabbed it, rewarding me with a sweet smile showing under his curly mustache.

Marie screamed. I came close to her, lightly touching her face, forcing her to stare directly at me. She stopped moving and looked into my eyes. The gesture created instant calm.

Together we dressed Marie and put her to bed. She collapsed, spent and compliant. "Thank you," she said, her voice calm. "You're a good daughter."

Rick glanced in my direction, and I thought, *Aha, the night may not be in vain. It's time to implement my plan.*

We returned to the whirlpool room to clean up. Once inside the door, I grabbed Rick by the shirt. Scenes in romance magazines filled my fevered brain. I pulled him into the seclusion of a darkened shower stall and began kissing him madly. He jumped back for a moment, startled, then returned my enthusiasm with a hard kiss, our tongues intertwined.

A moment later, he pulled back and held me at arm's length. "Whoa, slow down, girl. Not here. I need the job."

A rush of cold air hit my sweaty skin. "What do you mean?"

"I have a kid and bills to pay."

"I understand, I think, but does that mean you don't want to do it with me?"

"Oh God." He moaned. "I want to do it with you. Bad. Just not here, baby."

He leaned over the doorway. His crinkly smile illuminated his face. Green eyes captivated. His direct gaze warmed me in some incomprehensible way. *Well*, I thought, *I may still be in the running. Why not hit restart?* But if not here, where? My plan could not possibly be put into action at his house if his kid was visiting. Not cool, as Len would say.

Where then to advance my conquest? The dorm had strict rules. No men above the lobby. The front desk was watched over by a timid receptionist on the weekends. I thought he might be able to get past her, since she would be late to her post and school had not officially started.

On Saturday, I was alone. Len was busy with one of her lovers; it didn't matter which one since I was always confusing them anyway. Bottom line, she would not be back until classes began on Monday. I saw no evidence that either the receptionist or the dorm's by-the-book housemother had returned to work yet.

I took my chance and had asked Rick at work, "How about meeting at my place tomorrow morning to finish what we started?" His eyes had widened. He nodded once for yes but seemed hesitant. Before he could change his mind, I gave him directions and strict instructions on where to park, which door to open, and how to get past the lobby and upstairs to my dorm room without being seen. I made him repeat the steps several times.

At eight o'clock on the designated morning, Rick sat on the bumpy ledge of my single bed, door locked, his clothes already cast off, ready for action. The room's temperature measured well above ninety degrees. There was no fan or air conditioner, and the sweat above my upper lip dripped salt into my mouth as we began to kiss.

I wasn't sure what the protocol or steps were. I had received the bulk of my sex education from *True Romance* magazines, which featured way too much light kissing and very little actual physicality, other than phrases like "his member entered her core."

I decided to take an experimental approach. I got into the groove and stripped down as well. Naked, on the bed, I sat waiting as if it were a homework assignment.

A few sloshy kisses, a finger prod that made me jump as fingernails scraped along sensitive tissue, and the performance seemed to be underway.

Rick huffed and puffed like the wicked old wolf trying to enter the brick building. My room on the fourth floor aligned with the morning sun beating onto the lumpy bed. Rick's sweat poured over my neck as he kissed me. His fingers attempted to pry open the doors of my stubbornly closed "core." He was gasping hard. His "member" seemed pert and ready.

"What the hell."

He seemed exasperated and anxious, while I remained calm, observant, almost like a researcher taking mental notes on the possible outcome. He continued to mumble and struggle with entry. I sat still, watchful. It felt as if I were playing the ingenue role in some oddly distant movie with no plot, resolution, or eroticism.

Rick's amorous "key" seemed to be having trouble unlocking the "door" to my virginity. My cherry remained untouched. Mae would be disappointed, I thought. I gazed down at his efforts, and then it hit me.

"I'm a virgin," I confessed. "Maybe that's the problem?"

"Jesus, Sue, why in the hell didn't you tell me before? A problem? You think?"

He sighed, then with renewed concentration focused on entering the confined space between my legs.

For some reason, watching his obsession with getting it in and my body's response of "Good luck, buddy" struck me as obscenely funny. I began to laugh. No giggling in a girly manner but laughing outright with my whole body. Bursts of absurd guffaws erupted from deep within.

It suddenly struck me as odd animal behavior, something people put way too much emphasis on in poems and novels.

The laughing loosened me up enough so that Rick was able to slip-slide inside in one motion. The whole he-bang piece of his masculinity moved in and out a few times. He seemed distracted, in another world. His eyes shut. I watched him intensely, as if taking notes for a class exam. After a few grunts and groans on his part, my laughing subsided. In a few more moments, it was over.

"Is that it?" I whispered.

"Sorry, yeah." He jumped up and pulled on his pants and wiped his wet armpits with his T-shirt before throwing it on over his head. He slipped on flip-flops and began to walk to the door. He stopped for a moment and returned to my position on the bed, bent over, kissed me on the forehead, and said, "You were good, kid. See you at work."

"Yeah, I guess." I tried not to sound too disappointed. I stood up in a hurry, almost knocking over my nightstand. "Before you leave, let me check the hallway."

I stuck my head out, still naked, and could see no one. He opened the door and began running down the stairwell; the slapping of his flip-flops pounded each step as if he wanted to leap out of the building in a single bound. The noise echoed.

As the sound faded, a door flung open at the end of the hall. A tall female student turned to watch Rick flee down the stairs. Her head snapped back quickly to look at me. Her thin nose pointed down at my right breast flung over the doorframe.

Her face scrunched as if she had smelled the distinct odor of dead skunk. She pointed behind her at the tail end of Rick as he fled. She shook her head violently. "Disgusting." She slammed her door shut with dramatic flair. My gut clenched, not knowing if she would report this instance of my devirginization.

I dressed to take a walk. I needed to think, to stay calm and concentrate on what had just happened. The act seemed rather boring and prosaic. How had this inspired centuries of poetry, lyrics, love songs, and stories? After circling the dorm walkway and outer campus, I returned, thinking, *All's well that maybe ended well.*

When I entered the dorm, the housemother, receptionist, and tall tattletale were all standing in a line in front of the lobby. Expecting a lecture on the loose morals that led to sinful destruction, I walked inside warily. The housemother wore a shapeless muumuu to cover her lack of curves. A few pink foam curlers were still pulling at her black-gray hair.

"Did you or did you not have a boy in your room, young lady?" she asked.

I debated whether a once-married thirty-two-year-old man with a kid qualified as a "boy," but I could see from her face that she would not be amused if I pointed that out.

"We were studying." The lie seemed lame even to me. A

red rash of deception spread over my cheeks. My ears burned.

"She's lying." The tattletale hovered close to the housemother. "School hasn't even started yet."

The receptionist, who normally smiled a warm hello and gave me my room keys when I forgot them, now stared down at her bare feet as if checking each lilac-painted toenail. Evidently, she'd been napping in the back room when Rick arrived and was in trouble for dereliction of duty.

"You have twenty-four hours to get your things and vacate this dorm," the housemother said as she whipped her muumuu around her legs, while the tall tattletale grinned joyfully and followed behind her down the hallway.

The receptionist waited until they were out of earshot. She shook her head, her eyes sad. "I didn't know you were that kind of girl, Sue."

I didn't have time to retort. Twenty-four hours? Was she kidding? I ran upstairs to get dimes and quarters to use the hallway pay phone. I called the number Rick gave me. No answer. I left a message at the nursing home instead. He had to help me get out of this mess. We were in this together, right? The semester would start soon, and I had no place to go. I began packing my sparse belongings.

Rick called the dorm phone. I explained the situation, and the gentleman in him seemed to kick in.

"I'll find something and call you back."

Within two hours, he had secured an apartment in Syracuse's downtown inner city. His resourcefulness led me to amend my belief in his intelligence. He came back to my dorm late in the evening to place the few possessions I owned into his broken-down Thunderbird.

He pulled up to the curb of an alley behind a large brick

apartment building. The broken glass window eyes peered down menacingly at us. Men were laughing and swearing at each other in the alley. Women screamed for their kids to come to dinner. The whole place smelled like rotting garbage, cooked garlic, and stinky fungus-filled sneakers. I gagged.

Syracuse's nickname was "dog shit city" for a reason in the 1970s. This area of the city was littered with feral bone-thin animals—cats, dogs, rats. Syracuse's location, sitting within a valley surrounded by hills drenched year-round in a drizzle of seasonal downpours and snowmelt, caused sewage drains and neighborhood trash to fall to the hub of this downtown street. Rents were low, and the buildings were occupied with transient beings, such as me.

We walked up to the second floor. He had brought a few articles of clothing in an old, ripped canvas backpack. He slipped an old-fashioned skeleton key the super had given him into the lock. The door opened into a tiny studio apartment. The kitchen held a half-size refrigerator with one missing hinge, a bacon-grease-laden stovetop, and radiators covered in inches of dust and spidery mildew. The lone piece of furniture, a stained and ripped mattress on the floor, had rat droppings lining the seam's crevices. Although I had been raised in a small house with seven people, I was not prepared to think of this level of squalor as home.

"All I could find at the last minute," he said as if he had read my mind. He pulled a few towels from his bag for sheets, rolled up his jeans for a pillow, and lay down, exhausted. "I'd take you to my place, but it's too far from the city for you to get to school." He looked at me for the first time since he'd picked me up. "It's not an option."

He was right. I was running out of options. School was the

last thing on my mind that night. We lay together, unspeaking. The silence only intensified as sirens screeched in the street. Flashes of neon lit the curtainless room. Gunshots rang out in rapid fire as the bars closed. A woman's sudden scream made my heart pound. Then she began squealing in laughter.

For the first time in my life, I was voiceless. Out of shared fear and wanting some intimacy to cushion the night's blows, he made love to me, in a slow, easy, but what seemed to me joyless manner. I didn't stop him. I simply wanted a body to keep me safe from harm.

I asked myself, What had I done to deserve this punishment? Was it because I carelessly disobeyed, broke the rules? How did a decision made in a whirlpool room lead me to this rathole with a man I barely knew?

A seeping terror filled me. I began to cough. The coughing wouldn't stop. I tossed and lay awake most of the night while the sounds of errant gunshots shattered my nerves.

When I arose in a half stupor, Rick was already dressed to leave. My body, drenched in sweat, felt chilled. My coughing increased with every intake of fetid air. I felt something give way. I desperately attempted to sit up and hold back the feeling of illness filling my lungs.

"I've got to go to work," he said. "I shouldn't have stayed."

Barely able to move, I only nodded. "When will you be back?"

"I won't. I paid two days' rent to help you." He wouldn't look at me. "I meant to tell you. I'm going back home to my wife tonight." He picked up his bag, hand on the doorknob. "You're too young to understand why."

I thought, *Understand what? That he has a wife, as in he's still married? Really? What happened to being divorced? What else did I not know in my quest to lose my virginity?*

My coughing and nausea increased. The only money I had was from my scholarship and work-study that would not begin for another week.

"What about me?" I could barely speak. My throat ached. I shuddered despite a fevered heat washing over me. I knew no answer would be coming from Rick, the nice but not-so-smart guy who had a wife and kid. He opened the door and paused, hand on handle.

"You'll be okay." I could see his broad shoulders sink a bit. "You're a fighter, Sue. You can take care of yourself."

He left through the warped rickety door, shutting it quietly as if exiting a morgue. I sat in the towel-covered bed with my rolled jeans as a pillow and realized with utmost clarity that I would never hear from him again. I was no longer a frustrated virgin. I was, instead, an unduly punished penniless slut praying for redemption from the possible increasing difficulties that lay ahead. Deep down, a part of me knew I would find a way. Rick was right. I was a fighter.

I pulled my clothes over my drenched, sweaty body, then picked up my small bag, my violin, and my electric typewriter and plopped it all in the hallway. I turned, quietly shutting the door on my own innocence as I moved into the unknowable future, where I realized the instinct to survive resided only in the present.

10

Resurrection

That moment of bad decision-making in my dorm room kept returning to me. Had I purposely put myself at risk? I knew, in some way, no man would be homeless due to losing his virginity. Yet this one decision ran like storm rain growing into a destructive torrential waterfall of despair. I had believed that sexual knowledge would give me some magical power; instead I was paralyzed by self-doubt.

A band of shame squeezed tight around my chest. Coughing and weak, luggage in one hand, violin case strap slung over my back like some wayward rock guitarist after an overnight binge, I exited the apartment that next morning.

I staggered down the stairs, pockets empty, the violin case banging on every step. If I could only withdraw some money from the bank, a small cash savings from the nursing home job, I could catch a Greyhound bus to where my family had moved.

Another problem arose when I realized that no one in my family had bothered to send me an exact address. I knew only that the town of Canandaigua sat at the edge of the pinky digit of the Finger Lakes region. I remembered from my mother's last call that they had a "duplex close to downtown." No phone number given. I heard my mother's voice on the call: "You're busy. I'll send a card when we're settled. Besides, no one cares where we are anyway." *Well, Mom,* I thought wearily, *I care.*

Every cough brought shock waves of pain. I barely managed to get down the stairs, gripping the handrail and slowly walking step by step as my violin case bumped along the metal railing. I dropped my luggage and watched it fall over the last few steps, hit bottom, and split open.

A weariness possessed me. My bones jelled as if my entire inner structure was disintegrating. I repositioned my few possessions by shoving them back inside the small luggage case and braced myself to walk toward the local bank.

Each slow, careful step enabled me to catch my breath. I pulled my headscarf off to wipe away the sweat pouring down my forehead despite the gray skies. I calculated what it would cost to buy a sandwich and bus ticket. I knew I'd be arriving late at night with no idea of my family's address. All I craved was sanctuary.

I struggled with the bank's heavy glass door until a manager wearing a steely gray three-piece suit came to my rescue. I felt feverish and disheveled in baggy camouflage army pants, a ballerina-pink T-shirt, a torn and dirty gray jacket. He stepped back to give me a wide berth.

"May I help you?" His eyebrows scrunched together in a scowl.

"I need to get my money out." I plopped down in the nearest chair.

He began tapping his fingers in contemplation. "One moment."

He walked to a desk in the cavernous room's far corner and reached for what looked like a large phone book bound with

wire hanging from a hook on the edge of the counter. He returned and sat behind the desk, pushing his chair back to create
more distance between us.

"Name?" he asked.

"Yours or mine?"

He ignored me. I gave him my full name, date of birth, and
the amount I thought was in the account. I was able to pull a
torn deposit slip from my wallet showing the number. I had
opened the account recently for emergencies. As I attempted to
control another series of coughs, more beads of sweat slipped
down my chest, pooling inside my bra.

"I need about $20, I think, maybe more."

"Well, young lady, you have two problems." He lifted a finger
and used his opposite index finger to enumerate. "Number one,
your funds have not yet been processed into the accounting
system. We told you it would take a minimum of twenty-one
business days. Number two, you don't have enough money in-
vested to withdraw funds at this time from this specific type of
account."

I pulled off my bandanna and shot a big wad of snot into it.
He backed away another few inches. I cleared my throat. "It's my
money, yes?" He stared at my oozing handkerchief. "I have almost
$100 in that account. I'm only asking for some of it."

"Fund withdrawal for that account cannot be processed.
You'd essentially be borrowing your money with an interest fee
higher than the money in the account."

I didn't have the energy to argue with his twisted logic. In
reflection, I saw myself only a few days ago in a nice dorm room
with an absent roommate near the college where I'd once been
safe and virginal. Now I was deflowered, homeless, and broke. I
had nowhere to sleep and no way to get to my parents or to see

a doctor. From having witnessed my mother's walking pneumonia and my own illness when I was a kid, I knew I could rapidly deteriorate. I wouldn't make it past one night on the streets.

Tears began to gush in torrents. The sobbing made me take deep breaths that only launched another round of violent coughing. My whole body shuddered with both heat and chills. "The money is to take a bus home." I dropped my hand, and the violin case fell with a bang to the floor, strings resonating in its case.

He looked me up and down. "You need to leave right now, young lady, or I'll call the police." He grabbed the phone.

"Good," I said, "at least I'd have a bed and dinner tonight." I wiped my face, replacing fear with outrage, my fallback reaction to danger. "It's my freaking account. I earned that money for emergencies. This is an emergency."

He walked backward, hitting the desk of a woman next to him dressed in a satin blue blouse with a long bow tie and a gray swing skirt. The nameplate on her desk read JACKIE.

"Oh, for heaven's sake, Peter," said Jackie, "give her the frigging money."

"No way." He shook his head. "It's the principle of the thing. She needs to learn how to control her behavior and her funds."

"This is ridiculous." Jackie stood up and moved toward me. "Here, darling." She pulled out her purse and took a crisp twenty-dollar bill out and handed it to me. "You go on and catch that bus before you fall over and hurt yourself."

"Thank you," I whispered. I gathered my stuff, fearing if I stayed too long the manager would call the cops on me.

"Never mind about him. He's just a cranky old man. God knows some men don't make any cents," she said and drew air quotes around the last word, "and they sure as shit won't give a woman any dollars." She laughed at her own finance pun. I smiled as widely as I could muster in abject gratitude. "Now go shoosh, girl. The bus station is right down the street a bit."

I bought the ticket, with enough left over for a sandwich and Coke. Once on the bus, I promptly plopped into the seat behind the driver, slurped down the Coke, packed the food away, and did not wake up until midnight, when the driver touched my shoulder.

"End of the line, miss. This is your stop." Before he shut the doors, he winked and smiled kindly. "Good luck, young lady."

I wandered out of the empty bus station and down the quiet street. The murmurs of human voices coming from a bar across the street drew me. When I pushed open the screen door and walked inside, silence reigned. Everyone had stopped chatting to stare at me.

"I'm sorry to interrupt," I said, apologizing for what I did not know, "but I think my parents are new folks in town. I don't know where they live." My voice began to break. I knew I probably looked like a comic book orphan with my tattered dirty clothes and torn backpack. I felt ridiculous and wondered if I sounded like a lost little girl pleading, *Please help me find my mommy?*

The barkeep, an older man, wore a torn Grateful Dead T-shirt covered with beer stains. A long gray ponytail swished along his back. He held a dirty dishcloth over his shoulder. "Well, let me think," he said.

The middle-aged waitress, with a Dolly Parton wig out of proportion to her size, came over. "Well, now, young lady, just happens that I know a new family with three kids moved into Easton Street this week. My kids saw them a few days ago. They got all excited is how I know." She pointed out the door. "Just go down one block, take a left and then a quick right under the bridge. It's the green house. You can't miss it."

"Thank you. That's amazing." Relief washed through my entire being.

"Girl, not a lot of new happens in this town without everybody noticing." She turned back to the men leaning half against the bar. "Ain't that right, fellas?" A few looked up from their beers and answered with slow nods.

I walked down the street, first left, then right, and as if by a miracle, I dropped my luggage at the doorstep of my missing-in-action parents' forest-green duplex.

My mother answered my incessant knocking. Her eyebrows rose when she saw me. The glass of beer in her hand shook a bit. She looked both surprised and somewhat annoyed.

"What's going on? What happened?" She set the glass on the coffee table. "What are you doing here so late?" She rubbed the worry lines in her forehead. "I thought school started." Before I could answer, she added, "I just mailed a note to the dorm with our new address. How did you get it already?"

Instead of explaining my dismissal from the dorm due to my deflowering and my homelessness, I simply said, "I'm sick."

She picked up my bags. "Come in. You can sleep on the sofa." I could smell her half-burned cigarette and see two empty beer bottles sitting on the lampstand next to the glowing black-and-white TV screen, the sound down low. Once I moved within the flickering lights of the TV, I could see her eyes widen in alarm.

She shook her head, holding tight to the cigarette to keep the ashes from falling to the rug. "What happened?"

I had rarely ever seen my mother in a state of alarm. She kept her emotions, even upon the death of family members, under control. Her response increased my anxiety. How could I explain my present circumstances brought on by my own choices?

"Long story." I was too fatigued to continue. "Bottom line, I have no place to live. I'm sick. I just need a place to sleep for a few days."

She pulled my boots off, put my feet on the sofa, and laid a worn gray flannel blanket over my shoulders, tucking me in as one would swaddle an infant. In an odd way, it felt too intimate a movement for my untouching mother to make. I knew then that I must appear far sicker than I imagined.

She returned from the kitchen with hot mint tea and a bottle of Tylenol. My sisters and brother came down the stairs in their pajamas. "You're here!" my youngest sister, Julie, exclaimed as she threw herself over me for a hug. She was barely seven years old.

My sister Sharon, a senior in high school, observed dryly, "Wow, you look like shit."

My brother, now a teenager, simply nodded and said, "Hey."

I pushed Julie away, not wanting to give her my germs. I turned into the sofa's overstuffed arm as another coughing fit began.

I have few memories of the rest of that night and the following days. I remember waking up four days later in my sisters' upstairs bedroom. Evidently, the town doctor prescribed morphine to force me to sleep and heal. I have only vague, dreamy recollections of eating, shuffling to the bathroom, and then returning to the lumpy single bed for more glorious sleep, interrupted only by soup.

At the end of the week, I was able to stand. I gave my parents a condensed version of the eviction story, handily leaving out my dedicated plan to lose my virginity as the reason. My mother listened, said nothing, and turned her head as a clever dog might, wondering what was missing. She pushed away a few flying hairs from under my bandanna and held my shoulders.

"You'll be fine. You're like your grandmother. A fighter."

No hug. No kiss. But, instead, a confident smile that returned a belief in myself that I desperately needed.

I had a new college counselor who believed in educational opportunities for working-class kids like me. I became one of her causes. I had called to warn her of my homeless circumstance and my desire to find a place to study. I did not get into the details of my sexual misdeed. Nor tell her how this had happened due to misplaced trust in a married man.

She made a few calls and kindly set me up in a house above the Golden Pet Cemetery close to campus. To sell the owner, she told him that I had a biology background, had experience in dissection, and needed a job. Free labor for them. Free room for me.

I shared the house with a few other students as well as the remains of beloved dead cats, dogs, birds, hamsters, and gerbils. The forever smell of formaldehyde permeated the building and my skin again. I was back to square one—drenched in *eau de death*. After my bungled first sexual experience, though, I was ready to pull away from the dating scene entirely. This time, I didn't mind the off-putting smell. It kept me safe.

The apartment held a suite of rooms with a shared kitchenette and open space with only a coffee table, a gray-green shag rug covering the wood floor, and a broken reclining chair stuck in the reclined position.

Pet preservation took place directly under the living room. The smells associated with freshman year biology class returned like an old friend, embracing me in memories of scientific curiosity. The odor of destroyed corpses bore my fate, my resurrection. The landlord put me to work immediately digging miniature holes for canary and parrot graves. In this manner, the first semester passed quietly as I studied during the day and prepared animals for burial at night for the mourning pet owners who would dutifully arrive every weekend to attend a short ceremony. I would watch daily from my lab bench as visitors' heartfelt tears fell to the small mounds of soil, absorbing all sorrow.

11

Predator-Prey

To supplement my faltering income, I had signed up as an art class model. The pay seemed incredible back then. Less than twenty minutes of posing paid for an entire week of meals. I couldn't pass it up. Problems arose though. I had to stay still for up to ten minutes at a time, something adverse to my energetic physical nature. And I had to pose nude. My slight increase in knowledge of the sexual world; my fascination with biology, anatomy, and physiology; and my need to eat all made it an easy choice.

Luckily, with a female professor present I felt a degree of safety. She wore gauzy flowing gowns through which you could see her nipples. (No bra.) Her long braided hair had frizzy henna-tinted grayish-red strands that curled along her forehead. She had a way of moving as if in a fog that gave her the air of a lost fairy godmother. I sat half-draped on clean sheets that smelled like clover.

One day she asked me if I knew of another woman who might pose nude. I automatically thought of Len, my former roommate. That night when I pitched the idea, Len said, "Do what I do every night *and* get paid for it? I'm in."

We modeled together, trying not to laugh at the fact that we now earned more money than we ever had and all for the sake of art. The professor posed Len on all fours. Len glanced up at me and winked. "We are on a new journey of sisterhood. Who knows where this will lead?"

"Hush, please," the professor said as her gauzy scarf fell over both of us. The dark green beaded tassels tickled our chilled bodies. She had me lean over Len, my pendulous breasts grazing her back with my arms around her tiny waist.

We stayed as still as we could, stifling giggles. "This will make us popular," Len whispered.

"Or at least notoriously labeled bad girls," I whispered back.

My mind wandered. I dreamed of a luscious spaghetti dinner complete with freshly baked bread and tiramisu from the cash earned from this one pose.

After our shift, we eyed the sketches. The renderings seemed more like the exquisite black-and-white landscapes of Ansel Adams, with undulating flesh falling like human hills into the canyons and crevices of each other. My fear that we had unwittingly posed for soft porn evaporated. This was art.

The following day, the professor selected a poster-size photo of me with my head lifted and gazing upward, elbows rising in a V. A discreet cover of gauzy fabric hid my identity. Len remained unseen. I could not imagine who had taken the photo among the many in the class, but the professor wanted me to own it. She rolled the precious photo into a tube. I knew I would carry this photo with me for years as a reminder of a moment's rebellion. I had posed without scorn or shame, and I had the poster to prove it.

A few days after our session, Doug, a young man in the class who had drawn my body as an ink-and-pen abstraction with no resemblance to the real me, asked to borrow a textbook I had left in my apartment. I didn't think to question how he knew that I lived directly behind the art building. Tall and good-looking behind frameless glasses, he seemed to possess an artistic and sensitive demeanor.

We walked back to fetch the book between classes. I rummaged around and dug up the *Anatomy of Art* book for him. He lingered in the living room, sniffing the scent emitting from the basement embalming room, and scrunched up his nose. Although the clock struck four, the sun started to fade from the west-facing window. Only a dim glow lit the darkening room.

Since my roommates were eating dinner in the cafeteria that night, I had decided as a friendly gesture to offer Doug some instant coffee with creamer, both pilfered from the college shop. He seemed genuinely relieved.

I sat on the rug and crossed my legs, draping my wide skirt between my legs. He sat next to me as we thumbed through the anatomy book. He removed his glasses to focus on the overlays of female nudes rendered in pen and ink.

"Fascinating artwork," I offered. "The nudes capture the beauty of our animal bodies."

"Yeah." He breathed heavily. "It turns me on. Like that photo of you nude. You posed so easily, as if it meant nothing to you, as if it were all normal."

I stayed silent, not knowing how to respond. I glanced at the corner where the poster roll tube leaned against the closet. I wondered if he thought my posing nude suggested loose morals.

His words broke the giggling freedom I had earlier felt with Len that morning in the chilly art room. A cold fear replaced the joy.

Nothing is going to happen, I told myself. *Anyone could walk in.*

It's still daytime. I glanced at the sun peeking through the blinds. *Bad things, like abandonment, happen only at night*, I told myself.

Something in me said, *Get up, say goodbye, send him on his merry way with the textbook in his sweaty hands.*

But before I could get off the floor, he grabbed both my arms and threw me down on the floor in one swift motion, as if he had already measured the distance and practiced the move— hunter to prey. The back of my head hit the floor, stunning me. I tried to turn, but he pinned my shoulders down flat to the floor.

"What're you doing?" I tried to clear my head and twist my body but failed. "Get off me."

"Why? You let me in when nobody's here. You gave me this sexy book. Everybody knows what kind of girl poses nude. You were even laughing, enjoying it. I saw you. Stop being such a cocktease."

"What are you talking about?" I managed to say before his hand covered my lips. The calluses on his palm scraped the corners of my mouth. I tried to bite his hand. He twisted my neck as if with one more struggle he could snap it in two. I was stunned, motionless, confused.

Then survival kicked in. I wanted desperately to live. I relaxed my body into frozen passivity. I recalled once seeing how a fox's teeth gripped tight near a rabbit's jugular vein. The rabbit, by simply freezing in place, had been released and survived that cold morning years ago. Would I? Tears formed. I forced myself to remain still. I closed my wet eyes and concentrated only on breathing through my half-covered nose.

"You want this, and you know it. Don't play coy. Why else would you bring me here?" He opened his palm, waiting for me to respond.

Air rushed into my lungs; I was unable to fight my attacker

with anything but words. *Words*, I thought, *might reach his reasoning brain.* Words, I hoped, could reveal him as the artistic and basically kind man I thought him to be.

"Please take the textbook," I gasped.

He leaned in closer, holding my arms with one hand as he pulled down his pants. "Move and it'll be much worse for you."

I saw from the corner of my eye his twisted smile and unblinking stare. I could smell and feel his salty sweat fall on my exposed neck. My gut twisted. I thought I was going to be ill. His approach felt practiced, a series of movements performed in the past. How many times had he used this trick? How many others had he raped?

My exposed shoulders in the summer dress began to shake in cold convulsions. My brain could not register. I shut down.

He would win this battle. If I stayed disengaged, I might be able to protect myself. I repeated an internal mantra, "Stay calm. Freeze. Live."

My forced passivity, so unlike my true nature, grew to a plea. "Please," my voice barely above a whisper, "please don't hurt me. Please let me go. I won't tell anyone."

"Of course you won't. Who would you tell? No one would believe you against me. You looked straight at me when you were on top of that naked girl. You came on to me. Everyone in class saw that."

In desperation at what he might be harboring within his sex-fueled, addled brain, I said the most realistic, unromantic, and true thing I could think. "I'm having my period."

"No problem." In seconds, he yanked up my dress, tore off my panties. He pulled out my blood-drenched tampon and threw it across the room. It hit with a thwack against the opposite wall.

I watched the blood-streaked clumps of mucus run down in

uneven, slow patterns from wall to floor.

I struggled. The full weight of his knees pushed my now-spread thighs into the itchy dark green shag rug. He held my hands pinned over my head. A sideways glance shot from his fevered eyes. He looked like some manic god destined to destroy. I knew if I looked too directly at him, he'd see it as a threat. He had extra weight and muscle.

My mind crashed. A catatonic stupor overtook my nervous system. I felt nothing. I concentrated on breathing. Waiting. Praying nothing more violent would befall me in my frozen state.

He shoved himself inside me with one lunge. My body clenched. No movement. No reaction. I played the rabbit waiting for the fox to tire and be gone, looking for better prey. Within a minute that seemed eternal, he got up, zipped up his pants, and ran out the door.

I stayed unmoving, stunned on the floor as darkness descended.

Time passed in abject slowness. Day slipped into twilight. Glued to the rug, blood trickling down my thigh. Coldness hit the room.

How late was it? I sat upright, picked up my clothes, and cleaned up the bloody remains from the tampon on the wall and floor. My attempts to scrub the rug free of the blood seemed useless. I pulled the lone chair over the dark spot as if a broken piece of furniture could erase the memory.

Memories, both good and bad, I told myself, *pass. It's over. Forget about it.*

Being kicked out of the dorm, evicted from an apartment, and assaulted in a safe zone in a pet cemetery, I faulted only myself. My desire to live freely, to experience the sensual, held unknown dangers. Guilt swirled through my gut. Perhaps in some way I *had* led him on as he said. What defense could I utter if someone asked? Reporting assault at the college would most likely terminate my education, something I valued more than this momentary painful experience.

I took a hot shower using soft slivers of Ivory soap to wash every crevice clean. I stayed in bed that evening. The next few days blurred. Could I explain to my parents, to a college counselor, to classmates, to myself? The only call I made was to Len. She never answered. I prayed she stayed safe in the arms of either her boyfriend or her married lover.

One sunset slipped into another, plunging me into a soul's darkness. After a few days, both hunger and boredom reached my empty gut. I got up, turned on all the lights, ran a cold shower at full blast as I cried in a heap on the tile floor. Rivulets of tears, chilled like a spring rain that fell to the animal burial plots, broke my stupor.

I began a cutthroat self-interrogation. Did I cause him to rape me by posing nude? Did my playing femme fatale by staring at him unknowingly hold untoward consequences? Did I deserve this treatment in some way by inviting a man alone, someone I barely knew, into the suite? I knew reporting it to the college would only lead to more questions about my motivations. It would be one student's word against the other with the evidence of me posing nude and alluring my attacker.

A few days later, my roommates began to wonder why I, normally so chatty, had turned morose and bone-weary. I overheard them whisper what to do. On day three I shrugged when they asked me what had happened. "Bad period." One handed me a hot water bottle and aspirin and went about her business.

On that third night, a death-shrouded sleep ensued. I barely moved. It felt as if cement encased my soul. When I woke up the next day, a renewed sense of energy emerged. In a flip-flop, after one good night's sleep, I became the predator ready for revenge.

Something clicked. I turned from victim to avenger. *Let it go*, I told myself, but with each passing hour, my shame lessened while rage and anger grew. I marched over to the campus art class where my rapist sat contentedly painting.

I grabbed his easel and flung it across the room.

"You fucked-up son-of-a-bitch rapist piece of shit!" I spoke loudly enough for the entire class to hear. "If you ever come near me or any other woman I know, I'm ripping off your balls and shoving them down your throat. Do you understand me?"

"Jesus, you're a crazy bitch." He attempted to laugh and looked around the room at the stunned faces for support. "Crazy bitch, right? She's lying. She's nuts. Who are you going to believe? Me or this slut?" He asked his questions as if he stood in some courtroom TV drama with the class full of students as his nodding jury.

I stepped closer. "Did you freaking hear *me*?" I yelled the last syllable directly in his ear and loud enough to be heard in a stadium.

He slumped, looked down at his desk, nodded, and returned to his notebook.

I left the room without a glance at the shocked students and frightened professor, slamming the door behind me with a force that shook the entire hallway. Pure anger filled me with an absolute strength I'd never thought I possessed. Never again would I allow a man to force me to have sex against my will. *This is my call. This is my life. This is my body. My decision. My choice.*

The very act of confronting the rapist publicly in his own art class empowered me. I transferred my self-hatred onto Doug, and to Rick, transforming fear to fury.

Men were not the only objects of my focused rage though. I also despised the housemother and her belief in a system of double standards where men were allowed to behave any way they wished, walking away unharmed, whereas I, a woman, needed to be punished for every sexual encounter, even those against my will. I believed I stood alone in my rage, and this aloneness gave me a force to defy the odds.

With steely determination, I set my sights on the future. Yes, I realized that the world was a dangerous place, but I had a plan. I would study. I would travel. I would dance. I would find my tribe. I would make my own joy, erasing memory and time.

I would never return to the innocent and ignorant tomboy of my youth. I packed to move to higher ground. Safety for a sexually evolved woman living on her own would never be guaranteed. Reversing roles seemed the only answer. With that realization, I turned the rabbit prey of my former self into that of the predator fox, unleashed to roam.

12

Witness

I reentered the shared living room suite, barely glancing at the faded bloodstains. Ever the pragmatist, I realized my first move would be to find a better job. Only then could I leave the suite with its nightmare memory and start anew.

I vaguely thought of earning a living as a journalist. Upon the advice of my counselor, I had applied to transfer from the community college to Syracuse University. After being offered the Newhouse School of Journalism scholarship, I moved the next semester into an apartment on the hill above the university campus with two other female students. Unfortunately, the scholarship did not pay for room and board, and I again found myself desperate for money.

The local ads listed a job opening at the *Syracuse Post-Standard* morning edition. The hiring assistant I met did not seem to care that my father had been blacklisted from this newspaper room only a few years earlier. All she wanted was a low-paid typist whose fingers could fly across the keyboard. Luckily, by the time I was eight years old, my blind grandmother had taught me to type. She voraciously wrote letters to global pen pals, some as far away as Australia and the Horn of Africa. I

Sue Camaione

would type dictated letters, reading back the text to correct errors.

I silently thanked her for this one important skill that allowed a young woman to survive in the 1970s—typing. I was a natural. I had years of experience, far above my peers. From years of typing her letters, punching each key separately with precision, I clocked in on the typing test at ninety-six words per minute with only one error. I got the job.

Every Friday to Sunday in the 5:00 p.m. to 1:00 a.m. slot, I dutifully typed reporters' copy and scanned sheets into the Photon machine for the early morning edition. I had no social life, but I knew the job title of copydesk assistant would look good on a résumé.

In the hyperactive newsroom, Associated Press wire reports spit out constant clicks from the machine. Reporters ran back and forth ripping paper ribbons that fell to a basket below. Interview questions shouted by local reporters into mouthpieces could be heard across the room. The frenetic pace intensified as the night shift wore on past midnight to hit the final deadline.

I sat at an electric typewriter near the far edge of a horseshoe-shaped editorial desk. The managing editor, a serious but rather good-looking middle-aged man who wore his power regally, sat amid worker-bee editors. He would casually throw blue marked-up copy into my inbox to type out the final story to be scanned. He never gave me so much as a sideways glance. Instead, he referred to me as "intern," and the only words directed at me were demands: "Intern, type this . . . Intern, scan this . . . Intern, where's the copy?" I answered in grunts, taking galley sheets and handing them back across his desk.

By the journalists, I was referred to as Cub. They would spend Saturday nights at the only restaurant open past midnight,

Eggspectacular. I would sometimes sit with reporters to soak up stories of how they hit the city streets racing to beat the police to the most recent crime scene. They spent most evenings in cop cars or following arrests, calling the mayor's office, and filing stories with the king of the newspaper copy desk, the managing editor.

Across from the managing editor sat his lead editor. Her flat brown hair was trapped in a tight mesh bun. Eyeglasses with thick black frames slipped along her thin nose. She remained steady, studious, focused, and, I couldn't help noticing, quite pregnant. It was difficult to tell how far along, as she rarely rose from her perch.

She terrified me with her piercing glances behind the severe glasses. Her glare seemed to say that if I so much as made one typo, her disapproval would cause dismissal from the coveted copy desk. A tut-tutting sound demonstrated what she thought of my stupidity whenever I erred. She would hand the marked copy back to the managing editor. He would glance at it and throw it my way with a flick of his wrist.

They worked well together, exchanging side glances whenever someone asked a silly question or handed in inferior work. I was in awe of their intellectual connection. Both held a disdain for those not as sharp or experienced. I hoped to learn from them. I wanted to impress them. I asked if I could write a few obituaries, and they agreed to "try me out."

Every Friday evening, around eight, a beautiful blonde woman, also very pregnant, would sweep through the doors holding a picnic basket of freshly baked bread for the editorial crew. She was the wife of the managing editor.

He would shift nervously in his seat upon seeing her and glance at the lead editor across from him with a slight tilt of his head in his wife's direction. In a shadow of a second, the lead editor would shake her head, mirroring his gesture, and then return to the copy in front of her, glasses slipping slightly, her nostrils flaring. I didn't think anything of it. The two of them had exchanged many shared private moments. The rest of us ignored them.

Nodding in gratitude to the wife, I wolfed down the fresh bread, delicious and still warm. Because my scholarship didn't cover food, I was always ravenous. Most nights, I combined ketchup packets in hot water with pepper and crushed saltine crackers—all stolen from the newspaper cafeteria—to create a makeshift tomato soup. The wife's homemade bread tasted heavenly. I never knew her name, as she was never introduced. Like some fairy naïf, she left as quickly as she had arrived in lithe steps despite her pregnant state. She would look one more time over her shoulder with a big hearty cover-girl smile. Her wheat-colored locks swayed down her small-boned back in undulating curls. Her husband waved her away as if swatting a pesky gnat.

One night, I had to hustle to make the last bus back home. It was getting late. The nightshift bell rang. I raced to gather my bag. I had rewritten the last obit numerous times to make it perfect, so I was running late. I glanced at the clock. 1:12 a.m. The only way to make the 1:18 a.m. bus would be to run out the back stairwell that opened in front of the bus stop. I ran full speed, clutching my bag.

I jerked open the handle. The door clanged into the metal rails. I jumped the stairs two at a time. As I turned the corner of the second floor, I almost slammed into the managing editor. He stood, holding the lead editor in full embrace, their arms wrapped tightly around each other.

I tried to break my downward fall. "Oh, shit." Not knowing

where to turn, not wanting to miss my bus, I slipped, then jumped over a rail onto the floor below them.

I could hear the lead editor behind me repeat, "'Oh, shit' is right."

Pens and pencils had dropped out of my bag and scattered down the stairwell. I had very little money. I was making $1.85 an hour. I couldn't afford to replace them. I stooped to pick one up that had fallen to the stairs below. That's when I saw the managing editor glaring at me. The three of us froze.

With that, I left the pens where they'd landed and jumped down the last few steps to the first floor like some crazed action hero. I slipped and fell, banging my knee against metal, but somehow managed to roll over and end up back on my feet. My dress caught on the edge of the railing post. From the bottom step, I grabbed the skirt and ripped the hem.

Once free, I ran as fast as I could out the door to the bus as it started to move forward. The bus driver saw me, shook his head, and braked. I was heaving great gulps of air as I dropped into the first seat behind the driver in the empty bus.

"Hey, sister girl," he asked, "are you okay?"

I breathed in again and finally got myself under control as the bus rolled down the dark street. "I'm okay now. Thanks for waiting."

He nodded and stared straight ahead, studying the contours of the broken pavement.

At my stop, before opening the door, he looked up and down the street. I was the only rider that night. "All's clear," he said. "Now, go home and go to bed." I nodded in gratitude. He knew these city streets better than I did, and I appreciated his fatherly concern.

Once back inside my apartment, I felt happy to be swaddled

in the confines of my narrow bed. I tried to calm my nerves. *Just freaking ignore what you witnessed*, I told myself. *Forget about it. Certainly, they'll want to forget it ever happened, right?* The more self-talk I engaged in, the more anxious and worried I became. The alarm clock ticked 2:01 a.m. I knew the reporters were still putting the last of the paper to print. I needed someone to talk some sense into me. I needed a mentor.

I shoved a few coins into the hallway phone slot and dialed the news desk. Howie, a reporter at least a decade older and much wiser than me, answered. In a rush, I told him the torrid tale and how freaked out I was about losing my job.

He laughed lightly. "Calm down, Cub," he said. "Let's meet with a few others at Eggspectacular for dinner tomorrow. We can discuss a strategy to help you stay in the den." As if anticipating my concern about paying for a meal, he added, "My treat."

The next day at work I averted my eyes from everyone, my attention focused solely on the keyboard. At break time, Howie motioned to me. His lanky-limbed body walked toward me, and he placed his hand on my back to usher me out the door. He had a light and casual touch. His smile lifted his bushy brown mustache that lightened my spirit. His hair shot out of his skull in a wild array of curls in what he fondly referred to as his Jewfro.

He waved to a few others to follow us to the restaurant. I wanted to enjoy the inclusion in this force of formidable reporters, but my nervousness increased with each step. Once seated, I left my omelet uneaten, and Howie asked me to repeat what I had witnessed the night before.

I finished and said, "I'm kind of worried that I walked in on a private moment between the only two people who could have me fired."

The table roared with laughter. Howie lifted both palms out

to the table. "I won that bet. Pay up, suckers!" The others threw five-dollar bills at him, an ungodly sum to me at that time. They were joking that he was "too jaded" and "an observer of dastardly deeds." My dreadful fears had unleashed a series of insider jokes I couldn't comprehend.

"What bet?" I asked timidly since I didn't want to seem too inexperienced.

"Well, Cub, I bet a few months ago that those two brainiacs were having an affair. Everyone else thought I was seeing things." He lifted a handful of bills. "So, now, omelets all around on me!"

They cheered and dug into another round. I still felt terrified of the consequences of what I had witnessed on the stairwell. I knew a terrible secret. I had eaten the pregnant wife's yummy bread. Then with sudden fearful clarity, I remembered that the paramour, too, was pregnant. My head felt light. Fear of losing the job overcame me. I started to cry right there in the restaurant in front of the very people whose respect I wanted to gain.

Howie stopped joking and put his fork down. He leaned over and asked, "What's wrong, Sue?"

It was the first time I had heard anyone at the newspaper other than the human resource manager use my name. I became distraught. "I'm going to get fired, and I really need this job. I have no money. My scholarship doesn't cover much."

"Yeah," he said, "that's good old Syracuse for you. Been there. Done that." He paused. "You're not going to get fired. You know something he wants to keep secret. You have all the power. You just have to give him a subtle reminder of that."

I had no idea how to use, in a subtle or even overt manner, what I'd witnessed. The managing editor had power over me. He was my boss. Not the other way around. The pursed lips on the lead editor's face had signaled she wanted me gone. For good.

Listening to Howie trying to reason with me, I realized he was the first man I might be able to trust. He had a gentle yet focused way about him. His ability to get people to answer questions by pointing out "subtly" that not answering would lead to bigger consequences was his strong suit.

"Besides," he said, "they'll probably ignore it ever happened or deny it. I doubt they would ever bring it up. You're fine. Let's eat and forget about it."

Nevertheless, each day that week, I wondered when I would be fired. How could I survive? Where would I go? Another move seemed premature. I was barely settled. A week passed, and I realized that Howie was probably right. They wanted to forget about it. I returned to my weekend job at the copy desk the following Friday. No one said a thing.

Saturday afternoon, though, as I was getting ready to take the bus to work, the phone rang. It was the deep male voice of the managing editor. He coughed lightly when I said hello before introducing himself. He had never called me before. *Stay calm*, I told myself.

"Sue, I know you work hard and are trying to do well at the copy desk, but after consultation with others, I must say that it appears you're not working out satisfactorily."

I was stunned. Others? What others? I tried to steady my breathing and sat on the floor with a heavy *ka-thunk*.

He cleared his throat. "You may be in over your head writing obits. You may not be doing enough research, and you're not taking a respectful tone." He waited a moment and added, "I'm afraid I'm going to have to let you go."

I stood up immediately. This was exactly what I thought would happen. Anger replaced fear. *How dare this man, this cheater, force me to go hungry? Who does he think he is? What did*

Howie coach me to say? Oh, yeah, let him know I know. Subtlety be damned.

I took a deep breath and said in one rush, "You're not going to fire me."

Complete silence ensued for a moment. "What do you mean?"

"You're not going to fire me," I repeated calmly, "and, furthermore, you're going to give me a raise."

He cleared his voice. "Why would I do that?"

My mind envisioned that moment on the stairwell as I ran for the bus. I needed this job. I could hear his breathing grow more labored. I inhaled to calm my nerves and hoped Howie was right. I held the upper hand.

"Because"—I paused—"I like to run out the back door to catch the last bus."

"I see." Silence for a few seconds, then *click*. The phone went dead.

I slammed the phone down and went straight to bed. I would be at work tomorrow whether that cheating ass liked it or not.

Late the next afternoon, I took my place at the copy desk's typewriter. The managing editor, without a word, came over and gently placed an envelope over my shoulder and onto my keyboard. He returned and sat back down on his copy desk throne surrounded by his adoring copy editor staff.

At the first break, I went into the ladies' room to open the letter. Expecting to see "Please tender your resignation," I found instead a letter on my promotion to junior copy editor and a note on the raise from $1.85 to $2.25 an hour starting that day.

I smiled. Howie had given me excellent advice. I owed him

for sure. I placed the note on the countertop to wash my hands, which was a mistake, when the librarian—a slight-boned, exceedingly thin woman who spent her days hunched over paperwork to fact-check the reporters' copy—glanced at the note. Her face turned bright red; purple veins in her scrawny neck bulged.

She moved her head toward the mirror, as if looking at me straight on would cause her to have a stroke. She pointed to the letter. "How in the hell did you ever get a raise? What did you do to get that raise? Tell me."

"Nothing," I whispered, afraid to enrage her further and certainly not wanting to explain.

"Christ. I make $2.20 an hour, and I've been slaving away at this place for almost a decade. Who in the hell gave you this raise? What did you do to deserve it?"

I turned to ensure no one else was in the bathroom. I glanced at the door, hoping to flee before her anger exploded further. "Nothing," I repeated.

"Bullshit." Her hands grabbed the letter, and she crumpled it up and threw it at me. "I know exactly why you got this raise."

I began to shake. I could feel sweat accumulating under my arms, staining my blouse. Had she observed the managing and lead editor mid-tryst too? Did she imagine I had some other role in this lowly soap opera playing out before both of us in the newspaper room?

"It's obvious." She paused only to inhale. "It's because you've got big boobs." She pointed at the offending orbs. Her accusatory finger aimed straight at my double-D breasts as if they could speak volumes of agreement with her.

I feigned embarrassment, looked her in the eye, and said with some relief at keeping this torrid secret while retaining my raise, "Yes, of course, you're right."

"I knew it!" She turned and huffed out of the bathroom, trailing paper towels behind her.

I had become first a witness to deception and then a victim of jealousy. I was learning much about adult life and human desire. I was grateful to Howie for the strategy session. I bent down under the sink to grab the promotion letter, smoothed it out, carefully folded it, and stuffed it into my pants pocket for safekeeping. Now, I only needed to thank my mentor.

13

Rocky Mountain High

I converted Howie's role from senior mentor to lover. Our hesitation to commit fully kept us both at an emotionally safe distance. In this way, the semester passed in a dishevelment of work, school, and unkempt beds. Between the newspaper desk and classes, I could barely keep up. My grades began to slip. The university sent a letter. Financial aid would be cut by a third due to competition with other students on their wait list with higher grade point averages.

Sleep eluded me. I could no longer concentrate on lectures. An imperceptible restless need to move, to leave, to explore overtook me.

Saviors and knights in shining armor daydreams faded into the void of old fantasies. I was grateful for Howie's tutelage as a reporter. Although I wasn't particularly attracted to him physically, I fell into his warm, secure embrace. This contradiction gave me the awful sensation that I could use a man who cared about me simply to stay safe and stable.

Yet a constant ache to travel, to move on, to witness the world, to view more vistas grew. Travel became my obsession. In movement, I could conquer fear, find lovers to charm, replace nightmares with unknown fantasies in faraway places. The cold, dreary, smoky sky that shrouded Syracuse made me long for warm breezes and endless blue skies.

Staring out the window at the gray, Howie said, "I gotta get out of here before it's too late." His desire to expand his horizons matched my own. The time to explore beyond our origins led to a thirst for a different place, a challenge. With shared goals, we began the drive across the country, on the pilgrimage to see America that was so prevalent in the 1970s.

I packed my transcripts. I liked the idea of picking up again out West, in any college where I could secure financial aid. Howie quit his job and was ready to test his skills as a reporter westward. We had no destination planned other than seeking the warmth of another clime and creating an adventure. We had a simple agenda: keep moving west, until money or luck ran out.

I told my parents, half expecting an argument. Instead, we said calm goodbyes via the hallway phone. My sisters and brother came on the call for a few seconds, almost annoyed at being interrupted. Everyone seemed wrapped up in their own life destiny. My guilt at leaving them behind dissipated after that call.

Once again, I found myself carting luggage, violin, and typewriter. This time, I added the rolled-up poster-sized black-and-white nude photo that symbolized my first taste of sensual freedom.

I struggled to keep the load light and envied the male ability to ignore all the accoutrements women pack—makeup, bikini shaving kits, and birth control pills.

Our first stop was Howie's childhood home in Pennsylvania. His parents had attended Cooper Union College of the Arts in New York City. They were artistic, open-minded, and accepting.

Howie's dad welcomed me with generous and open arms. Father and son looked strikingly similar. I could see in a snapshot what Howie would become. His mom, a petite, thin fireball, performed for us a string of nonstop semi-dirty stand-up jokes. I liked them both.

For a moment, I realized they might see me as a future daughter-in-law. A twinge of guilt hit me. Shaky self-talk started spinning anew in my brain. Was I stringing him along to ensure a safe sanctuary to travel freely? Howie seemed content to have a traveling companion with bedtime benefits. He asked no questions.

We drove past flat fields and distant farms, stopping at motel hamlets every evening. It took a week to reach the waving wheat fields of the Midwest. Eventually, plains rose into hills, which shifted into mountain chains. The sheer size and beauty of the West entranced me.

Travel passed in slow, steady streams across America. Through the Chevy Camaro's scratched windshield, we saw sordid half-blown-out neon bulbs flashing vacancy signs in epileptic fits above the motels we frequented. Each motel housed nighttime wandering cockroaches. The combined smell of Lysol and moldy cigarettes masked the odors of death that I still associated with my work at the pet cemetery.

It wasn't until we approached Denver, Colorado, that I saw the great reaches of America's mountainous terrain.

Howie planned to interview for a job at the newspaper as I dropped off my transcript at the local college to see if any scholarships were available. Our motel funds were running low. To save money, we decided to buy a cheap two-person tent and used sleeping bags purchased from the downtown Goodwill store.

We drove halfway up the Rocky Mountains that hovered

over the glittering city. The roadway twirled around various peaks and zigzagged sharply along ridges. Once we were up in the lush thick pines and quaking aspens, we unpacked and set up camp. Stirring a can of beans over an open firepit never seemed so enticing.

Despite the end-of-summer warmth in Denver, in the mountains the temperature dropped precipitously. Suddenly, shadows covered the land. A wayward chill crept into the breeze. By nightfall, an array of stars never seen in the enshrined cloud-covered cities of our past now sparkled across the sky. The Rockies possessed an essence of starry romance.

Vistas of flat expanses lay below mountain peaks. Ragged swells of hills reached the sharp fingers of rock pointed to the dimming sky. The temperature dropped further. The mountain began to be engulfed in drifts of light flakes. Unlike the snow of Upstate New York with its musty factory smells and dreary clouds, Colorado's snow shimmered pure and clean as ice, clearing my lungs and mind, making me dizzy.

The fire burned out. A cold breeze swept through the mountain range. Howie unzipped the sleeping bags to combine them "for more body warmth," he said.

He patted the zipped-up bags and turned to me. "Have you ever had an orgasm?"

In a moment, I realized that the female orgasm had eluded me. Other than Len introducing me to the *Joy of Sex* with its illustrations of hairy hippies in different artistic positions, I still knew nothing of the ecstasy promised by the authors. I didn't feel passion with Howie, only comfort and gratitude.

My heart jumped. I felt personally attacked. Although his manner remained gentle and his voice soothing, I didn't know how I could possibly answer something I knew nothing about.

"I really don't know," I said, blushing hot with embarrassment for the ignorance of my own body. "Some confession, huh?"

"Oh. That's my fault. Not yours."

Even in my heightened state of naivete, I knew Howie was being too kind. How many men had I ever known who took any responsibility for a woman's pleasure? Why couldn't I simply love this man? *It should be easy*, I told myself.

I clung to some ridiculous ancient belief that to achieve orgasm I had to be in love. What difference would it make if orgasm simply evolved from the sheer act of sexual exploration? Would I be "using" him then? I felt like some goofy-headed teenager still hoping fireworks would go off with every kiss.

"I've got an idea," he said as he started to roll up the bag we used as a pillow. With great care, he laid out the sleeping bags, one under the pillow. "Please lay your hips down here." He pointed to the makeshift pillow. "Take your time. Place the small of your back on the roll." When he saw me hesitate, he added, "It'll be okay. Promise. Trust me. I'll be gentle."

I had no doubt he would, but it seemed an unnatural angle for a human body. My bottom was raised while my shoulders and head were cradled by the cold ground. I was young, limber, athletic. Eager to finally reach the climactic pleasure noted in literature, I fell to the sleeping bag, unraveling my torso into the suggested position. Compliant. Ready.

He placed my feet into his cool hands and began massaging toes, inner arches, left, then right. I started to giggle.

"Am I tickling you too much?"

"No, it feels wonderful. I was just thinking of something my father once said to me when I was a girl."

He smiled. "What did he say?"

"That you can't trust men. That they start at the feet and work their way up."

"Hmm, I never thought of it that way. He may have a point. Let's try that technique."

"I'm game."

The night's chill made me shiver. Howie noticed and stopped to place his sweater over my exposed chest and shoulders.

"What a gentleman." I sighed.

In silence, and before I knew what was happening, he ran his hands up my thighs. *Maybe my father was right*, I thought. Howie kneeled beside me, licked his fingers, and went to work.

At first, I was jumpy and cold, but within moments, warmth shifted from my face and neck to my abdomen. I instinctively lifted my hips to meet his swirling fingers. Heat rose in my limbs. I threw the sweater aside. I could feel red-hot fire sear my skin. The heat spread across my chest as he increased his movements to a rapid side-to-side motion with one hand while a few fingers of his other simply slowly caressed the labia outside my vagina.

What was this man doing? I didn't care. I wanted more. This feeling of surrender ran counter to prior experiences. My breathing increased. I felt as if I were running the start of a competitive sprint. Upward I climbed, higher than the Rocky Mountain peaks that rapidly enveloped us in their secretive folds of darkness.

I lost track of Howie. I lost track of time. I lost track of myself, of space, of consciousness. Then, suddenly, *pop*, my whole body began shaking and quivering in involuntary spasms. My hands grasped the sweater.

A rush of joyful pleasure washed over my physical being. Again and again, I exploded as he first increased, then decreased, then slowed his finger movements.

What wild, magical sorcery is this? I knew I was making animal noises. Loud animal noises. But I didn't care who heard me or why.

I began to slowly decelerate in fits and spurts from the high. Howie slowed down to a bare touch of simply sliding fingers, then holding them still on my now-swollen labia.

My body gave in to quick electric zaps of slowly decreasing movements until finally I collapsed.

Sheer ecstasy. Incredible pleasure. Heightened awareness. A secret euphoria unveiled a joy within my soul. I decided then and there that this activity, whatever you called it, was worth pursuing as one of life's unrelenting goals. I was sold! It was here where the heat of desire and my need for release boiled over until it dropped to an intense shivering.

Instead of seeking his own pleasure, Howie slipped into the bag with me and covered us both with as many clothes and towels as he could find. Despite the cold night, my body memory of intense pleasure kept me warm.

"Thank you" was all I could mutter to my benefactor. He held my hand, kissed it gently, and nodded as the owls hooted above us and the distant coyotes howled at the rising moon.

14

Tucson

Eager to travel south to warmer climes, we left Colorado's red rock canyons and landed in Tucson. An enchantment with the university town began the moment we entered its half-mile high gates. The circling chains of the Rincon, Santa Catalina, and Santa Rita Mountains stood as sentinels watching over the academic city with its lyricism of multiple languages and diverse environs. Eons of erosion had created Tucson at the northern rim of the Sonoran Desert, the only desert in the world where the saguaro cacti, the symbol of Western movies, grew naturally.

Nothing prepared me for the distant soaring heights and cloudless brilliant azure sky. Even the names of the surrounding peaks intrigued me—Cathedral Rock, Gates Pass, Prominent Point, Thimble, and Elephant Head Peak.

Enthralled. Enchanted. I fell in love.

I embraced the area's geology, in awe of the ancient seabed, the hieroglyphics of Hohokam Indian cultures embedded in stone, the yowls of coyotes on the hunt, and the screech of hawks searching for prey. I wanted mountainous arms to embrace me fully, to love me back.

The Zapata Hotel sat next to the El Minuto Café. From our

room, we heard sounds of Mexican mariachis and people shouting back and forth in border Spanglish. The air filled with delicious smells of hot queso and jalapeño sauce.

I set off early in the morning toward Tucson's heart, the University of Arizona. The admissions lady swept her long black braid over one shoulder, the tassel end brushing against her elbow. Bent over, her finger on each line, she read my transcript. Her finger lifted in midair over my GPA. She glanced up. "So, you held a 3.85 average? In biology? Not bad, but you'll need proof of residency. I need a Tucson address."

"I have a temporary place." She laughed when she saw the name of the motel. "Any chance of some financial aid before then?"

She flipped through a large book with tables of federal grants. "Pell grant. Work-study." She counted on her fingers. "Loans for sure. Scholarship after a year of residency. Can you do that?"

I nodded yes, a little taken aback by the speed at which she operated. I wanted to hug her.

"Fill out the paperwork and get it back to me tomorrow, and I'll stamp it so that you can start the semester. Here, take this. It's a course catalog. Start at second- to third-year courses."

This, I told myself, *proves that a moment's risk-taking can be rewarded. A moment of chutzpah. This is what love is all about. A soaring unconditional high with a healthy dose of ego bursts. I am home.*

In my infatuation, though, I had left behind the companion who had so graciously led me to this place and tutored me in the fine art of desire. Howie knew it would be a struggle to find a reporter job in a town that required the skill of fluent border Spanish.

"A New York Jew hardly qualifies as a native speaker," he said as he scoured the job listings in the *Arizona Daily Star* without success.

I wanted to hold and comfort him. Ignoring that he was more than a decade older, motherly instinct that I had honed from years of helping raise my own siblings marked my behavior in relationships. In the days that followed, Howie seemed distant. He wanted to move westward. He hoped I'd understand. Once I moved into the dorm, we said our goodbyes on the lobby steps. I felt a guilty joy in wanting to begin anew and only slight regret for losing the one lover who had taught me about the location of a woman's secret bliss.

The loss of my sweet, sensual Svengali was replaced with surprising energy. We were at different stages of life, and parting seemed best. I knew now he would carry on to other adventures without the burden of a girl barely out of her teens. Our goals had changed; we had changed. Howie wanted to explore further, to move westward. We hugged, and a few tears unexpectedly fell to his cheek.

I never heard from him again.

For a moment, I felt like a man who'd used a woman for sexual favors, then moved on without regret. Discarding the past gave me an overwhelming feeling of absolute freedom. Armed with newfound sexual knowledge, a supply of birth control pills in my purse, and the secret circle of joy that leads to female orgasm, I was ready for further exploration.

The co-ed dorm housed undergraduates in rooms arranged in a horseshoe-shaped building. The women's east side received glorious cool morning light. The west side's harsh afternoon sun pierced through the shaded windows of the men's residences. Although men and women were not next to each other on every floor, the rules were lax. Students roamed freely. By midnight, the hormonally driven were supposed to return to the safety of their same-sex haven. They rarely did, and no one ever questioned the spontaneous sleepovers.

A sense of freedom aligned with my goal of becoming a worldly hostess who would entertain an intellectual salon of writers, artists, musicians, scientists, and engineers. I created this nonexistent home in my fantasies, a place where joviality and sophisticated wit would flourish. Little did I know that the average student on this campus spent more time playing ultimate Frisbee and getting stoned than opening a book.

The university housed an odd array of serious graduate students along with the undergraduate party animals. Some undergraduates seemed to consider themselves "rejects" from East Coast Ivy League colleges. Their rich parents willingly paid the out-of-state tuition, which in turn paid for scholarships for students like me. The socioeconomic class of redistributed scholarly funds suited my ambitions perfectly and allowed me to further venture forth seeking amorous trysts with a smorgasbord of available men.

Enlightened by the dorm's lax standards, I met several men of different ages, orientations, ethnicities, and races, as if trying out a dessert cart of sensual flavors. In less than a few months, I had become what was referred to as a *liberated* woman. Within a few weeks of dating a man, it seemed that my rather noisy sexual energy was inspiring chosen male targets to declare "I think I'm in love with you," and a few blithely proposed to marry on the spot. I dismissed them all. I embraced free love without a thought to its aftermath.

Kai, my roommate, originated from the Ganado trading post on the Navajo Indian reservation. She called the quickie marriage proposals I received a version of the *Taming of the Shrew* syndrome. Her mother taught English literature on the reservation. From her descriptions, the tribal schooling system seemed a more cooperative educational environment than what I had experienced in a competitive public-school classroom.

She saw competitiveness as philosophically unsound. In my caustic East Coast fashion, I at first mistook her patient listening and waiting to respond to mean she was a shy introvert. Like me, she was a voracious reader, staying up late every night with her nose buried in a book. She saw me as the shrew from Shakespeare's play when I left for one more date while she stayed behind. But not tonight. Tonight, we were having a girls' night.

Kai stood no taller than five feet. She rarely wore anything to cover her feet other than brown leather sandals that flapped as she walked. Her flowing pima cotton blouses worn over camouflage army pants created a yin-and-yang style. The line of straight black hair swayed with every step she took. Men followed her. She seemed oblivious and simply flew above them as her mind wandered elsewhere. I thought of her as the Goddess of the Desert Dorm.

Kai pulled a turquoise beaded feathery necklace around her shoulders. "You're not going to play that watch-me-catch-the-men game again tonight, are you?" she asked with a tinge of sardonic humor. "I think the girls are all tired of losing bets to you." Her smile gave a downward pull. "Besides, you already made your point. Multiple times." She stood up and tossed the heavy Shakespeare compendium on her bed. "The moral of the *Taming of the Shrew* is . . ." She lifted her hands and began air drumming. ". . . that humor and innuendo outpace physical beauty." She bowed for theatrical effect.

"I don't think you need to stoop to my crass techniques to

gain a man's attention. You're a beauty." I put my arm around her. Her shoulders loosened, and she allowed the hug but kept her arms at her sides. Rarely did anyone make me feel so tall, so protective. "Although I do think if girls were taught, shall we say, the direct approach, we could rule this campus. Hell, we could rule the world."

She shook her head. I know I should have been a bit embarrassed by the coarse dealings I displayed with the opposite sex. But since I was always short on cash, and to prove a point when women complained about how men only wanted model-pretty girls, I had made up a betting game to prove that bravura had more power over men than mere physical beauty. I'd walk into the Old Towne Tavern, the bar closest to campus, with Kai and a few other girlfriends and ask them to check the room for the most beautiful woman.

They at first thought the request insane but had dutifully agreed out of sheer curiosity.

Later that night at the bar, I made the bet. My friends looked around and discreetly pointed to the most beautiful woman in the room. Checking through the haze of tobacco and marijuana smoke, I spotted her too. Tall, lanky, strawberry blonde. I almost dismissed her as a stereotypical model. It never occurred to me that my harsh judgments could be wrong. I watched her gaze over the crowd as if she were standing on a dais at a beauty pageant awaiting her crown. She ignored the male admirers surrounding her. Half the men were vying for her attention without looking around the room.

I studied the scene, taking notes like a field biologist. Glints of the fading purple sunset fell in drifting waves of smoke whenever the door opened. She half smiled, tolerant yet annoyed by each suitor who dared to approach her.

The young men, half-bound ponytails grazing their T-shirt collars, followed her every gesture. They moved as she moved, in harmony like a colony of worker ants, first left, then right. At the bar, a few fell into a territorial fight of pushing and shoving each other to get her a drink with the hopes of being allowed to touch her sacred skin.

"Ladies, listen up." I took a swig of cheap Mexican Tecate beer, its acidic aftertaste lingering on my tongue. "All bets are on whether I can pull every single one of those salivating testosterone-laden admirers away from the beauty in less than five minutes." I glanced at my target again. "Make that within four minutes."

"Oh." Kai was the first to speak up. "You are so on. There is no way anyone is going to bother with a pipsqueak like you." They laughed. None of us stood taller than five feet four. We were obviously no match for the model.

"Let's up the ante another buck," I said. I reviewed the situation, counted the number of men watching with fawning eyes, following every curve of her perfect body, every tiny pore of her exquisite skin. "If I fail, I lose, and you keep your money, and drinks are on me. But if I get their complete attention and bring them to you, the kitty is all mine. Either way it's a win."

"The whole kitty? Really? This is way too easy," Judy said. She was a slightly chubby girl with pink-tinged braids, bedecked in a camel-colored leather-fringed vest draped with peacock feathers. I liked her unique style and daredevil manner. "I'm in," she shouted.

They all followed her lead and threw dollar bills into the table's peanut bowl. I allowed one more moment to examine the men along the playing field. I checked the number to decipher who was the weak link, the followers, and the alpha male. A tall man, perhaps an alpha, stood closest to the model.

"Judges, start the clock. Let the game begin!" Judy said. "Three minutes and fifty seconds and counting."

I charged, not sauntered, across the room. Physically, I had only my brashness, my blue-green eyes, and my curves to help me. I was no match for this amazing specimen of womanhood, and I knew it.

I stepped closer to listen to what passed as conversation by the failing flirts encircling her. I stood a bit outside the inner circle. No one seemed to catch her fancy. She impatiently looked around for bigger fish. For all her beauty, she seemed nonchalant, almost careless in her lack of regard for the men surrounding her. I decided to use a straightforward tactic—direct sexual innuendo.

"You're so hot," one man said to her as she turned away dismissively at the insult that he didn't even know he had uttered.

"Hey, buddy," I retorted, "every lady in this room is hot. Smell that?" I waited a second. A few men turned, looking puzzled, but no one answered. "The very air in this place is steaming with sensuality."

All five men looked directly at me upon hearing the word "sensuality," like so many Pavlovian-trained sex-starved dogs.

I continued. "Hot will only get you so far in this bar, in this life, boys. Wouldn't you rather seduce the possibilities? Be brave. Take the chance to be burned with desire for one amazing night."

I moved closer to the circle. "Ah, but that might be too much for you boys to handle." I stared into the eyes of each, focusing on the one closest. He flinched, then waited. The others stood behind him. Experience had taught me that men fell into hierarchical structures. Whatever the alpha male wanted, the others would follow.

"What do you mean?" He smirked.

"Look across the room, gentlemen. Do you even see those ladies?" I pointed to my dorm girlfriends. "Every one of them is waiting with a loving open heart to be courted, and yet, here you stand in a circle of schmucks hoping for a few leftovers when real possibilities await right over there." I shook my head. "So sad." I gave a slight pout and shifted my left hip out ever so slowly, exposing my bare waist above my hip-hugging jeans while the extra flesh of my breasts barely slid into the inside corners of the halter top holding them precariously in place. Every eye was upon me now.

The beauty glanced down at me. She waved her hand dismissively as if she could make us all disappear. Obviously bored, she moved on. The tall man ignored her as she disappeared into the crowd. That's when the followers' circle smelled failure too. My words held some lure of imagination, a power of possibility. Their fantasies altered in seconds. They looked across the room to where triumph seemed a more calculated viability.

The men followed me back to the table with the empty broken-peanut-shell dish full of dollar bills. I winked at Kai and nodded to the other women. "Take it away, girls," I said as I grabbed the dish of cash, shells spilling out in all directions. The women, except for Kai, could not believe the parlor trick they'd just witnessed.

I left the crowd at the table to order my dinner feast of quesadillas with salsa.

Kai stepped up to the barstool. "Please. No more game playing. We're all going bankrupt watching you flirt your way to victory."

"Watch and learn," I retorted.

"I'll confess," Kai said as she sat down beside me, "it's satisfying to watch. It's like an anthropology field trip. I admit it's a bit of a thrill, but I wonder if competing for men's attention at the expense of other women isn't a bit unkind if not harmful to all women?"

Kai had become that whispering therapist of sisterhood, enlightening me on how I might be causing community harm without realizing it. I don't believe she meant to pass judgment on me. She simply wanted me to understand her personal discomfort and that the game could imply a lack of sisterhood.

A bright red flush rushed over me at the realization. I felt duly chastised and a tad shameful. Under Kai's kind tutelage, I learned how self-serving and decidedly harmful my behavior could seem to other women. For days, her calm pronouncement haunted me. Instead of empowered, I had become manipulative.

For the rest of the semester, I attempted to change. In solidarity, I threw my meager makeup kit and razors into the trash bin and joined the Tucson Women's Collective, a small consciousness-raising group of like-minded women who met at the university. I devoured feminist literature from Simone De Beauvoir and Betty Friedan to Camille Paglia and Gloria Steinem. I kept the wire-rimmed bras safely in place though. Given my sizable ta-tas, I wasn't about to suffer physically for any politically motivated group.

Soon, my newfound awareness gave birth to a different style of arrogance. I pushed aside my former penniless, homeless, sick girl weakness. *Goodbye to naivete and good riddance to virginal lack of knowledge*, I thought. All I needed was protective gear.

Volunteering at Planned Parenthood was my first political statement and where I met Mena. She tutored us on how to discuss birth control with patients. Her presentations were comical and flawless; her Newark, New Jersey, accent gave an air of toughness.

"Condoms come in all colors. A sassy black number." She laid it along her smooth light brown skin, the hairs rising from static electricity as she slid the condom down her forearm. "For passion, perhaps a raspberry red." I was enthralled by her performance and bravado.

"We have purple and orange, the colors of an Arizona sunset, ready for your next camping trip at Gates Pass." She winked at me directly.

Gates Pass formed into a perfect V shape that marked the connection between two mountain ranges looking west. Locals smoked cheap weed, drank even cheaper Mexican beer, and became lost in passion every evening after the sun's rays were swallowed by the horizon.

Mena's tone became serious. I focused on her words. "The choice is yours." She stared at each one of us. "And no one else's."

She seemed wiser than I could ever imagine being. Birth control meant freedom. Taking ownership was not some ephemeral wish. It was a choice.

I looked back with gratitude. Howie's expertise had demonstrated an unparalleled ecstasy. *Bold experimentation*, I told myself, *can cast aside centuries of female punishment for the mere pursuit of sexual pleasure.* I would no longer be stopped or shamed. Or so I believed.

15

Recruitment

The only job I could find was as a waitress in a cowboy bar called The Range. The bar resided on the northern outskirts of town. The owner, Orville, had taken a chance on hiring me even though he was not a fan of college students.

"Damn rich kids get it all," Orville once told me. "House, truck, boat, girls, and they ain't even got to work for it. They never get their soft hands dirty. Pansies." Orville and his compatriot cowboy clients had colorful, albeit sexist, ways of expressing themselves.

Orville did not give a rat's ass, as he would say, for political or social discussions in his bar. He tilted his sun-bleached cowboy hat to me as a hello to the new waitress willing to serve his rough crowd.

Despite his anger at students' seeming privilege, Orville was smart enough to know his in-debt cowboy drunks, relatives, and friends would never grow his business, much less pay the monthly bills. He needed a student influx of cash. I helped him write an ad to post in the college newspaper, claiming free spaghetti dinners for anyone with a student ID on Friday night. The beer prices would double, but students would never know that. Within twenty-four hours of publication, skinny, hungry, horny male students overran The Range.

Unlike the cowboys, who leered at me and made crude remarks but left me alone, these drunk frat boys saw me as their toy, their prey, their low-class object of desire. And so the grabbing began.

While I was carrying two large pitchers of beer, a guy slapped me from behind. Before I could catch the pitcher, I tripped, sending ice-cold liquid down a local cowboy's back. He erupted from his seat ready to swing but realized what had happened when he saw my face and the student's.

Orville lifted his finger at the grabby student. "You playing with this here girl?"

The pimply guy smirked and nodded yes.

"Where's your manners, boy? This is our New Yahrk girl," he said to mimic what he thought of as an East Coast accent. "I run a nice establishment here. You boys ain't from here, so's maybe you don't know we treat our women like ladies."

I tried not to laugh, since I'd seen the occasional barroom brawl with the cowboys' wives screaming obscenities at their husbands to come home and their violent reaction to that request. But I stayed silent, watching in fascination.

The student, not reading the situation well, threw the first punch, which gave Orville the excuse to take his class anger out on the boy.

A melee of fists, kicks, broken glass, and pent-up anger broke out. Cowboys sought revenge for years of working in the dirt. Frat boys looked for adventure so they could regale their buddies back at the dorm.

A strong arm surrounded my waist. With one quick move, someone pulled me out of harm's way. I looked up to see Raul. I recognized him from my Spanish class. He spoke fluent border lingo as well as formal Spanish as his first language. His family, going back generations, hailed from both sides of the border. I remembered asking him why he was taking a class in a language he already spoke. He smiled and answered, "Easy A. Why else?"

My relief at being in his protective embrace surprised me.

"Lay low," he said. "Follow me before the cops get here."

We escaped out the kitchen's back door into a night filled with the smells of rotting meat and stale beer. A full moon lit the path. We hopped into Raul's old convertible Mustang. Huge fuzzy dice swung from the rearview mirror as we drove back to the dorm.

The night air cooled the sweat along my neck. Wind rushed through my tangled hair. I fell quickly from my role as stalwart feminist to romance novel heroine. That night, within the confines of his small single dorm room, I demonstrated my gratitude. He rewarded me in physical kindness.

A few days later, I realized why Raul had a single dorm room. He had a string of lovers—particularly naive white girls, like me, from the East Coast. I overheard him brag about the *gringitas* who fell sway to his Latin lover routine.

For the rest of that first dry-heat desert summer, I vowed to experiment, to test my own sexuality using a smorgasbord of male talents. If men like Raul could live such a freewheeling lifestyle, why couldn't I?

Enter Ron from my Third World American Studies class. The literature focused on Ralph Ellison's *The Invisible Man*. Ron was a gentle accountant by day. His deepest dream was to be perceived as a wild Black Panther by night. I wanted to help him, but his lackluster and limp performance would need more than my own skill set could provide. I lost patience and moved on.

Ashwin, originally from New Delhi, quickly faded as a lover since he seemed to have an extraordinary fear of certain female body parts.

Then I met sweet Carlo. Unlike other students, he was already a professional architect on sabbatical finishing his master's degree in environmental design. He seduced me with balsa wood models he'd crafted. The smell of freshly painted veneer, and the visual beauty of his detailed drawings, appealed to an artistic sensibility dormant in my soul. Sadly, he rarely spoke. My attention waned, and I began to understand how a lack of communication skills could sink an amorous conquest.

In my own subconscious battle, I weighed the good girl versus the randy, roaming bad girl and chose the latter. Various aspects of the sex act and the Candyland choice of available suitors became my tutorial. Still, I knew I had a lot to learn. Single life represented wildness, while marriage seemed a conforming bondage.

One afternoon, as I confidently walked past the hallway displays where male students hawked their clubs and memberships to passing students along the university's open corridor, I stopped.

There, at the Model United Nations table, stood a tall young man with long wavy black hair falling well below his shoulders. Thick eyebrows and super long eyelashes covered soul-searching dark green eyes. I took one look at the other male staffers and marched over to the soulful-eyed god.

At first, he nervously gave his pitch on the importance of global cooperation. He rambled on about the history of the League of Nations and Eleanor Roosevelt, then rounded it out with a synopsis on the post–World War II inception of the UN. After another ten minutes of facts, I gaped at him in silence.

He must have thought my silence indicated an interest to be

further informed. On and on he went as he touted his left-leaning hippie vibes. I only half listened. His captivating eyes and sensually long-limbed demeanor held my attention. I did not catch his name, but I immediately signed on as a volunteer, infatuation guiding choice.

At my first Model UN meeting, I glanced around the crowd but didn't see the Adonis who had recruited me. Then I looked toward the stage and saw him.

He introduced himself as the secretary general of the entire western corridor of Model UN disciples. Awestruck and focused, I watched his every move. Sexy, sensual, and smart. I had hit the trifecta.

As I stared in wonder, a red-bearded young man next to me began chatting about his boat. I barely heard him as he attempted to persuade me to go on a sailing trip with him to Baja in the Mexican Sea of Cortez. As romantic, if not daringly questionable, as it sounded, I barely listened.

Then Adonis appeared. He gave us a quizzical look, his head slightly tilted. "So, is Peter giving you guidance on your Security Council position?"

"Um, I don't think so," I said. "Peter, I believe, is guiding me to ignore my own instincts about boarding boats with strangers. I think he believes a sailboat ride equates with his getting laid." I paused and turned to him. "I believe that's your position, yes?"

Peter laughed and good-naturedly said, "Busted."

"Ah geez, I'm sorry to have interrupted." The unnamed Adonis seemed bashful. His green eyes flashed bright.

"Sorry about what? That I'm not open to Peter's attempt to get me on his boat?"

He smiled. "I'm Andy." He extended his hand, and I could

not help noticing his long, elegant fingers as they wrapped around my hand.

"Sue." I nodded. "So, Andy"—I decided to take the bold approach—"are you asking me out on a date?"

To give him credit, instead of blushing or stuttering, he moved closer and said, "Yes. When and where?" He continued to hold my hand lightly. "Are you available to discuss your interest in our Model UN Saturday night?"

The only problem with accepting was that I already had a date with Carlo, who had made reservations at a very nice Italian restaurant on the edge of campus.

"Oh, sorry. I'm not available."

"Not available on Saturday or not available ever?"

"Oh, only Saturday." I could see him grinning under the beard. "Sunday works, unless you have religious restrictions I should know about."

He laughed. "I think if you knew me, you'd realize how crazy that question is. I'm a scientist, a chemist to be specific, and an atheist. You?"

"Agnostic." I paused. "I like to hedge my bets. You might say I'm a chicken-shit atheist." I was enjoying the opportunity to engage in smart-ass quips without worrying that I was insulting someone for once. "And you, Dr. Godless, why are you the head of this Model UN organization? Global politics is messier than science."

His tone became serious, academic. "I have three majors. Literature and philosophy as well as chemistry. I'm kind of a renaissance man, I guess," he said without a glimmer of arrogance, and an almost uncompromising self-appraisal.

"My, oh my," I teased, "aren't we ambitious. Are you sure you live in Tucson? You do know this is a party school."

"I've lived in Tucson for a few years. I'm open to partying when necessary. I'm a border rat," he added without a shred of humor, as if stating a local fact. It was the first time I heard the term. "I grew up in the Mule Mountains of Bisbee on the Mexican border. I spent most weekends during high school on the other side of the border."

I didn't think to ask him why he was border crossing. Instead, I was charmed by his internationalism.

"Given your tall, dark, and handsome good looks, I would expect you to be named Guido or Luigi or something. Not Andy." I put it out there. A line with a hook. Corny or seductive, only he would be able to tell me.

He smiled widely. "Good guess. I'm half Sicilian. My mother is first generation. She grew up under the pope's Catholicism until she married my dad, a strict Presbyterian Scott. She rebelled in her own way."

"Really? I'm half Italian, half Anglo." I was a bit surprised to find this ethnic combo so far from the state of New York— America's supposed European melting pot. "I bet your mom is proud of you, Mr. Secretary General."

"My mom died of cervical cancer when I was eleven."

"Oh, I'm so sorry." He had reported it as if this was one item on his "get to know me" list. For a second, though, I could see something sad in his eyes—a motherless child—and I melted.

"It's OK," he answered. "I survived. I have three brothers and a sister. To be honest, I was my mom's favorite." His eyes glazed over a bit. "She was one of the first women to ever graduate with a degree in pharmacy at Berkeley. So, as a chemist, I'm kind of following in her footsteps." His respect for his mother's intellect and achievements warmed my heart. I smiled and had to do everything in my power to hold myself back from hugging him.

His fingers slowly loosened their grip. A warm feeling to protect him washed over me. I had never felt such a strong affinity for a man.

"This is a lot to take in," I said. "Let's continue this chat. Sunday will be our first date then?"

He nodded, and I watched him walk away into the crowd of students.

"Now how did that nerd score and not me?" Peter said, jarring me. "He doesn't even own a boat."

The rest of the week, all I could think of was this motherless man-child. Try as I could to rationalize a mere physical attraction to him, my inner good girl tugged at my maternal instincts.

My thoughts were consumed by Andy's story. So much so that on Saturday I didn't realize how rude I acted toward my date, Carlo, who'd just said something to me on our date. I shook myself when I heard his calm voice in the distance asking me, "What do you think?"

The restaurant had a beautiful layout with large sycamore trees lining the outdoor patio. A tray of tiny candles sat on the table between us. Moonlight fell in waves between the shadows.

"I'm sorry," I said. "Can you please repeat that?"

"Okay." He inhaled. "We've been together a while. I want to know if you are ready to make a commitment." He paused. "Because I am."

Before I could clear my head to understand what was happening, Carlo got down on one knee in front of an entire patio of patrons and waiters. Time stopped. People stared.

His deep sable-brown eyes stared into my face. He opened a jewelry box with a small diamond ring. It glittered, blinking at me.

I began to giggle. Almost hysterically in a nervous fit. I couldn't stop. The odd glee made me sound insane. People glared. One woman shook her head. Here I'd been thinking of another man as Carlo, in front of me, was seriously asking me to marry him. I panicked.

"That's sweet of you, but we've known each other for only a few months. I'm sorry, but no."

The corners of his mouth shifted down. He stared at me in disbelief. I cringed and wondered, *What kind of woman daydreams about an upcoming date while being proposed to by another?* In a moment of clarity, I knew that in my pursuit of sexual freedom, I had become unkind.

In the morning, I found a note in my mailbox from Carlo: "I am glad you got such a kick out of my marriage proposal, but I was serious. I loved you." I did feel ashamed of my response. The guilt dissipated when I realized he had used the past tense— loved. But before I could think what to do to make it up to him, I realized there was another note: "Pick up at front desk."

A large array of wildflowers planted in a homemade clay pot, with a "Happy Birthday" card perched among the daisies, awaited me at the front desk. Who even knew it was my twentieth birthday? Inside, the card read, "I may not own a boat, but that doesn't mean we can't ride the waves of life together. PS, if you're wondering how I knew it was your birthday, remember that you signed a membership card with me last week. —Andy."

In the coming weeks, I taught Andy what I had shamelessly learned from other men about the intricacies of my body. As an in-kind reward, he taught me the fine art of substance-induced pleasures learned from his teen years of dealing drugs along the Mexican border.

Instead of being appalled or frightened, his risk-taking excited me. The combination of artistic intellectualism, political philosophy, and desire enthralled me.

I repeated to myself that this was simply the excitement of temporary pleasure. In the days and weeks that followed, I couldn't discern if I was falling ever more deeply in love with a man, a symbol, a need for stability, or the sheer excitement of blindly following someone off a very short cliff.

16

Sitting with Scissors

I wanted to be closer to the community, to the excitement, to Andy. I had quit waitressing at the cowboy bar after the brawl. It was too far out of town and a bit more dangerous than I had anticipated. I volunteered at the mobile Planned Parenthood unit in Tin Town, with Spanglish the language of choice. My birth control ambassador, Mena, handed me a box of condoms and a circular packet of birth control pills. I told her that as much as I enjoyed volunteer work, I needed a paying job.

"I have something," she said, "if you don't mind working for me."

Mind? I was ecstatic. "Sign me up."

"I'm the office manager in the Bureau of Geology on campus. I need a good typist, but before you say yes, I've got to tell you geologists can be a bit crude. Most are misguided urban cowboys."

"I'm a great typist," I said. "I spent the last few months prying drunk cowboys' fingers off my butt, so I think I can handle geologists."

"We'll see." Mena wrote down the address. "It's minimum wage but flexible to fit your class schedule."

Her life seemed so much more fulfilled and rewarding than

mine. Only seven years older than me, she already had two young kids and a house. Her husband, the lone Black prosecuting attorney at that time, had a reputation as a firebrand. The local press loved them. I learned that they were seen as the Black power couple. I admired them and knew I had neither life's exposure to daily racism nor the courage to deal with it.

The need to feel safe still haunted me. It kept me locked into a mindset of a cautious conventional life despite my feminist philosophy. Yet, for all the safety seeking, something gnawed at me. I wanted to experience the fullness of the emotional seesaw between desire and danger.

The job entailed typing, reading, summarizing, and editing final page proofs for geological survey field guides. To educate me on the material I was proofreading, the geologists invited me, the lone woman, to a field trip on the outskirts of town.

"What do you make of the rock formations along this gully?" said the lead geologist, a small but lanky older man. He pointed to a canyon filled with boulders the size of a Volkswagen.

"Always educating the co-eds, eh, boss?" A much larger man behind him winked at me as he spoke. He sported one of the largest wide-brimmed ten-gallon hats I'd ever seen. He held out his hand. "I'm Big Billy."

He wore a braided bolo tie with a large turquoise Aztec-inspired Quetzalcoatl feathered serpent that wrapped around the leather strings. His three-inch large copper belt buckle decorated with a matching serpent shone like a spotlight around his girth.

I looked away and released my hand from his.

"Ahem." The leader cleared his throat and ignored Billy to continue his lecture. "The water during the few weeks of rainy season is so torrential that it literally picks up these two-ton boulders, throwing them into the canyon below." He lifted his hands to the surrounding suburban community. "The neighbors think of the rocks as decoration. Some even have gardens around them."

Billy chuckled. "Yeah, the suckers have no idea they're in the path of destruction and spent a helluva lot of mortgage money for nothing."

"Unfortunately," the guide continued, "Billy is right. It's just a matter of time before the water picks the boulders up again and tosses them straight onto their back porch or worse."

I nodded. The idea that the sheer force of a spring rain rushing down the mountain could lift these rocks like toy sailboats and throw them into the canyon astounded me. Listening to their discussion of geological formations and why one peak looked like a castle rook and another like an old bear's face fascinated me. I wanted to feel part of their knowledgeable comradery. It reminded me a bit of being included in the reporters' circle. It felt good to find a tribe.

"It's getting late, and I'm starved," Billy said to cut off the long-winded explanations of the other geologists as they tried to educate me. "I vote we all get a bite at the Stuck in the Mud."

There were a few murmurs of consent, but all eyes were on me. "Want a real Tucson experience, co-ed?" Billy asked.

"Why not?" I shrugged. It seemed a good day to learn the local ways.

The outside of the restaurant sported silhouettes of seemingly naked females. The sign over the door was missing letters. Someone had blurred with a magic marker the S and T and left the UCK, creatively editing in the initial letter F.

We walked inside. I attempted to adjust my eyes to the dark

interior. A rancid smell of pork rinds, spilled beer, and pee covered with Lysol spray hit me as soon as I walked in the door. I heard scratchy sounds of a worn country music record. When my eyes focused, I saw three women with sparkly pasties over their nipples and uncomfortable-looking G-strings hiked up their waists lounging around a ceiling-to-floor pole. Paint peeled from the steel rod. The women were eating what smelled like tuna fish sandwiches.

"On break, fellas," one yelled out.

"We'll wait," Billy said. "We brought us here a little guest."

The strippers stared at me. *Don't be judgmental*, I told myself. *After all, stripping is a dance art form, worthy of admiration. Who am I to say? After all, I posed nude for payment.*

"How in hell did you guys rope that little calf into coming here? You guys ought to be 'shamed," said a woman with flowing curly hair in an unusual burgundy color. A crooked tiara holding on for dear life fell off the left side of her hairline.

"Hey, she's being a good sport. Show her what you got, ladies. It's her learning day." Billy paused and glanced at the barkeep. "Beer, pork rinds, and tacos all around. On me."

It was then that I remembered Mena saying as I had reached for the office door earlier that day, "Be careful. Field trips make those guys kind of rough out in the wild. They should mind their manners. It's Billy I'd watch if I were you. He's a blowhard."

"I can handle him," I said. As I listened to him brag, I knew I should've heeded Mena's warning. I placed myself in reporter mode. *What can I learn from the strippers?* I examined the scene and focused on the experience, almost like a critique of an art form.

I sat down in the booth and sipped on a lukewarm beer, telling myself to stop being a snob. I grabbed the handle of the mug and paused mid-lift. Beer sloshed around the rim. I'd found a cockroach inside. I scooped it out, setting the glass aside.

Maybe this is one way to examine the male psyche up close, I told myself. I'd noticed, out of deference to me perhaps, that the guys had chosen a booth some twenty feet from the stage. Such gentlemanly behavior. In the meantime, the "girls" were already up and working. Each gyrated in fits and starts along the grease-stained pole. Their bellies shifted. They swayed slowly, as if the effort to move was too cumbersome.

The dancing seemed perfunctory. They looked bored and put little energy into the action. I looked at one girl about my age. She stared back with black glassy eyes.

Billy noticed my stare. "Ah, she's high. Hooked on heroin probably."

They all nodded and returned to their "beers and jeers," as one called it. The burgundy-haired stripper sauntered toward the table, then turned around to show her thong and jiggling backside as the men slipped dollar bills into her costume straps.

Instead of witnessing this as a sexual experience, I had a vision of single mothers recovering from giving birth and forced to work at the bar, the only local job available to them. One of the strippers shot me a piercing glare as if she could read my mind. I looked away.

"What ya doing here, college girl?"

My face flushed red hot. Her sunken eyes wandered to the men at that table.

"Schoolgirl looks a little peaked," Billy said to the stripper. She laughed and wandered back to the tiny stage in the center of the barroom.

Billy was right. I did feel sick. The supervisor nodded for us to leave, my uncomfortableness evident and embarrassing.

When I got back to my dorm room, I ran to empty my stomach of beer, tacos, and pork rinds in the hallway bathroom. I kept thinking about the strippers. *There but for the grace of God go I*, I kept repeating.

The next day at work, once my head had cleared, I felt the visceral reaction fade, but the memory of her glassy-eyed sadness lingered.

As I finished proofreading a manuscript on porphyry copper deposits in southern Arizona, I felt an ominous presence approaching behind my office chair. I glanced at Mena. She looked alarmed but remained stone-still in her chair.

"Hey, college girl, you were in some fine tizzy last night. No strip club experience, eh?" I recognized Billy's booming voice.

"Nope," I said, not looking up at him, "and I doubt I'll return." I picked up the long industrial-sized scissors and started cutting the galley prints along the blue dotted lines, pretending to be lost in work.

"So, you lack experience?" Billy clapped his hands once. "Well, little lady, I got a cure for that. You curious?"

"Not particularly." I ignored him and returned to my task at hand.

"Billy, lay off her. It's bad enough she was stuck with you all day yesterday," Mena said.

"I wasn't talking to you, boss lady," he said. "I'm talking to this here assistant girl of yours."

He turned back to me and stepped into my zone to strategically place my face at his male bulge. "I'm guessing you've never been with a really big man?" He grinned at me. He wore his impressive and towering six and a half feet as a badge of privilege. He kept coming closer to mimic the oral act, with my face almost touching his pants.

You need the job, Sue, I repeated to myself, barely moving. I looked up again to see Mena sitting close to the edge of her seat, ready to pounce, but she remained silent.

The temporary office girl, Polly, also sat nearby, watching nervously. Her eyes darted from Billy to me and back again. From the few conversations we had, it was obvious she was being physically abused by a husband that she swore she loved and relied upon financially. Her entire body began to shake as Billy slid closer to my head. I glanced over to see her watching me and shivering. She seemed to roll herself into a small ball behind her desk. I became intrigued, more by Polly's fear than my own safety.

"I hear tell, Mena, that you and this one here"—he pointed his thumb toward me—"want a raise? Minimum ain't good enough for the likes of you two. So, I'm asking you, girl, and look up when I talk to you, what you going to do to earn it?"

I had almost forgotten about our request for higher wages when first hired. In confusion about my hourly wage and what that request had to do with Billy, I laughed. He moved closer, seemingly angry at my lack of response to his insults.

In that moment of him stepping too close, the memories of being frozen on a suite floor pinned down by a much larger man overwhelmed me. I could feel the bloody tampon being yanked from my body and thrown against the wall. I could still feel the violation, my shock of disbelief, and my inability to act as he proceeded to enter me. *Not again,* I thought, *not ever.*

I casually placed my hand in a strong grip over the long, sharp scissors. I glanced up to see Mena's eyebrows shoot up momentarily and a slight smile enter her face. In one quick movement, I lifted the sharp end of the industrial-sized scissors and held the razor-sharp tip at the base of his bulge.

Billy saw where I was holding the scissors, my grip powerful, my intention focused. A moment of tell-tale fear crossed his squinting eyes as he quickly stepped back and hit Polly's desk. She jumped up and shrieked, stunning us all.

To regain control, Billy stepped between our desks. His cowboy boots turned for a run. But, before he left, he spit out, "You New York WOP bitch."

I was less shocked than bemused. I began to laugh again. Loudly. WOP, or With Out Papers, was such an old-fashioned ethnic slur that I had to check the calendar to see which part of the century we were in. I had not heard "WOP" or "dago" or "greaseball" thrown at me since childhood.

My laughter seemed contagious. The other women began laughing along with me. The three of us went from fear to mocking disdain for a man so out of date in his ethnic insults.

Mena stood up. She was, after all, the manager of the office. "Be on your way, Billy." She waved to dismiss him. "Or you might be missing a few body parts that you'll have to explain to your wife."

Billy snorted upon hearing the word "wife," then backed up into the doorway. His raging eyes never left the pointy scissors in my hand though. For a minute, I stayed in attack position, ready to destroy the enemy if he came any closer. I stared at him, un-flinching, as he walked backward out of the female office he had once dominated.

"Bitches. All of you!" he shouted from outside the room before disappearing.

"Thank you for the compliment, Billy. Yes, we are bitches," Mena said, her voice calm. "Strong bitches, and don't you for-get it."

She returned to her desk and began typing as if nothing had happened. I fell back in my chair, suddenly exhausted from my constant guardedness. It seemed that some men, like Billy, believed intimidation and rape their birthright.

Mena and I learned a few days later that Billy had told the owner of the company, "It's going to be over my dead body before I'd give either that N bitch or that WOP bitch any raise."

I was shocked, appalled. Mena only shook her head upon hearing the extent of Billy's racist and ethnic taunts. "He's a weak piece of crap and he knows it," she said. "Being called a bitch is a compliment. Get used to it if you're going to keep using office weapons." She put her arm around my shoulders for a moment. "Billy's a blowhard. He has no other defense. His day will come, and you almost made it happen with that scissors bit. I tried so hard not to laugh. I thought he'd shit his pants for sure."

At that point, I wondered, *Am I really a tough chick or just a tired-of-this-sexist-shit chick? Or maybe this-is-the-final-straw chick? Or how about go-eff-yourself chick?*

For the rest of the fall semester, I traveled with the Model UN group visiting various Arizona high schools from Flagstaff to the Mexican border. Andy drove the van. I noticed he'd attracted an entourage of adoring female students.

I overheard remarks about him—gossip referencing his scraggly hippie appearance. One said, "I love a man with a beard. It's so manly." Or another, more direct, declaration would add, "He's got dreamy bedroom eyes." I heard a rendition of the male beauty theme more than once during those field trips.

Like a sociologist with clipboard in hand, I would write notes on female responses and groupthink. I learned more about myself than them though. Oddly enough, as others focused on the male object of my desire, my ear would follow to hear their assessments. By choice, training, or culture, I seemed to have made a draft pick in the way coaches do with a sought-after ball player. Being the other women's object of sexual desire enhanced his worthiness.

I never thought there could be a downside to infatuation based solely on sensual beauty. I remembered once asking my mother how she had decided to marry my father, given the fact she'd been dating another man. "It was a physical more than a rational decision," she stated. "There is some merit in marrying a handsome man. If by chance or time it goes to hell, you can at least stare at him all day."

I watched this young rebel of a man drive along the steep edges of mountain passes that hugged unstable red rock canyon walls. With each hairpin turn, he smiled under the ragged beard as if he owned the road, the world, and the entourage of adoring females riding with him.

There was no air-conditioning in his rattly old Chevy. We had to open the windows as we drove from the southern end of Bisbee's Mule Mountains, where Geronimo had once escaped, to the cooler foothills of Flagstaff. Fields of poppies bloomed orange red along the base of the mountains. Cream-colored cactus flowers bloomed in seconds if only a few drops of dew touched them along the flat dusty terrain. The giddy, sensual delight of watching Andy drive would be forever combined with the sharp, almost putrid, smell of newly blooming cactus flowers filling the valley.

Although Andy had left flowers on my birthday, he had continued to keep a discreet distance. A bit baffled by this, I assessed how to engage this man and make him my next conquest. As I watched the brilliant primary colors of flowering cacti blooming in disarray along the highway, I laid out my next steps. To ensure I hadn't misunderstood his intentions, I needed to be more forceful in my approach.

Every time I glanced at Andy, I knew that I was falling in lust. Fast.

The assessment technique, which I, and so many women at the time, had mastered in countless bars, was meant to ensure his focus was entirely on me. I felt empowered, capable of scheming my way to any romantic encounter, engulfing a heady drug of passion, both addictive and relentless, willing me to venture further without fear.

17

Stop, Don't Shoot

Courtship rituals danced daily between us, but I never could pinpoint who had taken the lead.

Andy's knowledge of the Southwest helped me to understand the culture and regional past. He spoke about the invading pioneers' cruel treatment of Papago, Navajo, Hopi, and Apache tribes. About how the Wobblies, or International Workers of the World, had attempted to unionize the copper mines. Sympathizers to the cause were gathered at gunpoint into a corral in the center of his hometown of Bisbee in 1917. Whole families of miners were displaced, forced onto railroad boxcars, and dropped into the New Mexico desert to die of dehydration. From him, I learned that Arizona history possessed a dark heritage beyond the Hollywood movie sets of Westerns filmed in Old Tucson.

He spoke in serious tones. His long black hair tangled in the wind. He moved in perpetual slow motion. The mere glimpse of a smile from him pointed in my direction, his thick-lashed green eyes fixated on my every move, intensified my desire.

We traveled together in small groups from the white-hot cement palaces of Phoenix, with its Cadillacs and gated communities, to Kai's Navajo reservation, with locals selling turquoise rings and illegal petrified wood by the roadside. The audacious wealth of skyscrapers in Phoenix contrasted against small adobe hovels. Once away from the city, barren red rock canyon walls with bullet-riddled signs warned hikers to beware of flash floods.

Air-conditioned comfort slipped away into an autoclave heat. Sometimes we would see silent migrants along the dirt-strewn highway seeking shelter among the shade of a few palo verde trees. Over the course of a few months, in every corner of the state, we witnessed displays of extreme wealth and abject poverty. An elementary school belief in the textbook propaganda of the American West soon dissolved into stark reality.

I asked endless questions about the terrain, geology, people, languages, and culture. In response, Andy invited me to hike the Rincons. "There's only one way to see the mountains in all their beauty. If you're open to it, let's drop some acid. It'll be your birthday celebration in the wild. LSD will expand your mind."

"You want to take me into the desert to get to know me, to take advantage of my lack of experience, or to make me lose my mind?"

"Maybe a bit of each." He laughed, and I found my defenses melt. "I promise to take care of you. It'll be your choice of what to take advantage of. Then, we can both lose our minds." His long fingers enveloped my entire hand. "I'll walk you through every step along the way. What do you say?"

Losing my mind, even if momentarily, did have an appeal. "But is it safe?"

"Remember, my mother was a pharmacist. I'm a chemist. Who safer to experiment with?"

Once back in my dorm room, though, I thought it best to ask Kai, who was far less enamored of the "hairy white boy who thinks he's God's gift," as she called him.

"Kai, how in the heck did I go from Carlo's solid marriage proposal to a rendezvous with a border rat to drop acid?"

She sat up, her torso twisting in the chair. "They're attracted to your wildness. This new guy thinks drugging you up will make you vulnerable. He wants to tame you. That's my take on it." She paused. "If it works, that's sad for him. And more so for you."

"Well, I haven't set a date for the trip. Yet."

"But you will. I can see the excitement in your eyes. You can't pass up a wild experience." She smiled. "It's why I like you. Just be prepared. It won't be what you think."

"How do you know, Kai?"

"Been there, done that. Drugs. Not hairy white boys. I'm not a relationship person."

"I'm in a relationship?"

She nodded. "I believe so. I think his bad boy quest feeds your adventurous streak. Tell me how it goes. But don't come back asking questions you already know the answer to."

I wanted desire to explode into a powder keg of ecstasy. I wanted to be that revolutionary woman willing to test the boundaries of sensuality, so why be afraid of a little LSD loosening my mind? *It's time*, I told myself, *to discard female passivity forever.*

We walked together down the path outside the cafeteria. I touched his arm. He stopped and turned to me. "I'd be delighted to embark upon this journey with you," I said.

He grinned and shook his head. "Do you always speak as if you stepped out of a Victorian novel?"

His statement had some truth to it, especially whenever I was nervous. Hell, I was freaking nervous. Anxiety made me pedantic. "I have no defense. Comparative literature is my major."

His bushy eyebrows shot up, and his eyes widened. Without a second's pause, he began to pontificate upon his honor's thesis on the hot new novel *V.*, by Thomas Pynchon. "The plot is that the bombings from the V2 rockets were within the control of an enlisted soldier's erections." He waited for a moment to see my response. I stayed stock-still. "Absurdity and satire are bonded together in this novel. Pynchon's writings are a bit like a drug-induced stream of consciousness."

It was then that I knew we were bonded through our love of literature.

That weekend we hiked along crumbling gravel and giant boulders that filled the dusty levees, steep inclines zigzagging the path. Andy seemed goatlike as he climbed and leaped over rocks, pulling himself over boulders along the dry riverbed. He turned to help me up the steepest rock ledges. His guidance came as a welcome relief. His long legs easily lunged from rock to rock, while my short legs held me back. He must have noticed because he halted every few steps for me to catch up.

"Isn't it great out here?" He shielded his eyes from the harsh sun.

I nodded, sweaty and out of breath. My cheap drugstore aviator sunglasses were useless. Nothing but relentless sunshine, a mirage of waves created by the heat. Choking dust swirled around us. I took out a bottle of water and swigged.

"Save some of it until we get to a spring," he warned.

"Oh yeah. I'm used to fog, snow, and drenching rain. Carrying all this water is exhausting. It'd be easier without the backpack." The sleeping bag hooked to the bottom of my canvas bag slid sideways, pulling me over. "Next time let's bring the mules," I joked.

I grabbed a rock only to scrape my hand along the spines of a Spanish dagger cactus, which seemed aptly named as I licked the blood from my scratched palm. "Oooooh, that thing's deadly."

"Deadly to any predator who wants to steal its water."

"Evolution is a b—" My foot slipped on the gravelly sand of an ancient lakebed, and I fell onto my left hip. "Crap." The heavy backpack, a canvas relic from Andy's Boy Scout days, shifted uncomfortably on my ample girl hips. I attempted to stand upright but found balancing to be problematic. It required a skilled dexterity I did not possess as a novice backpacker.

Repeat the steps he taught you, I told myself. *Place the backpack up against a rock or tree. Sit on the hard ground with your heels close to your butt. Dig into the hard soil. Pull straps around shoulders. In one fell swoop, lift, then hoist the weight of your next few days of sustenance, including two large and very heavy canisters of water, onto your back, and then miraculously somehow stand up.* I had yet to master the final step without Andy's help in lifting the bag onto my shoulders.

I wanted so desperately to engage in a rugged adventure, to explore beyond my physical limits, to become courageous and not simply conform to an indoor environment. As we hiked through the rugged canyon, I began to feel petulant. A child discouraged, complaining: "I can't do this anymore." What was wrong with me to trust a man with my survival? Was this what "falling" in love meant—a literal downward slide into a steep canyon with amorous myths fogging my powers of reason?

"I need to sit my weary ass. When do we stop?" I slipped on rocks, upturned like a dying turtle. Lusty fantasies dropped. "Are we having fun yet?"

"Definitely." He helped me upright and threw my backpack over his shoulder along with his own. It made me feel feminine, weak, but relieved.

Around the next bend, we finally reached the edge of the mountain pass. He turned, dropped the bags, then stopped to wait for me. He held out his hand for the last step. I waved him away and picked up my backpack. I refused to be some fainting princess.

We rested along the sand of the riverbed. I gulped water from my canister. Andy gently put his hand on my arm. "Might want to hold on to some of that water for the rest of the trip. It's mostly uphill."

I capped the bottle. The term "riverbed" seemed a misnomer since it became a waterway only a few weeks in spring as the mountain snowmelt rushed in fury down the canyon walls. Boulders larger than the height of a man and half the size of a garage stood sentry as evidence of the power of floodwaters—something I had learned from the geologists at work. That day, though, nary a drop of liquid could be seen in all four directions.

He handed me some homemade granola to munch on while sipping hot water from his dented canteen. I found it oddly chivalrous that he gave me his ration of water when we were both parched. As we hiked, he passed the time by telling me more about his childhood, how he had moved from the fruit orchards of San Jose to the cacti-riddled Mule Mountains on the Mexican border of Bisbee. I listened closely. There was something soothing in hearing his story as we rested in the canyon's cool shadow.

The desert held a holy silence broken by only a few wrens. I glanced skyward. "Why are vultures circling us?" I pointed to four large black birds, their long necks twisting back and forth, their white wingtips spread upward to catch the breeze.

He glanced up. "They probably see a dying animal."

"Could that be us? The backpack is killing me. Is there no cure for this slow, painful death? Or do I simply wait for the vultures to take care of my remains?"

"We'll sit a little longer to see what the vultures might do."

It took me a moment to realize this was his attempt at humor. It wasn't that he was humorless, but he displayed a stoic seriousness on most subjects that I took as evidence for his brilliant intelligence. I wasn't sure what to make of the humor yet.

I massaged my aching shoulders, glad to have a moment's respite, even as the midday sun bore down on us. We sat on a bedroll under the awning of a large rock, protected by a thin line of shade. He pulled out a joint and lit it up and offered it to me. I must have hesitated because as he held it, he began to confess how he was arrested as a drug dealer, luckily before he turned eighteen, and how in that moment in prison he had decided to leave town and go to college.

Mesmerized by his calm voice speaking of deep secrets that he was sharing exclusively with me, I believed I must be special to him. I never thought it might be a self-imposed fantasy.

"It was stupid, really," he admitted. "I sold half a kilo to a DEA agent at a high school dance party. Classic dumb teenage maneuver." He took a drag of the joint and handed it to me.

It was my first attempt at smoking marijuana. I tried to imitate his technique. Instead, I went into a long coughing spell. When at last I caught my breath again, I realized I was giddy as hell. I began laughing at how funny it all seemed: Man tells teenage tale. Woman laughs in encouragement. The laughing became uncontrollable.

We stopped at a hidden spring in the canyon's darkness to fill our canteens. He told me of his siblings, motherless children all, running the hills and valleys of the Mule Mountains. "We used to lift rocks to watch scorpions scatter, holding tarantulas in our hands, daring each other." The more he revealed himself, the more enchanted I became.

I glanced around at the stark landscape. I was hooked on this man and on the beauty surrounding us. Oddly shaped plants I had never seen wended their way through cracks in sheer rock.

"It looks like an ancient fairy land," I said.

"It's beautiful." He looked directly at me. "And so are you."

I lunged at him. Luckily, he was more than ready, hard as the rocks. I ignored my back scraping along sand.

In the grappling rush, we heard a gunshot.

He ignored it and mumbled into my hair, "That's normal this time of year." I found it soothing until the shots increased and seemed to close in on us, intensifying in sound.

He finished quickly, but I was not there yet.

"We've got to go," he said.

"But, but, but . . . I'm not done yet." I gasped and furiously attempted to finish the female part of this coupling activity with rapid hand movements, fingers flying at my nether parts. Luckily, since I'd played violin for decades, the dexterity and rapidity in my fingers made me a skillful and efficient artist.

"I admire your focus," he said, "but we really do have to go. The hunters are getting closer. We should flag them first."

"Hunters? Flag? The hell with that. Just shout out, 'Stop, don't shoot.' I'm almost there. Just hang on, for chrissake . . .'"

A shot rang out, grazing a rock behind us. That made me stop my intense jiggling momentarily. "Do we leap up and run?"

"No, they'll think we're deer. It's hunting season."

Frick, I thought, *but I'm not done.*

I'd only just discovered the West, men, and orgasm. I was too young to die, but I didn't want to stop until I came. Bullets went whizzing overhead. I didn't care. I wanted to finish what I started. My hand and fingers flayed in rapid motion, my body sweating in fits until, *pop*, a surge of joy streaked through my core. I stopped, satisfied, and opened my eyes to Andy staring at me in what looked like awe.

"That was impressive." He glanced over the horizon. "I don't think they see us."

I ripped off my white T-shirt, stood up, and waved it in the air. The shooting ceased as two grizzled overweight men with rifles in one hand and beer cans in the other smiled at the sight.

"You're an enigma." Andy shook his head and stared at me, neither smiling nor frowning. He waved to the men, then lifted both backpacks, one on each arm. In the next moment, we were climbing out of the canyon and into the foothills of the mountain ahead.

"Are you okay?"

Andy's voice reached out to me, almost muffled. The first tab of acid had easily melted on my tongue. I had no idea how much time had passed or if time even mattered anymore. I only felt a mellow lightness.

When we'd reached the higher elevation, I could see a huge meadow, a lush carpet of deep green waving in the breeze between two sharp peaks. Defying exhaustion, I began leaping casually from rock to rock and broken branches crisscrossing the creek bed, like a gazelle born to the shadowy edges of the mountain's ledge. Ponderosa pines swayed slightly in the breeze. The day's sun had begun to slip farther westward. Brilliant orange, purple, and fuchsia pink streaked across the darkening horizon.

A lightness of being took over. "I don't feel a thing yet," I answered.

"Well, we can cure that."

He handed me another small tab of paper with a blurred Minnie Mouse stamp on it. That first tab of acid I ingested had a bright orange sun bleeding into the thin paper. Minnie Mouse's face, on the second tab, smiled up at me, her comical image blurring the drug infused in the thin paper.

In my desperation to travel this new road with this new man, I had let down my guard. Maybe it was the wild coupling hours earlier in the canyon with bullets whizzing overhead that freed me. I wasn't sure. I knew that I wanted to impress this young man. I was falling in love. I could almost envision our open partnership, bravely dismissing conventional life. I wanted to impress upon Andy that I was different, bold, a free spirit. Yet a piece of my still-functioning brain flashed a warning. *Wait*.

The practical "I've got to survive" girl stopped and stared at Minnie Mouse's image sitting so calmly in his hand. I placed Minnie under my tongue. It dissolved instantly.

"Don't worry. I'll walk you through every step of the trip." His mouth turned a little crookedly. "If a bear doesn't find us first."

"Bear?" A primordial fear of being eaten alive while incapacitated reached into the lizard portion of my drug-addled brain. I jumped at the sound of a small group of coatimundis, animals that look like a hybrid cross between a wildcat and a raccoon, inching closer to us, heady from the smells of crumbling granola left carelessly along the trail.

"Don't worry." He shooed them away with a wave of his hands. The coatimundis scattered. "We wouldn't feel a thing if a bear attacks us right now."

"What's with you desert rats making fun of us innocent East Coast bunnies?" I began laughing. Then, suddenly, a complete sleepiness took over. "I think I need to lie down before I fall down."

All the experiences I encountered with Andy that night in the mountains were new, and I took this newness as evidence of his worldliness. I felt calm permeate my being. His knowledge and his long arms surrounded me, protecting me. I trusted him.

I stared at the night sky. We were almost seven thousand feet above sea level. The tree canopy opened over the meadow. Stars began to appear in clusters until millions sparked the night sky.

Never in my childhood had I seen so many shooting stars. Meteorites danced above us, appearing to touch the earth in fiery balls. I was mesmerized. I could barely move.

Time suspended. Stars evolved into blinking Christmas tree lights that shifted in ever-widening circles. We were silent as the acid's chemicals slowly wormed their way into every part of our circulatory systems, reaching into our brains, altering reality.

So, I mused, *this is what an acid trip is all about—pleasant, safe, introspective.*

I thought of that wandering bear or even a cougar waiting hidden in the tree line for us to lose our minds. But the fleeting thought disappeared as easily as it came, turning into dream images.

Tiles of exquisitely painted sapphire blue and shiny silver began forming all around me. It was as if I was the master builder centered within a historic mosque forgotten eons ago. Slowly I placed every tile one by one, building a stunning tower. My being, my mind, my body became part of a thin thread of pure silver glinting into the starlight, pulling me higher as I continued to create the mosque to its apogee. The structure narrowed as I built the tiles into the towering structure, one over another, each more brilliant than the last.

At the mosque's highest point, I became one with the silver thread, bursting through the tiny opening at the top while sparkling meteors showered all around. I never felt such elation and awe. I wanted nothing more than to stay suspended above earth, the wavering thread flying higher past the stratosphere. A floating tranquility took over my entire being.

I could hear Andy's voice as if from a distant canyon, asking me if I was okay. I didn't know why he kept repeating himself. I couldn't answer. My breathing increased. I was unfazed as his voice faded away. I could no longer hear sounds. I could not feel ground. I could not see beyond colors forming. Paralyzed, all I could do was be. Be the silver thread. Be the sky. Be the stars.

A calmness and vastness struck my very core. Such beauty in the universe. I attempted to lift my hand to it, desperate to grasp what was just beyond our reach.

Suddenly, the thread unraveled in great heaps. I began a deadly drop of such velocity that I knew I would break once I hit ground. My heart pounded. I went into free fall. Incapacitated. I had no control over my body.

Andy's voice rose from the din, guiding me, telling me to breathe, to relax, to trust him, to believe in him.

The sky filled with an angry swirl of gray mist that began to choke me. I needed water. I needed to reach the stream. I attempted to rise only to fall back again with a thud.

I wanted to cry out, "Get me out of here," but couldn't. I dangled into an abyss. A deathly mist curled around me, crushing my vocal cords. I would die here, in the mountains. The bears and cougars would have their meal. I wanted this to end.

Still, I hung on as I vaguely began to feel Andy holding me. He continued to talk me down from the horrors of the crash he knew was coming but had not alerted me to when we began this journey.

His care and safety created a warmth that slowly grounded and returned me to earthly existence. His gentleness, I took for caring. His experimentation, for adventurous risk-taking. His studiousness, for intellectual curiosity. His charm, for understanding. So many decisions were made that night. How many months, years, decades would it take to balance love's reality against that moment?

Later I would wonder if love became its own hallucination. But for that night, for that trip, I believed in love. All that followed in the coming years seemed to emerge from that illusory belief.

PART THREE

Reinvention

18

The Vow

Flashbacks from the acid trip continued for weeks. I became intimate with the term "freaked out." The creation of the intricate mosque that I had envisioned, and the subsequent crash, unglued my mind. Andy's calm guidance felt intimate and loving during those dark moments. His masculine riskiness under the towering pines and star-filled night held enchantment.

As the months rolled from autumn into a cool Tucson winter, we began a series of exploratory lovemaking, testing, tasting, desiring one another. After every completed-to-exhaustion coupling, Andy would repeat, "Move in with me."

Fearful of losing myself to a man once again, I remained cautious. I refused to lose my independence, until reality intervened the night that we spent hours discussing free will versus determinism.

"Sue, how can you think of choice as anything except free will?"

We had walked out of the university's library well past midnight. Our footfalls landed with an echoing *tip-tap* along the path. Our bodies created long shadows under the moonlight.

"Let me explain," I remember countering. "As a woman, so many stages of life seem already predetermined. Yeah, sure, I can try to break the pattern, but I won't get far believing in ultimate free will if I don't find a way around everyday restriction."

He shook his head. "What restrictions? You are an agent of free will."

He was growing impatient. He couldn't fathom how a woman's power to explore without barriers was limited by gender. The need to protect oneself against the ever-present potential for violence seemed foreign to him. How could he acknowledge constant danger if he had never experienced it?

"Free will exists," I said. "I do make choices every day. But I also feel limited by a biological determinism. Maybe these are theoretical restrictions that I've imposed on myself. In my experience, my choices to move about freely are limited by my sex."

"Will I insult you if I feel the need to protect you by walking you back to your dorm?"

I balked at the gentlemanly request to watch over me as if I were a delicate flower needing shelter from the storm. "I think I'm capable of the short walk on my own."

"I know you are, but as you just pointed out, there are restrictions to your free will that never affect me."

"Ah, then you agree."

"Hardly. I believe in the essence of free will. Even your choice to walk home with or without me is you displaying free will." He had a professorial air about him with an almost obsessive need to educate anyone who happened to be around him, to ensure he had the last word. To some, it may have felt pedantic. To me, at that time, it seemed a display of confident innate intelligence.

He placed his philosophy textbook into his canvas backpack.

"I respect your free-will choice to walk alone." His eyebrows shifted upward for a moment. "Besides, I have a thesis to write, and I'm stuck with an early morning teaching assistant slot in freshmen chem."

His kiss was a perfunctory peck. I hid my disappointment and turned to walk away, waving without looking back. A shroud of silence surrounded the university mall. Only the eerie glow of an almost full moon and a thin thread of walkway lights illuminated the path.

When I turned into the dorm alleyway, pitch darkness enveloped me. I had to edge my way along the brick wall, a technique my blind grandmother used—tap your foot on the sidewalk edge one step at a time to avoid a fall. Move with slow deliberation. Count each step. Touch the wall.

That's when I heard heavier footsteps hitting the pavement.

An inherent flight response set my feet into a sightless run, stumbling over rocks and scraping my arm against the rugged bricks. I clung to the wall, moving straight forward toward safety. Before I could turn the corner toward the lights blazing ahead in the dorm lobby, a large man jumped on my back, knocking me over. In one swift move, he had grabbed both wrists and pinned my arms to the jagged cement.

The smell of his sour alcohol-laced breath made me recoil. My heart pumped a loud drumbeat in my ears, an innate memory of the rape in the suite. In a second, the adrenaline rush of sheer terror overcame me.

"Stop moving, damnit." His voice was raspy, angry.

"Get off me." I arched my back and kicked violently. He slapped his hands over my mouth. I chomped down as hard as I could into his greasy palm.

"Jesus Christ, you bitch. You fucking bit me."

Something clicked. Fear turned to sheer rage. I responded by default, triggered by the memory of being pinned down, helpless. I had one moment to react and one moment only. The silent scream I had heard in my nightmares disappeared, and an instinct to survive engulfed me, possessing me with overwhelming strength. My howl of anger filled the night. I remember thinking, *You may be bigger and stronger, but I'm not going down without a fight. Not now. Not ever.*

When I screamed again, the sound seemed distant, but he reacted immediately and jumped back. I took the opportunity to turn to release myself from his grip.

He regained momentum, pinned me down again, and started tugging the waistline of my pants, yanking down on the zipper.

He muttered obscenities. "Bitch. Cunt. Whore." His hatred filled the empty walkway. He raged, insulted by my attempts to survive, spitting words in a litany of frustration. His raw language spewed forth directly at me, at every woman who had ever spurned him.

I had taken a college self-defense class. I remembered the police officer repeating, "Get away. Just run. Fighting back increases the danger." Every woman in the class knew that a man intent on harm, a man who sees women as objects, as his property, as a thing to destroy, could easily become inflamed if you fought back.

I had no choice. I had to respond. To choose to fight, to find a moment to run away, or to play dead and pray he wouldn't kill me. A free-will choice made in a nanosecond.

The attacker's obvious disdain for women and the words hurled at me in his pursuit of power and violation drove me to act.

No knight in shining armor would be coming to my rescue at this time of night. My body overruled my mind. I responded automatically, striking out, dodging his blows. I flipped over in one turn and slammed my heavy biology textbook straight at his Adam's apple.

He thrashed out furiously, screeching in pain. I hit soft spots only by sheer force of my fury. The relentless rage of memory struck out. I screamed. *This is not going to happen again.*

Jumping up, I began running at full speed, not looking back, my heart racing. I did not stop until I turned the corner and got inside the dorm. I kept going until I stood safely inside my bedroom. I flung my backpack onto the bed. Kai barely moved. I tried to calm my breathing, to think, to absorb what had just happened. I slipped quietly into the bathroom to scrub his smell off me. I dug the toothbrush into my gums to rid the grease and blood from my teeth where I had bitten him.

Once in bed, I began to berate myself for being so naive. How could I live by free will when I had to deal with such attacks?

I slept little that night. His curse words blew hot in my ear; his drool on the skin of my neck and his sour smell returned in nightmares. More than once, I woke up furiously wiping away imaginary spittle. I cursed myself too. Why didn't I let Andy walk me home?

In the morning, it seemed apparent to me that even with self-defense, buying a gun and learning how to use it, and never walking after dark, that fear might be forever present in my life, altering every decision. I didn't dare tell anyone. I didn't want to hear the questions: "What were you wearing? Why were you alone in a dark alley? What did you expect walking around alone at night on campus?" I didn't want to deal with anyone's shaming, real or imagined.

The joy of a solitary walk to admire the stars at night was

shoved aside, squashed, forgotten, destroyed forever. My craving for freedom had crashed into the brick wall of fear.

I reflected on what life could be with Andy. I ticked off a pro list of his best qualities. He seemingly cared for my well-being. He had asked to walk me home. He had treated me kindly and calmly during the acid trip.

Safety in his long arms held an animal primacy. The pragmatist in me knew it was much easier to survive with him by my side.

I accepted Andy's request to move in with him. *Once safe*, I reasoned, *I can pursue opportunities, form my own dreams.*

The move-in took place the following month. No questions asked. I never told him the reason for my quick change of mind. He simply handed me the keys. What I failed to notice at the time was Andy's lack of involvement in the process. Instead, I took his "you're on your own" approach to my moving in as his respect for my independence.

By semester's end-of-year break, he had insisted on flying to Upstate New York with me.

My mother, perhaps out of sheer boredom, flirted endlessly with him. Enamored by his dark good looks and starved for academic conversation, she met with him every night of our visit. He filled her in on existentialism. She listened intently, adding what she knew of philosophy from her readings. I watched her grow younger with each fresh discussion. I could see in her eyes that she'd longed for an intellectual's life, to have attended college, to be young and unencumbered.

Watching her reminded me of the time she told me to "always marry a handsome man. Then when all goes to hell, you can simply sit and stare at him." My father, upon hearing this, had said, "There it is. Honesty to the point of brutality." More than once, I realized that I had inherited her pragmatism, never questioning if the man involved felt used.

My sister Sharon came downstairs to the kitchen the morning before Christmas. I was reading the newspaper in the corner while Andy and my mother were at the dining room table chatting. Sharon yawned and went to grab the coffee pot percolating on the gas stove. She turned when she heard them. "Ma, are you still flirting with that boy?"

Without changing position, my mother retorted, "Ma is for goats. I'm your mother." She returned to her conversation, undaunted. Andy glanced from me to my sister and shrugged.

From the corner I could see my mother's light complexion blooming into a hot pink blush. She waved her hand, dismissing us both. She focused, instead, on Andy. I didn't question her motives. I knew her intellectual hunger ran unabated. I also knew she was less than sixteen years older than my beau. Her focus made me see him through her eyes—a protector, an intelligent, handsome, strong male.

After dinner that night, I took Andy to the neighborhood cemetery. It reminded me of my first illicit necking sessions nestled between the headstones of my teen years. The morbid evidence of the ephemeral aspect of life was scattered in graveyards with mostly nineteenth-century tombstones.

One man's headstone slanted sideways like a drunk ghost. It was surrounded by smaller headstones of several wives and newborns with identical death dates. Strolling among the graveyard from centuries ago, it became clear that childbirth sometimes became a young mother's death sentence. It was a reminder of the short time span of human existence. Oddly, it created an urgency in me to start my own domestic life. The stones stood as props, proof that marriage could come with a loss of life. Love never seemed to fit into the lines of these epitaphs.

The beauty of Andy, his kindness toward my mother, and the possibility of him as a mate made me realize love could be safe.

My gaze turned toward him. He had started to shake uncontrollably from the bitter cold. Enamored by the picture-pretty snow covering the bridge that overlooked a creek bed below, I could see him cast a suspicious eye at the ice shards at the water's edge.

In that moment, I fell in love with him, with his potential, with his vulnerable shivers.

Although personal choices can affect a lifetime, without hesitation, I said, "Marry me."

To build a bridge of my own, I had dismissed the dangers of sudden rock-solid decisions. Even stone, I would realize later, will crack eventually under duress.

I watched him translate the words in his head silently. Was he wondering what he would be gaining in companionship or losing in freedom if he said yes? He seemed to have been swallowed whole by the snowy path. I knew the question was a serious test of his precious free will that he so adamantly believed in. He looked at the ice crusting below, sparkling lightly in the lone streetlight. He nodded a compliant yes. Thin icicles from his beard slipped to his coat as he moved his head almost imperceptibly.

We both stared out into the frozen plots of dead souls. I wondered how many women had ever proposed to a man, much less in a cemetery. Most women seemed to wait forever in anticipation, giving hints along the way but never venturing forth to ask directly. Reversing gender roles gave me a degree of control and pride. A life together could launch a nonconformist adventure in partnering. We could shelter within each other's arms.

He realized I was waiting for a word, not just a simple nod. "Oh, of course." His voice was muffled by the soft flakes swirling around us.

"You're not just saying yes because I could plunge you to your icy death by pushing you off this bridge?"

He paused. He did not smile. His hat slipped forward over his scowling brow as he seriously thought about the implications.

I waited. Breathless. I could feel him weighing options. What were the odds that someone would propose to keep his bed warm during the difficult years of graduate school drudgery and long hours of lab work that lay ahead?

He sighed and threw his arms around me. The word "yes" finally reached my ears.

The next morning, if I had second thoughts, they fled.

Andy, hearing my father berate my mother, rushed into the kitchen as if to defend her. I followed but having spent my teen years locked in battle with my father's momentary bad moods and defending my mother since she refused to be bothered to engage with him, I wasn't worried. My mother would remain silent as my father raged. For all the days and months and years that my father hit us with leather belts and bare hands or shook us senseless, he never touched my mother. Even when she was in a drunken stupor and her finely honed sense of sarcasm flew at him with the knife-wielding accuracy of a circus entertainer, he never struck her.

"He shouldn't be speaking to your mother like that."

Andy dressed quickly to go downstairs to rescue my mom, his sense of honor high. I followed him, simply to ensure no blood was shed. When we reached the kitchen, we could hear my father bellowing swear words—about what, we did not know. My mother, sipping her coffee, looked up from reading the newspaper. She directed a dagger stare at him and slowly lifted her middle finger as if every second of motion held meaning.

My dad stopped shouting immediately. He backed away and left the dining room, pushing past us without looking our way.

I couldn't explain to Andy that no one could be saved from my father's moodiness. Yet, with one thin defiant finger held in the air, my mother had silenced him. Her power to deflect with the most minimal of movements fell into the realm of the domestic arts I knew I would never master. My mother's view of marriage was of practicality, not romance.

I remembered having met Andy's sister at Thanksgiving the month before. Her black wavy hair fell to her "arse," as she put it. Long dangling Navajo turquoise earrings in the shape of swooping hawks fell to her shoulders. She threw a casual remark my way. "I'm glad you're with my brother. Now I can stop worrying about him and concentrate on the three other lost boys." She had become the mother replacement to her four brothers when their mother died. I lessened her burden by being another woman, by taking care of another man.

The months after the proposal were marked by long hours of work for Andy. I relished the solitude. That spring, he won the outstanding senior award and was referred to in the graduation ceremony as the "renaissance man of his generation." My own graduation seemed unimportant, unworthy. I believed he was the super star. And in that belief, I continued the generational decision to become a mere helpmate, the other, secondary.

Marriage as a power struggle, with each opponent wielding tactics that worked only in certain circumstances, shaped my childhood. Where I had witnessed a war of control and dominance in the past, I believed marriage could exist between partners as equals.

Our wedding the following summer seemed to be the event of the season for my family. Relatives, some not even invited, turned up in droves to attend an outdoor ceremony at Sonnenberg Gardens, in Canandaigua, New York, while a thunderous downpour deluged the grounds.

Len, my college roommate, arrived wearing bell-bottom daisy-embroidered jeans, a lace cotton blouse straight out of a Mexican market, and a matching blue beret tilted jauntily to one side.

"Your maid of dishonor at your service." She bowed with a flourish, leaned in, and whispered, "Can you imagine how the clan would react if they could see our photos from that art class?"

I laughed, ignoring the confusion among the relatives who overheard us. They came for a show, and Len wanted to give them one. Sharon stood sentry at the entrance to allow guests onto the wet porch. Mark dressed in a polyester tan leisure suit attempting, at age fifteen, to look the part of best man. Julie flounced about, the youngest sibling, ten years old, grasping a bunch of daisies so tightly they'd begun to wilt.

Andy's Sicilian grandmother, his aunt, and a few female teenage cousins were the only visible family on his side. His own siblings could not afford the plane tickets to attend, which saddened us both. I tightened the tie of the light cream-colored halter-topped cotton dress I bought at a local Goodwill store. A large-brimmed straw hat with my sister's blue scarf flying in the wind acted as a veil. With my bridal attire, along with Andy's flowered shirt, jeans, and hiking boots, we posed for our hippie wedding.

During the ceremony, Julie slipped on the porch, hit her knee on the wood railing, and started to wail. Although in mid-vows, I stopped and hurried over to pick her up, almost as an intuitive reaction and much to my mother's chagrin.

"Stop babying that girl. Get back to your place next to your husband." I ignored my mother and hugged my sister to dry her tears. That's when I heard my great-uncle Guido's spitting words in a harsh dialect no one, except Andy's grandmother, could understand. She raised her voice, sharp prongs of unintelligible remarks in a Southern Italian dialect aimed at Guido.

Wedding guests turned from the bride and groom. Italian relatives watched with the anticipation of participants in a boxing ring, while my mother's Anglo relatives looked shocked at the lack of decorum.

Len caught my eye and tossed her head toward the commotion. From the flaying hand gestures toward the groom, I could only assume Guido's conversation held Andy in disdain. With the little Italian I could decipher, I heard something about Guido's assessment of Andy being a girl due to his long hair. The rest was lost in translation.

Without a second's hesitation, Andy's grandmother, Josephina, born and raised in Palermo, let loose a torrent of matching Sicilian dialect, saying that anyone maligning her grandson might want to take more care with his life lest he lose it. In one moment, my wedding became a stereotype of *The Godfather*'s working-class sequel.

I watched my soon-to-be husband's family matriarch destroy Guido with a few choice words and a well-placed hand gesture rarely seen in good company. Like my mother, she displayed a feminine power I did not seem to possess. I returned to my spot on the wedding dais next to Andy, who seemed more bemused than upset. *A good match*, I thought.

"Let me not to the marriage of true minds admit impediments. Love is not love . . ." I stopped. I'd lost my place, forgotten the next verse. I glanced down and saw mud edged around the hem of my dress, sandals streaked in brown as if I'd stepped into cow manure. *Why am I getting married? Because I am in love? Or because I need safety?* I stared at Andy. His brow scrunched up as if trying to solve a mathematical puzzle.

"Sue forgot her lines," my mother's voice called out, shaking me from my reverie. "Where are the cue cards?" She looked around at the crowd as if this was a poorly staged one-act play with mediocre actors. People laughed nervously. I looked out among the crowd of relatives from my childhood.

A panic began to set into my bones. *What am I doing? I'm too young.*

Oh no, you're not, I could hear my mother say. She'd been three years younger when she got married. I stared at the guests on the porch. The patter of heavy rain fell to the Italian rose garden beyond.

"Ahem." I cleared my dry throat and skipped ahead, altering my destiny. "I promise to cherish this, our *equal* partnership."

It was a simple belief. Nothing more. No promise for the future.

I would later learn that vows have a funny way of becoming lifelong dictates. I did not know at the time that those few words could make a difference in how one conducts a marriage.

By simply uttering words, it seemed, we had chosen a path to our own becoming. Words that could entrap us. Words that would take decades for either of us to decipher. A simple egalitarian vow symbolized, in a drenched garden with flattened rose petals sticking to the mud, that a vow expressed is a vow never forgotten.

19

Sea of Secrets

The wonder of the natural world excited Andy. Chemistry fit his perfectionist's obsession. Science became his methodical, patient, and calculating mistress. I could not compete with the hours it took to pipette from beaker to glass tube, each reaction jotted down into endless lab notebooks.

Fluorescent lights flickered late into the night as he wrote and endlessly revised his master's thesis. A vague discontent took over our lives. He wanted to push westward, and the seafaring life of an oceanographer became his siren call.

From pre-dawn hours until long after twilight, I organized the cleaning, selling, and packing. The day before his thesis defense, he walked into our empty apartment to find me napping on the lone piece of furniture in the living room—a half-deflated air mattress.

"You asleep?" He sounded tired and annoyed.

I opened my mouth in a languid yawn. "Not anymore."

I looked up to see him shake his head, his long shaggy ponytail swishing back and forth from shoulder to shoulder. He placed his hands on his hips and glowered at me.

"This place is filthy. Didn't you even sweep? How're we going to get our deposit back? We don't have enough money as it is since you quit your job a month too early."

"What do you mean? I quit when you said you were ready to move. I believed you when you said it." I sat up, alert, ready to defend myself. "If you haven't noticed, I've been dutifully packing so that you could be free to procrastinate writing your thesis." I knew I sounded snarky. My lower back ached from the hours and days of schlepping garbage bags and sleeping over a bare cement floor.

"My procrastination, as you put it, is to ensure everything is precisely done. Unlike you"—he waved his hands over the floor as if to make the dirt magically disappear—"I attend to details. Not the sloppy messes you leave in your wake."

I rolled to my right hip to stand. "May I remind you that you didn't help one bit. I did it all."

"Oh, poor you." He threw his hands up in the air, then grabbed the rolled sleeping bag from under my feet, almost making me slip. "I need to get some sleep." The bag dragged behind him like a bridal train, sweeping dust right and left, as he marched down the hallway to the empty bedroom. He slammed the door.

"The honeymoon is over," I shouted.

The door opened. I could hear the handle slam against the wall. *Well, there's damage that will reduce our deposit*, I thought with rising irritation.

He returned to the living room and loomed over me. "The honeymoon was over when you decided to move out in the midst of my finishing my degree."

"Move out? I moved out for all of twenty-four hours. Plus, that was almost a year ago. I apologized. Why can't you forget about it?" I remembered the dreary night I'd spent in a rented room. How could I stay? I'd grown unimportant in his life. He'd acted childish and petulant when I asked him to shift his lab hours to come home earlier. He'd shown a lack of concern about the serial rapist in the neighborhood and my increased anxiety. He altered his hours only after I had moved out. I thought all was forgiven.

"You left me when I needed you most."

It's just nerves about his thesis defense, I told myself, *nothing more.*

"Never mind. Just go back to sleep." He stated it as a command.

But he could not command me to return to sleep. With bleary eyes the next morning, I attended his oral presentation. I fell into a sleepy trance. The words "sulfur dioxide" and "manganese" floated past my foggy brain. Then, before I could register what had happened, Andy walked out of the conference room to triumphant applause and kudos from fellow graduate students and professors. I remembered my role and smiled dutifully, the ever-appreciative wife.

The silence between us intensified as we drove across the desert to Scripps Institution of Oceanography in La Jolla, California, where Andy would pursue his doctoral studies. Our 1957 Chevy pickup truck, nicknamed Old Guts, was laden with mattress, table, desk lamp, and reference books. Old Guts spewed smoke, chugged, and died in the parking lot, where we left it next to more colorful vehicles, like the flower-painted VW bug and red Mustang convertible sports car of our neighbors.

My images of California were forged from Hollywood musicals and the romance of the sea formed from Jacques Cousteau documentaries. For both of us, the coast seemed an uncharted territory of picture-perfect beaches and opportunities. It was a travel poster fantasy. My feet had never brushed an ocean's shoreline, much less experienced the crashing Pacific. Those first few days I walked up and down the La Jolla Shores Beach in solitude, watching surfers balance on the waves like glistening ballerinas in their black wet suits.

Andy's professor invited us to the weekly TGIF keg party overlooking the Scripps Institution of Oceanography's pier. Graduate students mingled to gain favor with advisers and align themselves with like-minded colleagues. While they chatted, my gaze fell upon the Pacific shore, my ears deaf to human communication. I listened to the sounds of the sea. And, in that moment, I understood Andy's desire to explore the ocean's depths, to watch dolphins follow a ship's wake, to go out to sea for months on end.

In the distance, I could hear Andy's voice. He seemed to be bragging about his outstanding senior award and his master's research while a petite female graduate student with pixie-cropped hair, tiny shorts flashing pink flesh above a distinct tan line, grasped a glass of beer in one hand and Andy's hairy forearm in her other.

I ignored her slight turn in my direction. By now, I was used to being examined as a potential rival to other women flirting with Andy. I waved a weak finger in acceptance, no longer bothered by the courtship rituals of graduate school seductions.

The sea's siren, on the other hand, beckoned. I wandered off down a crumbling limestone cliff. At the bottom, I flipped off my sandals under the lifeguard stand near the seawall and rolled up my jeans. I began to walk toward the foamy surf. I glanced up at the deck above to see Andy still engaged in conversation. I could see the crowd connecting, sizing each other up as possible partners, both professionally and sexually, a strange Kabuki dance of aspirations.

Surfers grasped long boards, decorated with curvaceous cartoonish female silhouettes, to their sculpted waists. They stood along the shoreline like a flock of majestic birds in black wetsuits, measuring cresting waves, rip currents, and distance with focused attention.

I picked up speed, running at a light jog to reach the shoreline, with the sudden desire to jump into the sea. I stopped at the foamy edge. Cold water surged up to my knees.

Suddenly, a wall of water slapped me broadside, knocking me to the wet sand. I began to roll and tumble. A current I couldn't fight picked me up and began carrying me out to sea. The shock of cold water and a billion rocky pebbles crashed over me.

I panicked.

Seawater churned in circles. Sand filled the soaked denim, cold on my thighs. The weight began to pull me to the rocky bottom. I tried to cling to the seafloor, digging into shifting rocks, when a cresting wave smashed over my head, and I fell into freezing water. My left arm scraped ragged broken shells on the seafloor. Salt water burned my foot. I felt before I saw the bloody gash.

It seemed a surfer had kicked off his board and the hard edge hit the heel of my foot, splitting the skin open. Pain shot through to bone. Dazed, I breast-stroked to shore as best I could.

It seemed I had blundered into an invisible fence of surfer territory, unknowing and unwanted. I began to flail, to get out of the way. Fleeting thoughts of blood attracting sharp-toothed barracuda made me scurry only to fall into the waves again.

Suddenly, a tug of a thin arm embraced my shoulder, and an

ethereal woman with wild to-the-waist red curly hair, wearing a tiny fuchsia-pink bikini, pulled me toward the shore. Gasping, I rolled over onto my back, desperate for air, and could only utter a throaty "Thank you" to my benefactor.

Shivering, I got up as best I could while my angel in pink guided me to the parking lot. She pulled the old blanket we kept over the torn seat of our Chevy pickup truck around my shoulders.

"Are you okay?" She gently lifted her hand to my shoulder.

"Yeah, just embarrassed."

"New to California, eh." It was a statement. "I'm from Texas dirt country. Waves freaked me out the first time too. After a while, it's just the same old boring shit."

"I don't think the beach could ever be boring."

She rolled her eyes for a second. "You came with the new grad student? Andy, right?" I nodded yes and blushed. In my embarrassment, it never crossed my mind to wonder how she knew his name. All I realized was that my childish and exuberantly stupid behavior had been noted.

"You're married, right?"

I glanced up and nodded again, feeling oddly exposed.

"I think you're going to find that you're an endangered species here. No one in oceanography is married—or stays married, I should say—except a few too-old-to-crap professors." She jogged in place a bit. "They spend way too many months out to sea." She shrugged. "And there's way too many opportunities."

"Opportunities?"

She dismissed me with a wave of her hand. Her multicolored braided bracelet swung in circles around her wrist. "Let's just say, you'll be studied here like some strange exotic fish." She laughed. "Call me Mescalita. Real name's Michelle. Got the nickname from a bar in Baja when I was drinking a little too much mezcal. They swear I ate the worm, but I have no memory of that." She winked. "Welcome to Sodom and Gomorrah." She turned to watch a string of male runners in tight speedos. "Enough about me. What about you?"

I said nothing. This move was all about Andy. Not me. I had no answer.

"See that cute hunk way over there?" She pointed to what looked like a tall, attractive guy in a wet suit, his brown beard shaking with seawater. "I'm dating that guy. Pablo. For now. He's a grad student and very sweet, but it'll be over soon." She looked toward the Scripps pier and waved. The hunk in question waved back. "Here, it's always over before it begins with these guys. But it's fun for a while."

"Over?" I repeated, feeling like some idiotic parrot learning a new language.

"Yeah, they go out to sea for months at a time. No communication. No letters. No calls. Nada." She stared for a moment. "Oh, but not everyone cheats. Sorry about that. Didn't mean to upset you. I guess if you trust your husband . . ." She let the words trail.

For a moment, I felt a sharp chest pain. She had appeared before me like a magician's assistant. Her lithe runner's body with few curves stood before me. Her hands on her slight hips, legs wide apart, her piercing green eyes flashed. She seemed assured of her worth and place in this world. In an instant, I felt like a nobody, an uncouth and awkward hanger-on to my husband's adventures. He would have "opportunities" while I had what?

"I do trust him. I guess." I heard my voice, too high pitched and not what I normally sounded like. "I trust him to be human."

For some reason, she found that hilarious, and her laughter filled the breeze around me.

"That's the best answer I've ever heard. If you're in an open marriage, you're in the right place."

"Well, maybe not open entirely," I corrected and glanced at where Andy stood, still busy flirting. "It's more of a quasi-open marriage." I shocked myself. I wondered if I was preparing for some future predilection for infidelity, mimicking my grandmother's maxim on every wife wanting to be a mistress, or if I was simply hedging my bets in case opportunities for me arose.

"I just moved here." I changed the subject.

"What do you do, besides trust your husband to be human, that is?"

Repeating that I was following my husband's lead sounded a bit insipid, so instead, I said, "I'm looking for a job. I've worked in publications, newspaper desk, geological survey, bookstore, that sort of thing."

"You work in publications? Hey, girl, call me. We're looking for an art production assistant." She lifted out a business card from a tiny purse tied around her even tinier waist. It was the first business card I'd ever seen. She handed it to me. "I'm a designer at the press. That's HBJ. The only shop in town. Anyone who jumps into surfer territory like you just did, clothes and all, has some guts. I have a feeling you're going to be fun to work with."

Before I could correct her about falling—not jumping—into the waves, tell her I didn't know a thing about surfer culture, and admit that "open marriage" was probably a misnomer, she waved goodbye. A big grin lit up her face as she ran back to the shoreline to catch up with her fellow joggers, her red curls swaying with each stride. I stared at the card with her name and number in large bold black type with the blue HBJ logo behind it.

In hoping to seem sophisticated, to fit into this new lifestyle, I knew I had to tamp down my anxiety. The "trust my husband to be human" answer had popped out. To live in this beautiful place surrounded by beautiful people and to be able to remain loyal to each other might be a challenge. Our vow to "cherish our equal partnership" shifted. Maybe it wasn't an equal partnership after all.

I watched from a distance my husband's attempt to make a good first impression. He walked in a casual stride toward the truck. His mustache drew upward in a private smile, his eyes shrouded behind dark sunglasses. My trepidations grew. He turned away from me to wave at a woman.

I later learned her name was Desiree, a PhD student like himself, and that she'd be going out to sea with him for many months. Trust would be tested.

At that moment, instead of being concerned about the stability of my marriage, I began pondering Mescalita's question: *What about you?*

Less than a week later, Andy headed for the *Ellen B. Scripps*, the scientific cruise ship that would carry him to Mexico's Baja Sea of Cortez and to freedom.

I followed up on Mescalita's lead. After checking local job agency listings, I realized HBJ, or Harcourt Brace Jovanovich, sat smack in the city's center near the San Diego harbor. I had read over the want ads, and sure enough, I saw the listing for art and production assistant. I jumped at the chance.

"Glad you called," Mescalita said as she escorted me into

what appeared to be a building made of glass. Brilliant rays of sunshine burst into every room. Large banana plants draped the gigantic foyer. She pointed me toward her boss Pat, the production manager.

"We got over five hundred applicants," Mescalita said. "Pat hates interviewing. Not even sure she likes people much. You're only the third person in line to meet her. I'm cheering for you." She walked over to another glass-walled office. I saw her lean over a large art table tilted at forty-five degrees, surrounded by miniature paintbrushes. Large pads of drawing paper with light blue markings over typed words bracketed in black margins were tacked all over the corkboard wall.

Pat remained in her seat, as if the very notion of greeting me at the door took too much energy. A half-burned cigarette hung from her cracked lips. The smell of smoke brought back memories of my time at the news desk in Syracuse. I felt instantly at home. She stared at me for a second before grabbing a handful of Hershey Kisses from a jar on her desk. She began unwrapping them, chowing down one Kiss after another, the cigarette miraculously staying in place.

"Okay, kid. Talk." Her Brooklyn accent momentarily threw me off. San Diego had a reputation as a health-crazed, outdoor-living, low-key, non-smoking, slow-talking Western kind of town. Yet here in front of me was a hard-driving New Yorker. I took it as a good omen.

"I'm your new production art assistant," I said.

Pat dropped the candy wrapper and stood up. I could see then that she was decked out in a man's crumpled suit that swam on her heavy body. She motioned me to come closer. I could see a glimpse of a sunset tattoo on her neck with a black crow snaking over her collarbone. "What makes you say that?" Her hazel eyes drilled into me in a way I was unaccustomed to from a woman.

Suddenly, my polyester cornflower-blue pantsuit with ruffled blouse seemed both too formal and too feminine. I coughed, my throat dry. I pulled out my one-page résumé. She grabbed it.

"I worked at the *Syracuse Post-Standard* in New York and the university publishing branch in Tucson. I've written several personal interest stories for local papers," I said, the rapid pace of nervousness rendering me breathless. I stopped, hoping she wouldn't ask me for the by-line articles, since most were from student newspapers. One piece covered the local ballet company, another an art museum opening. A third reported on interviews from the prison riot in Attica, New York.

"We don't need another wannabe writer." She jabbed her finger at the paper. "It says here that you won honorable mention at an Everson Museum of Art gallery. Have you done any artwork?" I nodded. "You got any problem with hauling boxes around, marking up galley proofs, and rushing around like a maniac to meet insane deadlines?"

"That's what the newspaper trained me to do." I smiled.

"Good, this saves me some time. I'm not up for any more interviewing of half-witted stoned surfers who think they can write the great beach novel. You're hired. You start Monday."

Work kept me busy. I forgot my loneliness. I took up that oh-so-California hobby—jogging on the beach at sunset every evening. I ran north to Black's Beach then south along La Jolla Shores. Magnificent flocks of seabirds filled the horizon as the sun disappeared beyond the Pacific.

In our semi-empty apartment at night, a different reality hit. I was awakened several times those first few months by a recurring nightmare. I attempted to deconstruct the symbolism of the dreams by writing them down. I thought back to my mother's introduction to Jung and *Psychology of the Unconscious* when I was a girl and waited for an epiphany. But my mind only churned in darkness.

In the dreams, I was perpetually climbing a steep ladder along a crumbling limestone cliff. Sharp outcroppings scraped my knees and tore open the flesh of my bare feet as I scrambled upward. Heart pounding, fingernails torn and bleeding, I gripped each slippery rung. One hand pulled upward, I could feel the possibility of making it onto the platform above, free from struggle, standing in open air to gaze upon a wide horizon.

A woman on the cliff stared down at me. "You don't belong here." She resembled Desiree, the student flirting with Andy at the TGIF. The woman smashed her foot onto my fingers clinging to the cliff. Bones cracked and fractured. Pain shrieked through my hands as I grasped the top of the ladder. Then the assault increased. Kicks to my face. Blood filling my eyes, I would start to lose my grip. I began a slow descent, falling but never landing. I would wake up drenched in sweat, shaking.

Some nights, I could not get onto the ladder without being kicked down immediately. On other nights, I made it midway. The goal to reach the top without help remained elusive. It was on these solitary nights that I missed my husband. But did he miss me?

20

Too-Hot Tub

When Andy returned from science cruises, we would reacquaint ourselves, touching tentatively, attempting to make up for lost time before the next cycle of absence.

Through Mescalita I had befriended a few graduate students who knew Andy. Pablo, her "for now" boyfriend, was a laid-back surfer from New Jersey who saw his PhD project as an excuse to ride the waves for the next six years.

Saturday evenings, Pablo and I sat on the wall overlooking La Jolla Shores, waiting for Mescalita to complete her run. Our late-night beach conversations floated through philosophy and storytelling, movies, and music. Sometimes our reveries were disrupted by fellow students. One asked, "Did you know your husband was seen with Desiree?" Every time my husband went out to sea, another man attempted to enlighten me about Andy's activities and female associates. I dismissed the rumors as male braggadocio.

Pablo glared at the recent interloper over his sunglasses. "Move on. You got the wrong lady." He stretched against the seawall.

"Pabs, can you believe these guys? Are they serious?"

He pulled up his foot into his hand behind him for his final stretch. He smiled, his big toothy grin flying up toward his laughing brown eyes. Despite Mescalita's declaration that she and Pablo were lovers "for now," their friendship had already lasted for years.

"Yup. They are dead serious in their clumsy way. You know, it doesn't help that you look like a rock star." I looked down, puzzled, as he explained. "You know who I'm talking about? The one who wears lacy lingerie and sings about being a virgin." He cocked his head and held up his fingers in a frame around my face, as he'd seen Mescalita do when she set up her photography equipment. "Yeah, I see it now. Except the virgin part."

"Very funny." I playfully slapped him. "You're not the first to tell me."

Suddenly Pablo grabbed my hand and pointed over the ocean's horizon. "Look. The green flash."

An illusory dark turquoise-green splash hit the sight line. I realized how lucky we were to share the same momentary phenomena that our ancestors had witnessed eons ago.

I admired Andy. I was in awe of his ability to combine an academic career with risky adventure. Southern California, home of movie stars, drug dealers, and sexual experimenters, tested human loyalty daily. I wondered how a man could go out to sea with so many adventurous and brilliant women without being tempted. To protect my ego, I held to the mantra that nothing had really happened. *No*, I told myself, *cheating is not possible in our "equal partnership."* If I remained loyal, so would he.

The science cruise ships returned in a flurry of activity, unloading samples and taking down temporary labs, only to rebuild them once again in the science office building.

For a few days, the two of us would settle down to a semblance of marital normalcy. Then the weekend would hit. Students and associates would gather on the deck in front of a beach house near Scripps. Free food. Free beer. An open firepit next to a huge hot tub filled to the brim, somewhat scalding water sloshing over the deck.

I'd attend after work. The food was already dispersed, beer keg spurting foam and running low. Intense flirting had been well underway for hours. My lateness made me feel like an outsider, but that didn't stop me from enjoying the bubbling hot tub, kicking men's attentions away from me whenever one moved in too close or decided to do an underwater dive to catch a glimpse or grab me "by accident." I held no grudges against these men in their awkward attempts. It became a game of dodge the drunk. While I was thus engaged, my husband was flirting along with the others. One night, I realized it may have appeared to others, with our separate entrances, that we did have an open marriage.

I warded off men who approached me. They'd seen my husband with so-and-so doing this and that on the rear deck of some ship or having disappeared in a woman's bunk space for hours at a time. Most seemed to assume we were in a quasi-open marriage. The quasi part also gave me carte blanche to flirt at will with no punishment or reward.

The Southern California scene in the 1980s glided in hip and enticing circles, without restraint. No drug went untested. Everything in life—bodies, minds, work—became an open invitation to explore social boundaries.

One night I arrived late. I stood back from the crowd, eavesdropping on lengthy scientific discussions while my eyes wandered, searching for my husband. Men around me grew bored, barely tolerating my inattentiveness, and moved away.

The party resided within a glass-encased beach home. A large pool sat on the deck. The party noise drowned out the sound of ocean breakers. Only whitecaps lit by the Scripps pier were visible in the distance.

A swirling hot tub beckoned in a dark corner lit only by candles. People were leaping from cold pool into steaming heat, all the while embracing on the sly.

I'm no prude, I told myself. *I can fit in among the hot tub crowd.* Before I had a chance to move into the pool area, I found myself trapped in the entryway listening to a woman ramble on about her knitting hobby. The click-clacking of metal needles unnerved me.

I feigned interest as I glanced around the party. My husband was nowhere to be seen. Since I knew that neither of us brought a bathing suit, I did not imagine he was in the hot tub. It wasn't until the knitter rose to leave that I sauntered out to the deck. The pool was filled with people splashing each other. I glanced at the hot tub.

That's when I saw him.

Andy's arm wound tightly around Desiree's shoulder, her hand massaging his thigh resting barely beneath the water.

So relaxed were the two of them that it would seem they were lovers. Both naked, laughing and chatting, while in an embrace as if alone and sharing a hot tub in the backyard of their private home.

A painful rippling of muscle seared my gut. I tried to breathe. I automatically backed away, attempting to render the scene meaningless, and caught myself on a deck chair before tumbling over.

Upon hearing the clang of the chair scraping the deck, my husband looked up.

He didn't move his arm from around her smooth, tanned shoulders. The graceful fingers of her hand remained on his thigh. In that moment, I was both visible and invisible to them, an annoyance, a mere passerby to an intimate moment.

"What's going on?" My voice came out louder than expected. I stared at Andy. He didn't move or flinch.

"We're enjoying the view," he said, his voice almost too casual.

Desiree laughed as if he was the funniest man she had ever met. Her blonde-streaked wavy hair danced to the beat of her bobbing breasts.

"Come on, Sue," he said, "don't be so provincial. We're all friends here. Be cool. We're in Southern California. Nothing unusual. There's even a hot tub on the science vessel. We're used to it. It's a good way to unwind. Come on. Relax. Besides," he added, "you've said whirlpools are too hot for you."

Even though I wanted to believe this was only a little flirtation, an escape valve for Andy to keep from exploding, I bristled at the words "too hot." I commanded myself not to react in some jealous fit as a "provincial" wife would. *Be cool, Sue*, I told myself. *California cool. Fit in. Enjoy the lifestyle, the casual decadence.*

I turned back to the living room, the knitter's *click-clack* of metal needles now getting on my nerves. Maybe out of suppressed anger or sheer boredom, I fantasized about what I could do. I needed to stand up for myself despite my feelings of insecurity, even if I couldn't be an intellectual equal to these graduate students and professors.

Unleashed scenarios flew through my brain. I thought of my husband and what we had in common—our backgrounds, our working-class values, our loyalty to family. Could I leave him? Could I earn enough to live alone? Did I want to live alone? It seemed like a superfluous question when I already spent half the year alone. What did I expect of myself in our "equal partnership"?

A feeling of revenge took over. I stood up and removed my halter top in one swoop, threw off my shorts and panties, and marched over to the pool, ignoring my husband and his "friend."

I had vowed if ever I should find someone who wanted me, needed me, loved me, I would be faithful. But now, watching my husband, I wondered, *What is the point of fidelity?*

I lifted my arms in the pose of the black-and-white gauze-covered photo I had modeled for years ago. Throwing my hands forward in prayer, I pushed off from the edge and dived into the cold pool. I gasped and spat out a stream of chlorine-rich water and rubbed my eyes to see waves of violent whitecaps crashing into the invisible dark sea in the distance.

21

Lost Band of Gold

Something inside me broke at the hot tub party. Did I really endorse this lifestyle choice? "Quasi-open marriage" were my words, not his. I assumed that meant flirtations were tolerated. Nothing more would progress. But now I wondered.

We were married. Our vows "to cherish our equal partnership" fell between the cracks of promises to love and honor. Was it broken if people semi-agreed to semi-open marriage?

Options seemed limited. I wanted to fit in with these adventure-seeking, freewheeling oceanographers, to live an unconventional life. I suffered from an underlying shame at my own weakness to adhere to their unwritten social codes. Instead, I waited in silence. For what, I didn't know.

Sexual expression in the marital bed became a tutorial exercise in new positions and techniques, oral and physical. I dared not risk asking where my husband had learned his new skills to please a woman. I simply enjoyed the result. Time passed. The rhythms of passion and disenchantment repeated endlessly through those three years of his master's and over six years of graduate school.

A bonding pleasure would wash over me after making love. In

those moments, I chastised myself for sentimental weaknesses, my longing to be safe. It was during one of those rare Saturdays when we were together that the seesaw of trust became unhinged.

We sat on the beach watching the seafoam grow along the shoreline. Winds blew the froth into rising circles. Waves crashed heavily, scattering rocks and sand. And yet a sweet calm overcame me, having time alone with my husband for the first moment in many months.

Swelling storm tides surged forth and hit the coast. Not a single cloud marred the sun's brightness that day. Yet at the edge of the horizon, glowering fingers of darkness spread. Surfers headed straight into the coming storm.

"I'm going in," Andy said.

"Those waves look dangerous." I stared at the wave line. "There's a riptide to the north moving south toward us." I'd learned to spot rips from the surfers as they stood along the cliffs overlooking the vast Pacific. One showed me what to spot when a riptide formed. A calm trough of water flowing, a gravity-defying river rushing back out to sea, while waves in the opposite direction moved inland.

Brash surfers believed themselves immortal. Long boards tethered to ankles. Muscular bodies outlined by black rubber suits.

"You're too cautious." Andy's voice rose. "I'm tired of your fearful conformism. I'm going in."

"They've got surfboards and wet suits. You've got a speedo and a small boogie board. I think you might want to wait this one out."

"I really wish you could be more adventurous, like Miriam or Mary."

"Or Desiree?"

He ignored me.

Without even glancing at him, I rose from my cross-legged position and stretched. "I'm not an oceanographer. I'm just the wife of one. A wife who worries about her husband's safety. Go surf. I'm not witnessing it when they drag your lifeless body out of the water."

I got up and began walking northward toward Torrey Pines. I jogged a mile, then out of concern, and a nagging sense of responsibility, I returned. I saw Andy, drenched and shivering, near the cliff overhang, his boogie board nowhere in sight. He waved his left hand at me and pointed to his ring finger as I approached.

"I lost my wedding band. The waves were too strong. It slipped off my finger. Lost the board too. I think it broke in half on the rocks. It's still out there somewhere." He waved his ringless hand toward the ocean. "I've been thinking about not wearing it for a while anyway. Especially when I'm out to sea."

"Interesting decision." I turned away, allowing sarcasm to be the only reply.

In the following weeks, I asked several times if he wanted to shop for a new wedding ring. He'd simply shrug. Then one evening as he watched me, I placed my wedding band inside a small jewelry box my little brother had painted for me when he was in fifth grade. The memento held sacred value. It reminded me I was once strong, a protector.

Andy watched me remove the ring. "Why did you do that?"

"If you don't have to wear yours, why should I wear mine?"

"I don't want my hand to get torn off by a machine. You don't have to worry about that. It's not like it's a big symbol." He paused. "Don't you trust me?"

"I trust you to be human."

"Whatever the hell that means." He shifted his stance and gave a half-cocked smile. "We're both human."

"Agreed."

"Is that a threat?" His voice rose a decibel.

"As you like to say, it's only a band of gold."

"It signals you're not married and open to date men, and you know it." He crossed his arms tightly in front of his chest, scrunching the marijuana plant emblem on his T-shirt into a green blob. He began to pace.

"While I live faithfully with a man careless about his vows."

"Why do you always have to be so freaking sarcastic?" He lowered his ringless hand to his side, signaling a change in tactics. "You know I love you. You're the most important woman in my life. We've got something special together."

"Then why pose as a single man and have the gall to dictate that I must wear my ring to advertise my marital status?"

"Don't give me any of that double-standard crap. You want to date when I'm away? Is that what this is really about?"

"I'm not following." I kept my hands open at my sides, forcing myself to stay loose, refusing to engage and mirror his anger.

"Let's examine. For one, your overuse of your *toys*. When I'm gone, I get it. But when I'm here, why?" He shook his head in a spasm. "You got your replacement husband in the bedroom drawer. No need to take off your ring."

"Let me get this straight." I forced myself to stay calm. "You want to seem single so that you can date other women while relegating me to dating a cheap Spencer's Gifts rechargeable vibrator?"

"No one's dating anyone." His fingers tugged on his beard as his frustration grew. "Don't confuse the issue, and don't be so naive about men. If you don't wear your wedding ring, they'll surround you like a pack of wolves."

"Only with the full moon." I could feel my left eyebrow rise in disdain.

He stood still, barely moving even to blink.

"You want to have your cake and eat it too," I said. "Old story." I knew the term was so clichéd as to be trite. But it also exposed emotional dangers, an unbalance of power. Saliva gathered in my throat. I wanted to spit out words, hateful words. I breathed once and attempted a rational tone. I swallowed. "If you don't wear your wedding ring, I won't wear mine."

"Fine." He pulled his backpack out of the closet and began to pack for his three-month trip out to sea, away from his argumentative wife.

"Let's place a bet to make it more interesting." I refused to let it go without first making my point. "Don't wear your wedding band. I won't wear mine. Let's see who gets a date first." I marched to the deck surrounded by plants, hidden from his view.

No more words were spoken that night.

Our polite silence continued for a few days. But by Saturday, before he boarded the ship, he was wearing a common gold ring on his left hand. He said nothing. I said nothing. Instead, I placed my own ring back on my finger. The tan line hadn't even had time to fade.

This became the stalemate on our unspoken open marriage, until our final days in California. Our vow, uttered almost a decade earlier, swirled in my mind, mocking. I wondered how equal, much less cherished, the evolution of this marriage could hold.

Andy returned a few months later in triumph. Listening to him describe his experience, I realized his first love was not for women but for the world of exploration. With nothing more than an emergency $10-a-minute ship-to-shore ham radio operator call, there had been no communication, no letters, no calls while he was out to sea. I imagined him experiencing a heady combination of a scientific mindset with a heated sexuality in every port. I envied him. In his place, I realized, I would probably feel the same.

But, I wondered, what plan did I have for my own life other than to wait for him? It seemed my feminism had flown away with the desert Santa Ana winds, swept out to sea with my husband.

Myriad excuses for being away from home, once he returned, emerged daily from Andy. Some were legitimate. He packed an entire lab on the ship to prep for onboard experiments. He'd return home exhausted. When the ship came into port a few days later, he'd be off for long hours, unpacking, and the cycle continued.

Sex became rushed, perfunctory. I still enjoyed orgasms. I cherished the vibrator that I'd bought at a beachside stand from a local woman who had a penchant for cocaine and an array of surfing dude lovers as backup. In an odd way, autoeroticism kept me faithful. The old joke "Don't knock masturbation; it's sex with someone I really love" repeated nightly.

Each new cruise led to more months of loneliness and silence. No emails or Wi-Fi existed back in those days, and I held no lover in my arms. Despite the battery-operated nights, I grew increasingly lonely, needy for companionship.

Andy would return happy, fatigued, regaling me with tales of his time out to sea, his ventures in the submersible *Alvin*, diving miles toward the ocean floor, discovering life among deep seamounts. He slipped on occasion, noting a woman he had dined with onshore in La Paz where the ship had docked. He stopped abruptly when he realized his mistake.

"So, tell me what happened to you while I was gone," he said.

I told him about Pablo and Mescalita, my boss Pat, and my jogging excursions. He half listened as he swigged his black coffee and read the *Los Angeles Times*. I kept talking, desperate for human contact. He treated me like a pesky fly until he needed—wanted—sex again. I couldn't blame him. Our worlds were so divergent. Compatibility seemed out of reach. And yet, I felt determined to engage him, to stay married to the man I had professed to cherish.

Time slithered by in this fashion. What should have been the glow of youth turned to an early midlife-crisis marriage. I began to despise myself for living this way. Waiting for my man. Unable to plan for myself. Anxiety increasing every time Andy went out to sea.

To meet some fading emotional need, I attempted to engage men. A clunky courtship would commence. Others were more forward with come-ons like "You're going to need a man to make you feel better, babe. Try me."

I barely registered what was happening during these short encounters. Sometimes, I didn't even bother to learn their names. I flirted to feed my lagging ego. It seemed that the men knew secrets about Andy they only hinted at, like some California code I couldn't decipher.

The only reprieve I had from my ruminating mind was my job at the publishing company. I grew fond of my colleagues and spent a few evenings with Mescalita and Pablo on the other side of the border near Rosarito Beach in Baja. It was while sitting in the back of Pablo's van and gazing out at the pilot whales returning to give birth to a new generation that I was introduced to cocaine.

Rolled dollar bills and a quick inhale gave me clarity about my situation. I lived among kind souls in a land of sheer allure. Salt air filled my lungs. Emaciated feral dogs wandered over rotting seaweed. Smells intertwined in sharp contrast.

"This is the life," I said. "Birth and death right here."

"You got that right, sister." Mescalita pointed to a line of dark gray small pilot whales breaching. "See how the females band together? That's to keep the males from harassing them."

"Harassing?" Pablo stretched out on the dark sand. "The boys just want to get laid. Give 'em a break."

"Too late for the boys," she said. "The females are ready for labor. Give the ladies a break." Pablo stood up and reached over and hugged her tight.

I watched them in envy as the white powder's magic began to swirl through my brain. I felt invincible. I jumped off the tailgate with a Broadway-style pirouette, and I added a cartwheel that landed me flat on my back. I felt light, airy, alive. They both clapped.

"Well, kiddies, time to go back to the States. It's a school night." Mescalita gathered the food wrappers into the picnic blanket.

I wanted to stay, to play with my friends, to swim with the whales, but they took me under each arm and dragged me back to the van. The sound of tires on gravel intensified as we drove back north to the Tijuana border.

About half a mile before the invisible line between north and south, Pablo stopped and said, "We need to finish off the goodies or we'll all end up in a Mexican jail tonight. Not my idea of fun." He handed me a straw and a credit card with white lines of powder.

"Why not just dump it on the sand?" I began to open my door.

Mescalita reached past me and slammed the door shut. "Because it leaves a residue they can trace. Plus, this stuff ain't cheap. Let's finish it off."

Once finished, we headed off across the border. No one stopped us or asked us what we were doing, but I did giggle when the guard asked if we were bringing anything back. Mescalita grabbed my knee to shut me up.

On the drive home, a rising paranoia took over. After they dropped me off, I stayed up the entire night pacing, thinking about Andy. *What is he doing? What am I doing?* Without any sleep, I drove to work at eight the next morning.

I spent the day pulling galley sheets. In my haste, I tore a cover ready to go to Singapore for printing. There was no duplicate. It forced Mescalita to redo it. She forgave me, but I couldn't forgive myself. *How could I be so clumsy? What is wrong with me?*

I cried. Not the feminine dabbing-the-corner-of-one's-eyes crying. The outright sobbing and bawling. Everyone turned to look. A few people emerged from offices. Pat ran over to me, lifted me roughly around my shoulders, and practically threw me into her office.

Still, I couldn't stop and continued to apologize.

"Pat, I'm so sorry. I'm so stupid."

"Sit." She pointed to a chair. "Shut up. Stop crying."

"But I screwed up." I thought of my drug-induced lack of sleep, my inability to control myself. I began to understand why my husband might have wanted someone else. I began to cry harder.

"Oh, for heaven's sake." She jammed a tissue in my hand. "Stop crying. I don't care what your reasons are. A woman crying at work is a professional death knell. I mean it for your own sake when I say stop it. Don't ever cry again in the workplace.

Do you understand me? It's important to all working women."

I wiped my eyes. Black streaks of mascara painted the back of my hand. I attempted to rub my lids with the tissue to remove any makeup. I could only imagine what my face looked like. "But, Pat, what am I supposed to do if I feel like crying?"

She paused and sighed. "You do what men do."

I sniffled. "What's that?"

"You cry in the car on the way home. Now compose yourself and get into your car right now. I'll see you tomorrow. Get some sleep. And don't go to Baja on a work night ever again."

That night, I cried in the car all the way up the San Diego freeway to La Jolla, as a man would. As a woman, I got home and continued to cry on my sofa for hours. I cried in the shower, hot water scalding my face. I cried in bed, my pillow soaked in my own salty tears.

This, I told myself, *is what happens when you're broken.*

22

Banished to Boston

L ate October in 1984, on the eve of my thirtieth birthday, we attended a party at Desiree's home. I floated about the room making small talk, thinking about our impending journey to Boston, when Pablo tapped me on the shoulder.

"Want to share a toke for old time's sake?"

"Sure, why not." I glanced around the room. "Where's Andy?"

"He's not here, but don't let that stop you from having fun."

Mescalita waved us to the back door. Purple tips tinged her red hair. I followed her colorful bouncing curls as Pablo opened the door with a gallant flourish. We sat near the firepit, passing a pipe around.

"What time is it?" Mescalita yawned.

"Time is of the essence," I said as the smoke swirled past the eucalyptus trees. "Time after time. Time and chance happeneth to them all. Time waits for no man." I started to giggle. "Or woman. Especially not for disappearing hubbies."

Pablo stretched out his legs to push a burning log back into the firepit. "Been more than two hours since he disappeared with Desiree."

I saw Mescalita kick him. Pablo winced as her face contorted, angry, something I'd never seen before.

My mind churned. Where in the hell was Andy and what

was he doing? It was well past midnight. People had begun filtering out and leaving Desiree's place sans Desiree. I sat in a funk. I could not return to our apartment. The car, with my husband in it, was among the missing.

The sweet fog of drugs turned dark. Where were they? What was taking so long? I worried he was in a car accident. That something had gone horribly wrong. I refused to think of the obvious.

But only minutes later, both Desiree and Andy reappeared. A few remaining stoned people lounged on patio chairs.

Andy held out a rectangular bakery box. "Surprise." He turned to look at me. "Happy birthday."

Staring at the blank white frosting of the cake, I said, "It took two hours to find an undecorated cake?" I could hear the sarcasm in my voice rise.

Desiree stuck her finger into the side of the cake and swiped vanilla icing. She pushed her finger deep into her mouth. Andy laughed.

Without thinking, I slapped her hand away like an angry mother to an unruly child.

Desiree turned to Andy in shock. She placed those fingers along the flesh of her exposed hip above the ultra-tight shorts. "You told me she'd be grateful."

I attempted to smile. I could tell it came out more as a sneer. I hated crying, especially with Desiree watching. "I'm so damn grateful," I said, trying to regain a shred of dignity. "Do you mind telling me where you really were?" I knew I sounded petty, bitter, a jealous wife. The few remaining guests scattered quickly.

Pablo grabbed Mescalita's hand. I almost smiled when I heard him say, "I'd rather be naked in a room full of hungry pit bulls than get between a husband and wife in a domestic fight."

"Forget the explanation." I started for the door, leaving the cake sitting on Desiree's beer-bottle-strewn coffee table. Before I reached the door, I heard him excuse my outburst.

"Sorry, Des, you and I were out to sea on the day of her big three-oh. I think it bothers her. Maybe she got a little jealous."

She smiled, nodded, and gently placed her hand on his arm.

Is that what gratitude for an intimate moment looks like? I wondered.

Fall passed into winter. To hasten our exit in hopes of starting anew, I found myself editing Andy's dissertation late into the night for weeks on end.

With some sadness, in the moments before Andy finished his PhD defense in 1985, I stood one last time on La Jolla's shore. My eyes aimed for the furthest horizon. Endless waves in hues of blue and green with churning whitecaps. A lone surfer rode winter's dangerous swell. I envied him the adrenaline rush of an impending crash. To feel free enough to risk death seemed the ultimate liberation.

A U-Haul trailer, attached to our orange VW, sat in the Scripps parking lot. Andy had received two postdoctoral offers: the first, a prestigious fellowship to the Pacific Marine Environmental Lab in Seattle; the second, a research position at the Massachusetts Institute of Technology in Boston. I wanted to stay on the West Coast. Seattle offered twice the salary, placement in a world-renowned marine lab, free housing, and a counselor to aid the spouse in a job search. He refused to discuss his choices and insisted on taking the MIT postdoc with no explanation. It left me bewildered. No matter how I weighed his unilateral decision, it made little sense.

Questions gnawed at me daily. Why Boston? Why not Seattle? I demanded a reason, until one day, he burst out, "It's MIT. Important people study there. Smart, ambitious people you don't know." He shook his head. "Never mind. You can't understand."

Hurt by his dismissiveness, I reacted in the only way I knew to settle an argument with a man who refused to listen. I started to sing. I began singing tunes about the cold and ancient stasis of the East Coast; songs that extolled the virtues of California's beaches and laid-back lifestyle. While belting out the lyrics to prove my point, I pivoted, ballet-style; my leg extended in a swift outward kick to grand battement. I continued the musical gyrations until I was spent and hoarse—my singular passive-aggressive way of protesting the inevitable.

He held up a hand to stop the noise. "It's irritating when you answer in song and dance. It's infantile. You're not on Broadway. For once, I'd like an adult conversation."

"Like the deeply *intellectual* conversations you have on board a ship or in your lab or at a hotel conference?" I could feel my face twisting in contempt.

"Oh, grow up." He shoved his hiking boots into the suitcase and slammed it shut. "You're an agent of free will."

That old argument of free will versus determinism from that fateful night in the university's library reared its ugly head. I complained about my fate, yet I went along with every major decision Andy made from where to live to what to do. *Whose fault is that?* I thought.

"I'm asking one more time, why are we really going to Boston?"

His hazel eyes were shadowed by long lashes. My mother's dictate to marry a handsome man haunted me still.

"I told you. It's MIT. Woods Hole. World famous. What don't you get?"

"With half the pay, no moving costs, no help with housing or my looking for a job, and a boss who's a known alcoholic, when you have an equal opportunity in Seattle with a higher salary, paid moving, helping me, housing, and a nice guy heading the lab there." I paused, out of breath.

In a whisper, I asked, "Who is she this time?"

"Sue, I'm disappointed in your jealousy. You're my wife. I love you more than any other woman. Trust me when I say that." He returned to packing his bag. "Now, let's put our stuff in the car and get on the road. We can hit restart again. There's nothing here anymore."

"I'm disappointed in myself." I fluttered my hands to push away the resentment. Starting over again appealed to me. It gave me a shred of hope to move back East. It would be many years before I realized some men pull out the jealousy card to distract from the truth. Instead, his words made me crumble.

"I don't know what you can do in Boston." He looked up. "I always thought you'd start a business or do something different or important." He picked up the luggage. "I guess I thought you'd be more successful by now."

My gut clenched. "Fooled you, didn't I?"

I attempted to give him a Mona Lisa smile but knew it came out as a sneer.

I commanded my spine to straighten and myself to face the facts. I could almost hear my grandmother's voice: "You'll be called all kinds of crazy when you stand up for yourself." What did I stand for? I knew Andy's statement hit my gut hard. I had nothing. Here *or* there. Other than an outdated marital contract and loyalty. Equality seemed distant, unachievable.

Before he could utter a response that might destroy our marriage forever, the phone rang. We both jumped as if lightning had struck. I gingerly picked it up to hear a female voice badly mangling the pronunciation of my last name.

"We're calling to tell you that your grandmother Edna passed away last night."

No! Impossible. She was supposed to live forever. She guided me in times of trouble. I needed to see her one last time. It was my one incentive for returning east.

"What?" I rubbed my eyes in disbelief. I could hear the anger in my voice. "I mean—" I started to cough uncontrollably. My grandmother. My teacher. My mentor. The strongest woman I knew. Dead when I needed her most? I refused to believe it. "Excuse me, but why did you call me instead of my mother, her daughter?"

"Because"—she stopped, and I could hear paper ruffling in the background—"she listed you as first notification." Her voice became robotic then, as if reading a grocery list. "According to the most recently dated missive of record, it was your grandmother's last request. I'll read it. 'Sue shall be my primary contact. I consider her the most responsible and reliable relative you can call after my death.'"

The word "responsible" pierced through the fog in my skull. Of course. To Edna, I would be the oldest in my family, the one to call others, to stay calm. She had trained me, commanded me, to remain stalwart amid chaos. To stay the course. I'd a sudden vision of her standing up for me against my father's violence, my mother's passivity, my teacher's incompetence, and my siblings demanding attention as I studied. Edna's presence in my childhood had become a superpower, a protective shield of female strength. Her beliefs had kept me focused on pursuing an education, on moving ahead, on maintaining a goal beyond mere working-class survival.

With her gone, belief shattered.

That evening, I fulfilled the responsible and reliable role. I called and spoke to my mother, who drew in a quick breath when she realized that I was the contact upon death. "Of course you are." She sounded agitated. "It'd be just like your grandmother to dismiss her own daughter by planning out her own funeral." I could hear her turn to tell my father, then she came back on the line. "Well, you were her favorite. I'm guessing you won't be able to get here in time for the funeral. No, probably not." She answered her own question, then suddenly changed the subject. "I went to the library and read Andy's scientific article. I couldn't understand half of it, but I found it impressive."

A memory of giving my mother a newspaper article I had written for the local San Diego newspaper flitted through my mind. Instead, she had read Andy's academic paper in detail multiple times and wanted to ask him questions about the geothermal vents in the Juan de Fuca ridge. My article probably sat on the coffee table untouched or disappeared in the morning trash. "You didn't even glance at the article I wrote, did you?"

"Your local article is not exactly in the same league as a scientific journal. Be careful. Put your husband first or he'll be gone." I knew she was thinking of her own father, who abandoned the family when she was twelve. She blamed her mother for being too sharp, too demanding. In the knowledge of my grandmother's demise, my thirtieth birthday cake fiasco seemed trivial.

Not long after the call, I knew I had to get dressed for Andy's dissertation party, my mother's words echoing in my brain: *Put your husband first.*

A few days after his dissertation had been signed and stamped, we found ourselves driving in silence. To maintain an inner peace, I cast my self-indulgent ruminations in a metaphorical closet and slammed the door on any questions. Our exhaustive journey across America continued.

I knew I would miss California, but there were certain aspects of it that I hoped to escape. I thought, once we vacated the West Coast, that my husband and I could reconcile, deal with our quasi-open marriage, hit restart in a new place. The journey could be a rebirth, a restructuring of what it meant to be married. It never crossed my mind to ask if we wanted to stay married.

I had stopped taking birth control pills and begun using a diaphragm. I wanted my system to be clean of any chemical poison before even attempting to reproduce. Having children would change his outlook, would change us, I believed. After all, reproduction posed as the historical intent of legalized marriage. Love was peripheral to marriage's true purpose.

That year, the worst winter weather on record moved with us across the country. The orange VW I had bought used from my boss Pat broke down at every stop along the way. Andy cursed the car and me, the person who'd bought it. At least it felt that way.

My body's reaction to suddenly being released from the hormones of birth control pills sent me into a maelstrom of a bloody, anger-filled period.

Somewhere along the way, stuck in some motel parking lot, I needed an answer. "Be honest, Andy. Why are we really moving to Boston?"

He fumed and began muttering. I knew my irritating questions drilled into his being, but I refused to stop until I had an answer.

We drove from the cold Texas winds to the ice sheets of the Carolinas into the snowstorms of the Northeast. Childhood nightmares of excruciating pain from the cold haunted me. Memories of Grandma opening the oven to heat the room undid me. I began hormone-raging, endless crying jags.

What depressed me the most was knowing that he was so very eager, not just to go out to sea, to have his adventures, but to get away from me. And here he was trapped in a car going across the country with the one person he was trying to escape. As I raged, I secretly couldn't blame him for fuming in silence.

When we finally arrived in Boston, I found myself, once again, being measured as the straggling, unnoticed wife, hardly worth the effort. Every new meet and greet at MIT pounded home that reality.

Until the day I met her.

Kendall, his officemate, the one he referred to as "brilliant . . . incredible . . . she almost thinks like a man"—as if that was the highest compliment he could imagine.

Kendall did not seem nor behave particularly male in my assessment. Yes, she stood close to a man's height with her cropped hair and sharp features. She also wore tight clothes, low-cut tops, and spiked heels with makeup done to perfection to cover her adult acne. When we met, her eyes fell to squinty slits as she examined me up and down like some lab experiment gone wrong.

A slight shock hit me. From the look in her eyes, I suddenly knew she was the reason we'd moved to Boston in the middle of a blizzard. In the back of my mind, I always knew the motivation might be personal. Nothing else made sense. I'd simply not met the person behind the reason.

The final storms of winter swept across the Charles River. We slept on the hardwood floor of our empty apartment wrapped in sleeping bags. That year influenza swarmed our bodies as we awaited our furniture's arrival. We had no table or chairs and no kitchenware other than a small pot and a few spoons. The only food in our new pantry: canned soups and ravioli that we opened and left half-uneaten, then returned to shivering on the hardwood floor.

For almost a week, we were unable to do more than drink tea and swallow Tylenol. Still, I saw a silver lining. I felt closer to Andy in those moments of coughing fits than I had in a long time. I began to cherish every pain and ache and believe in the possibility that a better marriage might emerge in Boston, despite my fixation on his secret tryst.

Once we recovered, Andy launched his career as a postdoctoral fellow at MIT. He'd leave early in the morning, rarely returning before midnight. I busied myself with my job hunt. It didn't take long to find work at MIT's school of architecture as a marketing copywriter at their alumni magazine. The balance of art and engineering in building designs appealed to my creative side.

I studied MIT's building plans, getting lost in my research and prepping to interview students and professors for the calendar of upcoming events. I truly enjoyed working for the dean, an Australian native who'd spent most of his life in a missionary family in Bogotá, Colombia. The faculty and students hailed from every continent on the planet. I listened intently to their conversations, enchanted by their worldliness.

The oceanographers, part of Woods Hole on Cape Cod,

were led by a swaggering, aggressive, often drunk professor. I first met Dr. E in the corridor. He stood tall and menacing. To me, though, he was the same old same old male swagger. I still held in my mind those scissors that could put an end to any egotistical machismo, even if shrouded in the egalitarian left-wing rhetoric of the Ivy League.

One day, out of the blue, Dr. E mentioned his expertise with the ladies. "You might be interested to know that I've had well over two hundred women in my lifetime."

Without a pause, ignoring that this professor was my husband's ticket to advancement, I said, "Is it, perhaps, because no one could stand you for more than one night?"

He backed away after that, and I wondered how the sharp retort might have repercussions later. At that moment, though, I was simply tired of the gamesmanship. His swagger seemed a mere continuation of the dominant lifestyle of oceanographers.

Andy paced back and forth like an attorney in a courtroom with a difficult case. His long legs covered the distance of our living room in a short step before returning to where I sat.

"Hear me out." He placed his hands outward in an offering gesture I had seen him use on the presentation podium in lecture mode. "If we're apart for months, we will still have needs."

"Needs?" I tried to tone down the sarcasm.

"No, no, no," he said in a rush. "It's not like that. Marriage is an institution dictated by bourgeoise society, agreed?" He didn't wait for an answer. "We don't need to live by others' rules. We can invent our own rules like when we invented our own vows."

"You're quoting Sartre and existentialists to justify your behavior?"

"Simone de Beauvoir wrote that. You read the book."

The thought that none of the couples in these open partner-ships had children, nor ever would, crossed my mind. "Let me get this straight. You want to go out to sea, take trips without me, do what you will with whomever, while I sit like a dolt waiting for you at home?" I stood up. "Don't you want kids someday?"

"Of course I want kids." He sat down hard on the lone patio chair we'd found in the trash. "Someday." A sadness crept into his voice. "Be rational, Sue. For now, I'm just suggesting an alternative path."

"Or a 'get out of jail free' card."

"Never mind."

I paced, tapping my finger to my chin in an exaggerated thinking gesture, my stomach turned acid. "So, you're saying I could go to bed with whomever I wish while you're out to sea?"

"No." He jumped up, knocking over the lawn chair. "I mean" —he sighed—"you're a loyal person, Sue, I know you'll do what is best. How about this. The rule is if you're gone for a long time and traveling far away . . ."

His voice trailed off as he realized the hypocrisy he was proposing held a sharp double edge—in his favor. I knew I could not earn enough to live alone. With that reality, the return of a poverty mindset reared its ugly head.

"I'll think about it."

In an instant, I knew nothing I said would dissuade him. But maybe I could give myself permission to follow suit. I, too, could find a lover.

23

Ten Rules

During the week, I was busy working as a copywriter for the school of architecture. From the infinite corridor, I could watch small sailboats flow in bouncy waves near the Harvard Bridge, then twirl back toward the Longfellow Bridge in endless circles.

But weekends grew silent, and to alleviate the solitude, I spoke to strangers along the Charles River trail. A few emitted nervous smiles and nodded. No one stopped to engage.

My first foray into the city brought me near the crowds gathered at the Hatch Shell, home of the Boston Pops Orchestra. That spring afternoon, I saw a young woman in black leather pants with chain mail slung around her thin waist. Her raspy voice sang "Manhunt" from the movie *Flashdance*. I stopped to listen. Mesmerized by her kohl-lined black eyes staring directly at me, I swayed as she belted out the lyrics.

A few people clapped and walked away. As the band began to pack up, I walked toward them to place a few quarters in the donation basket. "Great rendition. Loved the movie." I added, "And I love to dance."

"Me too," the lead singer said. "A manhunt kind of reverses a girl's fate. Ya know? Kinda gives us a chance for once." She smiled. Purple lipstick stuck to her front tooth. "Haven't seen you before. We're here most Saturdays."

"I just moved here. I really don't know a soul."

"Well, then, girl, go on a manhunt yourself." She lifted her amber-colored glasses. "Want to come with us?"

"Oh, thanks, but I have to get back home." I paused. "I'm married."

"Don't let that stop you." She turned back to the band. "Boys, wave goodbye to the married lady."

They soon disappeared along the colorful tents, and I cursed myself, trapped by my own narrow thinking. What was I waiting for? Andy had a life without me. A life of scientists and exploration, while I remained ashore, rushing to a mailbox where no letters ever arrived. I felt dizzy. Nauseated. I sat down on a bench.

A manhunt sounded better than waiting in the wings, hoping to be wanted, begging to be loved. The singer could've been a soulmate, a mentor, a super heroine, if I had followed her. Families, lovers, friends mingled in tight groups, laughing and hugging goodbye.

Friendless and alone didn't fit the image I had of myself. In the past, I had envisioned dancing, conversing, enjoying other people's company. I could hear my grandmother rising from the dead to admonish me to "get a backbone," slapping me out of my self-indulgent stupor.

I drifted among the outdoor stalls. An oil painting of a wild ocean, shades of blues and greens tinged in gray-white caps, caught my attention. OLAS the title plate read. Waves. I could almost hear the crash of sea, envision the light and color changes, smell salty seaweed. The screech of gulls pierced my memory, and I could feel imaginary grains of sand digging into my toenails.

Suddenly, a group of teenage boys on chopper-style bikes rode around me in a tight circle as if they were vultures targeting prey.

"Hey, lady," one shouted, "over he-ah. You crying?" They all laughed.

Heat flushed my face. I began to sweat. The loneliness I attempted to hide in public seemed to be prominently on display. First the singer recognized it and now, in a more humiliating fashion, this pack of teenage boys. I waved at them, attempting a sardonic grin, and then walked over to the bridge and back to the dimly lit T station to board the red line.

Once I was inside my empty apartment, twilight darkened to night, and I collapsed, belly down, on the frameless mattress. I counted scratch marks on the old oak floor. Sheer boredom gave way to a new game—plotting that elusive "manhunt" in the song. When I'd planned to lose my virginity, I'd been gullible. *This time*, I told myself, *I have sexual experience.* I'd plan it in a more precise manner, monitoring any consequences, standing by my decision.

Freed from obligation and fear of reprisal, my fantasies fueled wild sexual exploits. In the weeks ahead, dreams of enticing men in odd places overtook my waking thoughts. Nights were accompanied by a variety of toys that vibrated and shook me senseless, releasing an intense pleasure. I felt like a sex addict. I could sleep only after masturbating. I began to wonder if the term "nymphomaniac" fit when one was overly active with oneself?

The more I tried to not think of sex, the more my mind focused upon it. Various permutations of sexual positions floated through my imagination. These were not the charming fantasies of female soft erotica. No, they were the relentless, harsh, driven, and hard thrusts of lust. I challenged myself to envision nameless men engaging me in various physical acts, in unlikely places and exotic locales.

I attempted to calm my libido with romance novels only to skip through pages and whole books in search of hardcore sex scenes. I researched and plotted with vigor where to overtake or be overtaken by a man. How about that bench in the park under moonlight or the elevator in Copley Place as it rose ever higher? Why not the corner of the bus stop or a quickie in Kendall Square behind the MIT offices?

Bright streaks of desire burned my flesh. I thought of little else. I remembered Mena saying, "Wait until you turn thirty. You'll be like a cat in heat." She was right. A cat in heat trapped with no way to climb out the window and mate.

I needed a man. Big in all the right places. Smiling and willing to take me in all my craziness. *Finding a man willing to deal with my present insatiable insanity might be easy*, I reasoned. Dealing with my guilt at being married faded with each fervent masturbatory delight. Irrationality ruled every decision. Strategizing a pursuit and the tactical arrangement, I believed, would ensure a positive outcome.

Prior to leaving, Andy had posed a vague open-marriage contract he termed "polyamory," a term I'd never heard. I dismissed the notion as marital destruction, conveniently ignoring the morality. We seemed to be operating under an unstated quasi-open marriage still. If he offered the suggestion again, I knew I would, without hesitation, agree.

How could I blame him for his peccadillos when I knew I'd grab the opportunity with gusto if given half a chance?

At work, I enjoyed the camaraderie of MIT students, faculty, and coworkers. We bonded together in a proud badge of nerdiness. Goal-oriented, results-driven, lowly paid staff fed the machinations of academe. The work pace relied on constant deadlines. I enjoyed the faculty administrator, Judy. She wore a "grunge" outfit, complete with parachute pants held tight by a turquoise wrap belt, with a silk T-shirt as her one compromise to office attire. Her earlobes held different dangling jewelry every day, such as a pearl skull in one lobe and a gem-colored kitten in another, in a force of contradictory defiance.

"The dean wants you to interview that architect from London." Judy pointed to the request form.

"Me? That's cool," I said, excited by the prospect of interviewing men famous for their practical creativity.

"Don't get your hopes up. The architect's probably another egomaniac like the rest of them." She shuffled through the folder. "Here's the background info. If you have any questions . . ."

Before she could finish, an attractive woman about my age, with black bobbed hair that fell in geometric precision along her prominent jawline, grabbed the office door directly in front of us. She yanked it hard; it crashed against the wall. Her dark brown eyes shot an angry glance at the door as if it were a personal affront. She barely lifted her lips in greeting. A slash of deep red ran across her full mouth, a front tooth edged by a gold-tipped crown.

"Door's broke," Judy said. "Sorry about that."

The woman marched directly to us. "Where's Rod?" It was more of a command than a question. She rolled the *R* as if growling like a crazed dog.

Judy shrugged. "No idea."

The woman turned and stomped up the stairs to the array of graduate student cubicles we called "the loft." You could see from below the shadows of what happened above. Her hands flailed over a desk, papers flying. She picked up one, then returned and banged harder on the stairs than her small stature would seemingly allow. She marched out the door.

"Whoa, you can see who's in charge there," Judy said.

"Who's Rod?"

"One of the grad students. He has a desk up in the loft. Works for Mike. Been an architect before, so he's a little older. But his wife. Wow. I'm impressed. I am going out on a limb here to say she's one of my people."

"What do you mean?"

Judy just cocked her head and grinned.

"How is that even possible?" I mused more to myself. "She's married to a guy."

Judy laughed at my naivete. "I'm telling you, my gaydar is up and running, and I'm rarely wrong. I've spent years in lesbian bars, and I calls 'em like I sees 'em."

"Well, this has been a learning day for me," I said, acknowledging my own ignorance. We both laughed.

A few days later, I met Rod. He jogged toward me, carrying a handful of floppy disks as I stood by the printer, awaiting the final copy of an article I needed to send to press.

He was a few inches taller than me with a lean physique, more like that of a soccer player than the typical graduate student. He wore a crisp buttoned-down shirt with fitted pants. He stood out as a rare sight amid the crowds of disheveled students clad in dingy T-shirts and torn baggy jeans.

Before he could crash head-on into me, I held out my hand to ward off his approach. I needed to finish the print job to get the interview into the newsletter.

"Excuse me," he said, a lyrical accent filling the air, "I believe it's my turn. Whatever you're printing can wait. I need to take this to my thesis adviser today." He lifted a floppy disk.

I could hear the lilt of South American Spanish drifting through my ears like evening jazz. I glanced up to see his tense figure, muscles tight and ready to spring, hair in wild sable curls.

"You can wait. I'm on deadline."

"My future depends on this thesis. I must go first."

I couldn't tell whether he was desperate, entitled, or joking. "Well, grad student, my ability to pay rent depends on this article." I continued loading paper. "I've got sole possession of this printer for now, so please step aside. Wait your turn in the queue."

"The queue? You mean as a student I'm last in line?"

I shot him what I thought of as my freaky-face look. "I'm printing now. I'm staff. You're a student." I slammed the paper tray shut. "Look, whatever your name is—"

"Rod, Rodrigo."

I didn't recall ever having met him before. I may have seen him dashing to his office loft. Like his wife who had crashed open the door and demanded answers the day before, he gave no introduction and exchanged no pleasantries.

"Well, Rod Rodrigo, it's lovely to meet you. I'm Sue, a worker bee, so yes, I get priority. I go first. You need to wait."

"So, you reinforce the hierarchy of MIT to get your way?" He paused, changing tactics. "Sue." He said my name in a calming sibilance. "I'm on deadline too. I need to get this printed if I'm ever going to graduate."

I sidestepped past him and caught a glimpse of curly hair

tumbling over his brow. His aquiline nose held John Lennon-style glasses. I sighed. "I repeat, you're a graduate student." His brown eyes tinged with green shards stared at me, unflinching. "Please remove your carcass. I'll let you know when my printer is free."

"The printer belongs only to you?" He shook his head, and a swath of curls crossed over one eye. "So territorial." He took a step closer and almost whispered, "Typical American."

It seemed more a political statement than an observation. I took umbrage. No matter how cute he looked, or how I knew I really should be sharing the printer, I stood at high alert.

"Typical?" I stepped in closer, almost touching. "Let me assure you I'm not simply a typical American. I am a quintessential American." I refused to back off physically, verbally, or politically.

Instead of anger, his smile widened. He began a soft chuckle. A natural charm rose freely to the surface of his eyes. I could feel his body heat, smell his cologne.

"Touché," he said.

"What's so funny?"

"I expected a different reaction. That's all. I admire that you stood up for yourself."

"You expected me to cower, back off, and feel guilty or try to show you how untypical an American I am by giving in to your demands?"

"Something like that." He lifted his hand from his pocket, and in one gentle motion, he placed my hand in his and kissed the back of my wrist while lightly caressing my fingers.

Despite my initial anger, I began to giggle like a teenage girl on a prom date. I remembered my mother's command: "Never giggle. Laugh. Guffaw. Burst out if you must," she would say, "but don't giggle like an idiot girlchild." But giggle I did. His appearance and reaction did not match up to my expectations. I felt entranced.

"Very gallant," I said, and tried to withdraw my hand from his caressing fingers, "but I'm still making you wait."

He held the palm of my hand, a light touch that kept the tight distance between us. "Of course," he said. "A gentleman always waits for the lady to come first."

"Come? Or do you mean go first?" I asked.

"Oh, my silly confusion with English verbs and all those double meanings. I must learn to focus." The word, with his accent, he pronounced as "fuk-us." His smile widened, and I wasn't sure if he was playing me or if his command of the language veiled his real meaning. "I am at your service," he added. "Please come, or rather go, first."

I couldn't help smiling. "You're correct," I said. "A lady always comes first in any endeavor with a gentleman."

"I'll remember to always be a gentleman then. Anytime we get into a power struggle, I promise that you will come first."

Instead of leaving, he moved closer, close enough that I could smell his Paco Rabanne aftershave, a burnished musk melded with his own male scent. His smile grew in a slow, ever-widening line that lifted his entire face. He watched me intensely, as if waiting for any reaction from me gave him joy. His quick laughter was contagious. I found myself smiling.

"I have to admit," he said, "I didn't expect such a clever response. I think we may very well enjoy each other's company." He cocked his head. "If we fuk-us on each other's needs, that is."

The pronunciation made me smirk. "I know this probably sounds insulting, but you have a beautiful accent, even when you're arrogantly making demands. Where are you from?"

"Chile originally. Argentina when I was very young. Then

we moved to LA. And you, the owner of all office printers, where are you from?"

"Upstate New York originally. Tucson a few years. Then San Diego."

"From the far ends of the Earth's poles and opposite coasts, at last we meet." He bowed.

I couldn't help myself. Perhaps it was the sudden change of tone, the lightened mood. Perhaps it was the combination with my desire for companionship. Or perhaps a lusty need reaching an apogee of horniness as I measured this specimen, a possible candidate for my manhunt. Maybe it was the way he saved face with humor, open to being taken by surprise, using laughter to find commonality in our small space of existence.

Whatever it was, he had broken through my tangled loneliness. I laughed. Loudly. I knew my braying style might turn a man off. Instead, he joined me in a shared humor, matching the decibel and tone, and gave me hope that I might be able to find a friend in Boston with a harmless flirtation on the side.

The workdays merged into anticipated joy. Where once I had waited for Andy's return from his ventures out to sea, I now found myself waiting for Rod's return to the office. Every afternoon, he would appear at my tiny windowless room with a quip, an interesting approach to a subject, a fresh cup of café au lait just the way I liked it. Something he knew only by paying attention.

"I confess I accidentally met your wife." He did not flinch, only looked curious. "I was wondering how long you've been married."

"I guarantee I've been married longer than you."

I perked up. A challenge I couldn't allow to pass. "Are you sure?"

"Absolutely. No graduate student here has been married longer than I have. It sometimes feels like I was born married."

"What makes you so cynical? Surely, you fell in love."

"Not sure about that. We couldn't come to the States unless we got married. She needed her papers. Her parents are conservative and demanded a legal marriage first. My parents were having their twenty-fifth wedding anniversary, and my sister was also getting married. We did all three celebrations at one event on the same day in Santiago."

"How very efficient. Sounds like North American pragmatism to me."

"Bite your tongue. Nothing about me is North American–like."

His eyes suddenly went dark, as if they held a difficult secret. It passed.

"How much," I said, "do you want to bet on who's been married longer?"

"A buck."

"Last of the big spenders."

"I'm a graduate student on stipend and scholarship."

"So, how long have you been married?"

"Longer than you, longer than anyone here, longer than life itself." He sounded exasperated.

"I highly doubt it. I met my husband while I was an undergraduate. I knew him less than a year when we got married."

"Okay," he said, "the deal is if I've been married longer, you take me out for coffee and tell me why you got married so young. If you've been married longer, I will give you the dollar bill for you to take me out for coffee."

"Wow, what a deal. How could I resist? In this case, you go first."

"Going first," he bowed, "as requested. I've been married over eight years."

"Nine." I clapped my hands. "I'm a competitor. You better show me the money."

He pulled a bill from his wallet and leaned over my chair and placed it in front of me in one slow motion, lingering against my shoulder. "Here," he whispered. I reached for the dollar bill. He held it until our hands touched. "Anyone who has survived almost a decade of marriage deserves a reward."

Something in the way he said "deserves" made me wonder if he had deciphered my marital distress or was offering his own. Glancing at his tight features as he placed the bet on the table, I realized we both displayed marital disillusionment. When he saw me staring at him, he recovered, flashing that disarming smile.

"I'll confess," I said, "I've attempted to learn Spanish many times. One thing that's difficult is the temporary versus permanent condition. *'Estoy cansada,'* I'm tired, temporary condition. Yet it's *'Soy casada,'* I'm married. Permanent condition. Forever."

"*Los dos,*" he replied, "both. Being in the permanent state of *casada* leads to forever being *cansada.*"

I laughed. "*Muy cansada!*" *Very, very tired of being married.*

During the following weeks, our friendship grew, and every day brought a new snippet about our backgrounds and personal histories. The flirtation intensified. Andy increased his time out to sea, keeping his officemate as his primary companion. I had no proof, of course, of any affair, only vague notions. I knew I could simply be rationalizing my own lusty behavior and innuendos that I knew would soon lead to a bedroom, if left unchecked.

Rod and I discussed our lives in abstract ways, as if telling someone else's story. He was born in Chile, migrating to the States when he was fourteen only to return to Santiago again at the wrong moment with the dictator Pinochet in power. His family promptly hit reset and returned to California. I wondered if his haste in getting married fell into the category of "arranged," but I didn't know enough about him or the cultural realities of immigration he may have faced to ask.

We met regularly, sharing a sardonic sense of humor with a sharp edge. It was a relief to enjoy a moment's hilarity with someone who would feel challenged by my observations. We enjoyed an endless round of sardonic humor and undivided attention.

It was in one of those moments that we discovered both of our spouses would be out of town for part of the summer. Andy would be working in Baja California with Kendall. Rod's spouse would be visiting southern Chile to see her family and former boyfriend.

Fate seemed to be dropping us into its adulterous arms.

"Should we step it up?" he asked.

We were strolling along the Harvard Bridge. I looked over the wall into the muddy swirls of the Charles River. Sailboats floated in slow, lazy glides. "Step it up to what?" I couldn't help placing a little coyness in my voice. "Whatever are you talking about?"

"I'm talking about what you're talking about as long as you're talking about the same thing I'm talking about," he said, slamming the conversational ball back in my court.

I wondered how many times this conversation had passed

between paramours on this very bridge. "What do you suggest?"

"That we hammer out an agreement."

"A nonlegal term of engagement"—I paused—"or rather, disengagement?"

"It would be smart to add an exit clause."

We both released a nervous burst of laughter. I glanced around.

Rod moved closer to me. "Where do you suggest we meet to continue this scintillating conversation?"

"Scintillating sounds suggestive," I said.

"I further suggest, given the complication of this conversation and to ensure we're in agreement, we meet for lunch to hammer out a non-contract."

I should've noted the red alerts. He was a plotter, a planner, an architect who wanted to think carefully before committing. But I was complicit, a practical seductress, unwilling to let details remain vague.

After a few minutes, he said, "Facts." He put his index finger into the palm of my hand. "First, we are both married and have equal amounts to lose if we're caught. Second, we can discuss rules for disengagement to cover any contingency, to know what to say, when to stay, when to go."

"Rules to protect our spouses, our marriages, or each other?" I asked.

He nodded, his finger circling the lines in my palm as if reading my future.

"Covering our asses for the seventh of the ten commandments," I said, and enclosed his fingers in my sweaty palm. "This tactical discussion has such a romantic ring to it. No shame or guilt. Just good planning."

He grinned, and his eyes glinted gold in late spring's harsh light. "We're simply setting up a foolproof system, together." His hand started to shake. "I've no idea how much luck has to do with our plan though. The fate of having met. At this moment in time."

"We both have a lot at stake." I withdrew my hand. "Let's take a pause. We can meet to agree on the process and decide whether to go through with it. I'm a pragmatist, not some virgin in a Victorian romance being seduced by a count. Yes or no, I'll understand either way."

"It feels a little like building a work breakdown structure for an architectural project instead of a possibly exciting love affair."

"Ah, you said the *L* word, 'love.' I feel completely secure in proceeding with full knowledge that we're talking about the same thing."

"Love," he said quietly, turning the idea over in his mind, shaking his head. "In Spanish we say, '*Te quiero.*'"

"I want," I translated from my elementary studies. "Not, '*te adoro,*' I adore, or '*te amo,*' I love."

"It's all the same, isn't it? We want. We adore. We love. We pursue. I think to want is stronger and more enduring. Love is too confining." His voice maintained a certain calm, as if he could force us both to stay on our short-lived passion track, then walk away from it easily. "We would not want to fall in love."

"Nothing more than a quick summer fling."

Maybe it was my imagination, but I detected a slight sadness behind his words. Half the fun of creating the illusion of an affair seemed to be in planning the logistics, strategizing the locale, making yourself giddy with anticipation, and timing the climax. Much like lovemaking itself.

"Rule number one, then, will be no falling in love." He held up two fingers. "With a corollary. Rule number two will be never to say, 'I love you.'"

"In either language."

We both laughed at the absurdity of falling in love. Our cynicism felt intoxicating, freeing us to plan the unplannable.

I held my fingers in a V formation. "Rule number two hardly seems an issue, since we're setting up rules for disengagement for an affair before we've even so much as kissed each other. Who knows? We may be so disappointed that we end it before it begins."

With that, he took my head in his warm hands and lightly feathered his lips along mine.

I was not much of a kisser, as my husband could attest, but the shock of newness and barely felt soft skin created waves of pleasure I had never felt before. I remembered reading once that a prostitute may refuse to kiss a paying John. The act of kissing was far too intimate. The prostitute's response made no sense at the time I read the article, but suddenly I realized with a visceral clarity why it did.

A few days later, we met for lunch near his office in Boston's Back Bay. His wife preoccupied herself with packing for her trip to see her old boyfriend. My husband preoccupied himself with packing for his trip to the Sea of Cortez with his female officemate. The timing for a seduction seemed too perfect. All parties accounted for and ready to go.

We sat down together at a quiet diner, sandwiches left uneaten in our excitement. Rod grabbed a napkin and Sharpie pen as we sat close together on teetering high stools to draft the ten rules on how to conduct an affair.

1. No falling in love.
2. Never say, "I love you."
3. The marriages are of primary importance and not to be discussed.

4. Don't reveal anything to each other that would jeopardize the marriages.
5. Never call the other at home.
6. Never stop by unannounced.
7. Do not touch each other in public.
8. Never confess, no matter how guilty you feel.
9. Don't tell anyone, not even friends or family, that you've had an affair.
10. This is a summer fling. It ends before the leaves of fall change color.

Simply stated in black and white on a used napkin—I wanted sex. He wanted sex. Nothing more.

24

Fault Lines

I knocked on the door once, and Rod immediately opened it. He held a large sunflower in his hand. I pulled sunglasses down my nose to get a better look at his tiny graduate student apartment, dwarfed by the sunflower. For a moment, I felt like we were rehearsing for a Broadway stage entrance. One step inside, the door closed with a soft click, and the show was on.

There was no going back.

I walked over to the window. "Wow, you have quite a view here."

"Yes, you can see the Charles River from the Science Museum"—his left hand reached one way—"to the Harvard Bridge on the other side."

He came up behind me and began stroking my hair. All those teen years of reading *Modern Romance* had prepared me for this moment. In the background, I could hear my grandmother's words: "Every wife wants to be a mistress." Being a wife seemed a big bore. Always waiting. But a mistress, I learned that night, held her own agency in her lover's embrace.

A crack of thunder reverberated; a slash of jagged lightning slammed into the Citgo sign across the river. Instinctively, I jumped and backed away and almost fell into a ficus tree. The leaves fluttered in protest at being used like an armless love seat.

The storm intensified. Lightning strikes illuminated the muddy water.

He started to undress me in a methodical way, his warm fingers working in slow strokes, slipping from my shoulder to my hips, caressing every surface of skin. With each new gasp escaping my lips, he increased the stroking. I moaned. Loudly. Like some klutzy romance heroine acting out the wrong storyline.

"*Mi amor*," he said, his voice barely heard above my involuntary half hums of pleasure, increasing in decibels with each new touch. "That's what I want to hear."

He led me to the aptly named love seat. I fell into the cushions. My head dropped over the seat's edge, my neck exposed. I arched instinctively. The ficus leaves brushed in sensual waves along my forehead with each thrust.

His fingers worked constantly, and the song "Magic Man" with his "magic hands" swirled through my ears, competing with the thunder. Lights flashed, I didn't know if from the lightning, the electric lights as power flickered, or my own interior explosions.

I gasped to catch my breath as he held me in his arms, both of us spent.

"A married man," I said between breaths, "makes a great lover."

"A married woman open to new experiences is a beauty to behold."

Our fairy-tale affair extended night after night. We clutched each other in gratitude with every exploration of lovemaking. The experiment of my life as mistress continued for six weeks.

Our conversations deepened. We laughed with each orgasmic delight, playful in intimacy, while ending with pillow talk discussing history, cultural differences, political beliefs, and our attraction to each other. No subject was verboten. Even our disappointment over having married young.

We extended our conversations late into the night, knowing our affair would end with summer according to rule number ten of our agreement written on a paper napkin.

"Would this be exciting if we were single?" I asked. "Or is it due to the illicit nature of an affair?"

"Different people, different results. Maybe as with all great love affairs, there is an element of fate."

"Fate has a ring of fantasy to it. I like it."

"I think we make love to talk, to connect," he said. "I love how open you are, how accepting. It's a new experience for me too."

"It's wild that we laugh during the act, kind of funky, unique, and fun." I brushed my hand along his arm. "Well, back to the real world tomorrow."

Before I could stop myself, I began weeping. An eternal sadness sifted through the air between us, almost a mourning. Instead of backing away, he held me closer, a moment of shared sadness at our predetermined parting.

"I wish I'd met you earlier," he said, "but I feel responsible for having brought my wife to the States. She really can't take care of herself."

Instead of abruptly pulling back or saying, "But she's an adult," I remained mute.

"Seems I'm a little too loyal."

I glanced at him sideways. "An affair seems one hell of a way of showing it." I got up then and dressed quickly.

He gazed at me with profound sorrow, then rose to dress. "How about a farewell walk along the Charles?"

I nodded. *Rules be damned*, I thought. *I'm in love.*

Ten minutes later we were sitting on our favorite bench overlooking the river.

"I want to be with you a while longer, Sue. Nothing more."

He began to tell me about his childhood in Argentina, his father in prison waiting years before returning to Chile. How close he was to his sister and how he felt he couldn't protect her, and it pained him still. The stories of his older brother helping him deal with bullies who saw them as outsiders. The three siblings holding close together to survive the turmoil of moving from country to country in a deeply troubled time.

There was something about his gentle charm, his kindness, and the soft and lyrical way in which he spoke about the people he loved. I knew I would miss his kindness.

Waves slapped in choppy whitecaps over the riverbanks. Canada geese squawked, fighting over food tidbits left along the water's edge.

I sat in mourning for the happiness I would soon lose.

A week after departing from my lover, I landed in Acapulco. The taxi dropped me off at a beach hotel. The stucco building with Spanish tiles rose from the sandy cliff, a quiet beauty once crowded with Hollywood celebrities. It had been two months since I had seen Andy.

I checked into the hotel room to drop off luggage. A note scrawled in Andy's script—"Be right back"—sat on the side table.

I undressed and put on the cotton robe hanging by the

bedpost. The big, open king-size bed, with the sea breeze making a ghostly flutter along the canopy of mosquito netting, seemed like something out of a B movie. I pulled into a fetal position as Andy opened the door. He held one long-stemmed rose. He seemed happy, calm, unusually content.

"How was your flight?"

"Easy," I said. "Was the cruise a success?"

"Oh yes. Kendall and I got a lot of work done. We were inseparable, scientific soulmates."

I wanted to retort, "I bet you were," but then realized having spent unlimited inseparable time with Rod made me a hypocrite.

"We're just friends," Andy added.

I lay back down. Without the precursor of kissing or touching, he took off his clothes and opened my robe. I responded with open arms, trying to stay in the moment, both of us in a dance of deception neither would admit. We finished in a rush, barely satisfied.

"Did you meet anyone in Boston while I was gone?" he asked, once he had dressed again.

I looked away, wondering if my eyes conveyed guilt. "A few people I work with."

"Anyone you were inseparable with?"

I froze. I missed Rod. I missed the easy camaraderie, something not evident with Andy. Perhaps he found as easy an association with Kendall or Desiree or Beth as I had with Rod. "Nope. Just friends."

The next morning, the earth moved. Literally. Floorboards swelled as if made of gel. Clothes in the closet swung back and forth like a pendulum.

"Quit goofing around, Sue."

"Are you serious?" I jumped up and began putting on my

clothes. "This, Professor Geologist, is an earthquake. Can't you feel it?"

He was awake now. "We have to get out of here in case there's a tsunami." He pulled on shorts and grabbed his wallet.

We waited in the doorframe of the bathroom until the next wave passed. Then we ran out of the building and up the hill as fast as we could. A few locals were already snaking up the cliff. We joined them. Many of the European vacationers stayed on the verandas, watching us and shaking their heads.

Above the horizon's sight line, we could see a large wave. We stood on the hillside, clutching a tree, watching as the wave increased in size, then crashed onto the edge of the veranda, making tourists scatter with the wait staff back inside the hotel. A few more waves hit the shore as the rumbling continued, then subsided.

In the hours following, smells of cooking fish mingled with the fumes of diesel oil and rotting seaweed. The shoreline receded at low tide. An eerie, silent calm surrounded the town. No one moved downhill back to the shore for a while. Our bare feet stumbled on sharp needles of cacti as we scrambled up the limestone cliff overlooking the beach. We dug our toes into loose sand in desperation to hold to the earth. As the tremors subsided, tourists and locals began the slow descent back to the hotel.

My grasp of Spanish was poor, but from what I understood, it seemed as though the smaller rumblings meant it was safe. We could see pavement tiles on the hotel walkway that had buckled in various directions and splintered from the quake's force.

We slept fitfully that night. In the morning, I bought a local newspaper from a young boy in torn huarache sandals. I slowly translated the short news report from Mexico City. It seemed there had been an earthquake, one of the largest in the populated city's history. The count seemed to be in the tens of thousands or more who had died and even more who had been injured or were without housing. Mexico City had been devastated.

Checking the map in the newspaper, I could see that although Acapulco sat smack in the epicenter of one of the biggest fault lines, the earth's crusting motions reached the interior, hitting Mexico City in a series of increasingly large undulations. The ancient lakebed upon which the city rested had become a sea of soil, crumbling large government buildings and poorly constructed housing projects in its wake.

We ran into a small group of scientists Andy knew who had been on the cruise ship. They seemed anxious. We watched them down straight shots of mezcal to calm their jittery nerves.

"Are you okay?" I asked the young woman. She turned a blank eye toward me.

"Mexico City is totally devastated," said the middle-aged man next to her.

"Oh no." I put a hand on her shoulder. She crumpled over, placing her head on the table. I glanced at the man. "Do you think they need people to help with the rescue?"

He shook his head no. "You can't even get into the city. On the outskirts you can see apartment buildings crumbled with body parts in the street." The woman kept her head down. "They're trying to get people out from under the rubble. Be glad you're safe here together."

We were lucky. Lucky to be alive. Lucky to be in Acapulco and not in Mexico City. Lucky to be together.

The dean of the school of architecture, who spoke fluent Spanish, had called the hotel and left a message. My mother, I found out, had telephoned everyone she could once she heard about the earthquake since she knew we were at the epicenter. It shocked me, because I didn't think my mother worried about me at all. I rarely heard from her, and when I did, she seemed almost dismissive about any turmoil I'd experienced.

In less than a few days, I had gone from the ecstasy of an affair to guilt for surviving. I thought I didn't believe in a vengeful God. Yet I couldn't shake the momentary and irrational fear that my own joy from those six glorious weeks with Rod had caused harm.

Andy returned to the ship to pack his equipment to travel to San Diego. I flew into Tijuana, my emotions in disarray. I had to reorient myself to get home, but no cabs were in sight. Darkness began to descend upon the desert. Orange streaks of sunset slipped along the distant mountains. I knew I had less than three miles to the border, where I could cross to take the trolley back to San Diego.

I'd begun to walk northward when what I thought was a taxi stopped. I didn't recognize the Pemex logo of Mexico's largest oil company on the side of the car. A good-looking middle-aged Mexican man smiled and waved me over.

It wasn't until I was in the car traveling a dirt road that I realized I had made a possibly dangerous mistake.

"*Adónde?*" he asked. "Where to?"

"La Frontera. The border gates."

He glanced at me in the rearview mirror. "*Está bien.*" Then in English upon seeing my worried brow, "It's okay. I'm an engineer at Pemex." When I remained silent, he added, "The big oil company?" I nodded. "It's along the way. I'll take you there. *Cálmate.* You're safe."

I clutched the door handle, ready to bolt if he changed direction, but I could see from the road signs that he was driving me directly to the border, only a few feet from the entry point.

"*Gracias.*" I pulled my backpack on. Gratitude boiled over. A few tears of relief fell down my cheek.

"*Tén cuidado, chiquita,*" he said, his voice low. "Be careful. You're a beautiful girl. It's dangerous at night in Tijuana."

I nodded, then noticed he continued to watch me cross the border before driving away. Suddenly, I realized how lucky I was. I could have ended up dead in an earthquake or disappeared in the middle of the Baja desert. Instead, I had been rescued by a caring and kind man.

After the date rape and the attack in the alley, I had believed I needed the security of a husband to survive. But that night on the border, I confirmed for the first time that perhaps only some men held evil intentions. What I learned on that unofficial taxi ride with the kindly engineer was that most men were good. As most women were too. Where we went off the rails, I surmised, was when we felt insecure and lonely. In those moments, we made decisions we regretted. Our intention to remain loyal to vows dissolved in a desperate need to be wanted.

Still, I did not regret meeting Rod, being intimate with him, or falling in love with him—or, perhaps, the idea of loving him. The earth rumbled within us. Evil or not, each choice was ours to make, and every hidden fracture in our fault lines held the capacity to destroy or reshape our lives.

25

Redemption

I missed Rod's intimate friendship, the tight embraces that suggested if he let go, he would lose me forever. The affair had been an addictive drug gripping on to my soul with gusto. The casual approach to married life afforded a degree of freedom. The open marriage that Andy proposed replayed in my head. Jealousy, emotional distancing, and gaslighting conflicted with my desire to connect fully, to be loved solely without competition.

Rod returned to the architecture lab to pursue his second master's degree. We had avoided each other for months. But one night, after the holiday party had finished and staff had gone home early for Christmas Eve celebrations, we indulged in one bad decision.

Alone with me, Rod leaned into my office. "*Amiga mía*, I have a proposition."

"Don't tell me." I cocked my head. "You want to add an addendum to the ten rules?"

He smiled, confidence shining on his face. "Perhaps we forgot it for a reason, but now the reason has changed."

I hated to admit it, but Rod's intriguing approach had a drug-inducing essence, melting my hesitancy.

"I'd add this," I said. "Something like 'Pretend I don't miss you. Pretend I don't care. Pretend I don't want you in my life.'"

I could see his hand shaking slightly as he held the door. "I missed you. I keep rehashing our conversations." He placed his hands on the chair back and turned me slightly toward him. "I missed my best friend. It would be awkward not to talk to you. I really think we can make our friendship work."

It was late. We were alone.

"Up to the loft." I said, "I don't mean to be bossy, but I want you, and not just as a friend. I want you to desire me, long for me, show me how much you missed me." I wanted to tell him I'd missed him too, that what I really wanted was his love, but instead I focused on the physical.

He nodded, his glasses slipping, giving him the look of a librarian startled by a group of loud teenagers. He glanced out the door. His deep tenor voice dropped to a whisper. "Whatever the lady wants."

We quickly jogged the short hallway and ran up the stairs two at a time together.

Without preamble, I began to undress only body parts needing attending. He sat back, his arms dangling over the chair's edge. He seemed stunned.

I didn't think of myself as alluring or captivating. I thought of my approach as full-on masculine, direct, unmitigated.

I walked over, sat atop him, and began moving in rhythm. My toes lifted and fell like a ballerina at a barre class. He held tight to my hips, waiting, as if any movement on his part would awaken him from this dream. The sheer will of desire captivated our tandem movements. I refused to stop.

Suddenly, the office door below us flew open and slammed into the wall. We both froze in flagrante delicto pose. We breathed into each other's necks to hide our gasps. Then we heard the muttering of the editor. "Where in the hell is it?" We could hear her rummaging in her desk drawer, then, "Ah ha. Knew it was here."

We stayed in position—me on top of him, him inside of me, our arms wrapped tightly around each other. Then just as quickly, the door slammed shut, echoing in the empty room.

"Maybe that's a sign," he said.

"A sign that we escaped notice or that we broke yet another of our ten rules?"

He looked puzzled.

"The first rule. No falling in love."

"No." He rebuttoned my blouse. "I'm not afraid of loving you, but we don't want to disrupt our lives with a possible baby."

"This wasn't planned." I added, "You were just there, available."

"Just there?" He gently lifted me off his thighs, and out came the body part and my now deflated and lost-to-the-wilderness orgasm. "I hoped I was more than a mere body part to you." He sounded hurt. "We should be careful. This could have bad consequences."

"I take full responsibility. My fault. I practically raped you."

"I wouldn't go that far." He zipped up his pants and left.

That same night, I made furious love to my husband to ease my frenzy, to cover my tracks, to fulfill a basic animal instinct. I knew I had sunk to a new low. Afterward, loneliness seeped into the atmosphere, shrouding me in its cold embrace.

I was almost five weeks late for my period. I carried around tampons in denial and somewhat in hope of relief from my stupidity and risk-taking. Then one morning in the shower on the sixth week, I began to cramp.

I doubled over and saw shreds of red-brown goo clogging the drain. I fell to my knees. The pain increased. Desperately I tried to wash away the remains, but shreds of humanity only stuck to the metal shower grill.

Lifting my bloody hands of miscarriage in horror, I began to cry uncontrollably. Andy heard me and stepped into the shower and glanced down. I looked up at him, ready to confess, to beg forgiveness, to cringe at his response. Instead, he walked into the shower fully clothed and bent down to hold me as I sobbed.

"I'm so sorry." I gulped air between words, trying to not look down into the red abyss.

"For what? It's not your fault. It happens." I could see his lip quiver, then tighten to stop the emotions within.

He gently covered me with a towel, ignoring the red stripes running down the drain, and pulled me toward him. "I know you told me you wanted a child. We argued about it. I wasn't ready, and I'm sorry I walked away from you, from us. I'll probably never be ready, but maybe this happening is kind of a wake-up call to right our lives. I love you."

The magic words "I love you" undid me. Our collective wrongness had undone us both. It seemed the sudden loss of this fetus might have released us from determining when the time would arrive, when we might be ready. Shivering, we held together tightly until a communal warmth slipped over us, while the shower washed away my repentant sins. Five weeks later I knew I was pregnant. Again.

I had counted with calm diligence six condoms in Andy's toiletry bag before he left with Kendall. I didn't know why I was torturing myself. Maybe it was the hormones or the ever-increasing size of my torso, but I had thought of pushing a safety pin through the package of condoms with a note that simply said, "Gotcha." I realized he would probably have used them anyway, and then decisions about another woman's pregnancy would complicate our lives.

He opened the bedroom door, glanced at the opened toiletry bag. I avoided questioning him about the missing four rubbers in his bag. He simply pushed it aside to embrace me. "I missed you." He placed a hand on my abdomen. "I'm happy we're having a baby. The miscarriage was a wake-up call." He grabbed his attaché case and pulled out a black jewelry box. "A little gift for the mother-to-be."

I opened it and stared at the turquoise necklace like those I had seen being sold on the roadside to passing tourists. I could feel the pulse in my thumb pound as I held the gift. "Did you enjoy your trip?" The words seemed to fall like chunks of ice driven into open cavities inside my embittered mouth.

He shrugged. "Halley's Comet was spectacular. You would've appreciated it. If you'd been there, you'd have been excited too. You're adventurous that way. Kendall sure as hell isn't. I had to wake her up. She was really ticked off since it was four o'clock in the morning."

"Woke her up?" I let the necklace fall to the floor, the silver threads twisted around the pendant. "What do you mean you woke her up? What did you do? Poke her?"

I sorely wished I had Wonder Woman's mythical golden Lasso of Truth, but it didn't seem I even needed it, so at ease was he with sharing his amorous adventures he didn't even bother to lie.

He froze in place for a second, then recovered and began to reenact his story.

"No, no, I got up and went to her hotel room and then banged on her door." He demonstrated by rapping his knuckles on the coffee table with a quick succession of increasingly loud raps. "Our rooms were next to each other." He kept up the charade, demonstrating by physically rising from his imaginary hotel bed, getting fictionally dressed, and banging on her door, leaving out any reference to banging *her*.

"Sue, you wouldn't believe it. She got so pissed." He paused on an intake of breath. "Really, all I could think of was how much better it would've been to experience it with you. It was complete darkness. Not much out there but the dry seabed."

"And Kendall," I added.

Evidently, the streaking lights that formed the rare sighting of the comet seemed to have cooled their passionate moments. He retold the story in a way to cover his tracks. Once again, I had to remind myself that I, too, once had a lover. Shared deception encircled our marital bed. Who was I to stop my husband?

The wife and mistress labels entwined once again. Could I really return to the social confines of wife? I had played my parts secretly, as so many women before me. No apologies were given or needed. Desire's duality served me well despite the omnipresent sexual double standard that drove the nail of necessity into my cheating heart. *Bury lust*, I told myself. *Remold the broken parts, crystallize our separate identities, and pull the shards into a recognizable form of marriage that can be held in the chambers of an empty glass heart.*

The phone rang, and Rod's melodious voice fell like a soft breeze, surprising me. He had broken rule number five: *Never call the home number*. I hadn't spent any time with him after that fateful moment in the loft.

"I'm leaving Boston." I could hear his voice catch. "If you ever need to talk to me, any time of the day or night, I have an eight hundred number. It's secure."

I grasped the phone tighter. "Rod, I know you believe we can be friends, but I think my attacking you in the loft should tell you that's impossible. Once we touch each other, we have no control." I took a deep breath. "I'm going to be a mother now. Everything's changed for me."

"Has it changed for your husband too?"

Silence. He waited. I had no response, no assurances. I only knew that my quasi-open marriage must end now that I was pregnant. I believed the emergence of a child would change me, would change us all. My husband and I could concentrate on being parents. But I knew if I uttered this belief to Rod, I would sound delusional.

"It doesn't matter what happened between us," I said. "I choose to change."

I could hear him sigh. "I understand. I'll miss our friendship. Please call me if you need a friend. Sometime in the future, I'm certain, you'll need me, and I'll need you."

As I said farewell to my lover, my heart compressed a bit. I cared for this man, maybe even truly loved him. The biological imperative to continue life, though, was stronger than mere desire.

26

Renewal

"It's one of the only nude beaches here. We go there a lot."
Kendall's husband, James, said over the phone. "Come with us. It'll be fun."

He seemed eager to have me join them. It was midsummer, and I was seven months along. I almost laughed thinking of lounging on the beach in Rhode Island in my obviously pregnant state.

"I'm not exactly bikini ready." I was more intrigued than anything else as to why the husband of Andy's lover would even call to ask. "Oh, what the heck," I said, "let's shake things up."

"That's the spirit." James paused to clear his throat and added, "Maybe you should know that Andy asked Kendall to watch over you while he's out to sea. I'm not sure why she just didn't call you herself."

"I wonder too." Curiosity about their marriage overcame me. Did they also have a quasi-open marriage? I'd never know unless I went along for the ride.

Block Island on a Saturday afternoon in late August was littered with all types of bodies—heavyset, ultrathin, young, old, tall, small, but mostly human and distinctively not of the

California, Muscle Beach physique. I felt at ease with my bulging-with-baby anatomy.

Waves lapped in the distance. I glanced toward the shore and laughed when I realized that I couldn't see my toes. I felt like a biologist observing animals mating in the wild. I mentally documented each nuance of Kendall's behavior, any change in response to her husband that might help me to determine what Andy meant to her.

I closed my eyes and fell into a light sleep until I heard Kendall whisper to James, "She looks like a beached whale."

I opened one eye, a slit behind my mirrored aviator glasses.

"She looks fine," he said.

"Well, if you like that type. If you ask me, she was already too curvy with those big breasts even before she was pregnant."

Her words of envy confirmed my suspicion. But I realized I wasn't in any position to judge Andy's mistress.

"Well, I think she looks beautiful with child." I could see him push his hat over his eyes to end the half-whispered discussion.

Kendall leaned over and punched his arm. Hard. I heard his "Ouch, Jesus," but he didn't move, as if used to physical harm.

As I prayed that the sound of washing waves, screeching gulls, and laughing children would drown out their bitter exchange, I revisited the reaction to my first memory of public nudeness in 1960. I still could hear the words of Trudy, the local prostitute on Fage Avenue, when my sister and I walked down that city street, "You're going to break some hearts," and the disapproval from neighbors labeling me "a little hussy . . . shameless girl . . . seductress."

From my deflowering in a humid dorm room to posing for an art photo that led to my being raped in a college suite, my body seemed to be defined by others. Even after discovering the secret of ecstasy from a kind man who had stroked me into the high of my first orgasm and the warmth of my lover's attention, I'd struggled to own my physical being. But now, I embraced my body's ability to produce new life.

Rather than feign deafness, I stretched and rolled over, hoisting my breasts with nipples the size of saucers. I pulled my leg in a provocative posture across my burgeoning torso—a "Marilyn Monroe by the poolside" pose, complete with upward lift of my arm for all to see in my naked transparency. I shifted my sunglasses and winked at James.

"This whale needs to get out of the sun," I said. "I want to thank you for taking care of me, but it's time to go home."

Kendall shot a sideways glance at her husband. He grimaced and shook his head. Once in the car, the couple bickered in sharp whispers over every imaginable sign of their distaste for each other, from James's driving style to Kendall's choice of picnic food.

In an unmitigated streak of cruelty that defined Kendall, she snapped at her husband, "I refuse to apologize. Fat people should know others are uncomfortable with seeing them on a nude beach in public."

He sighed. "That defeats the purpose of going to a place where everyone is accepted. You'll understand better soon."

Something about the way he phrased it triggered my memory of the beach. I had watched the shift of Kendall's hips. With clarity, I realized she, too, was pregnant. I counted down the months from the last field trip she and Andy took together and knew why she was freaking out about maternity.

"You're pregnant," I said from the back seat. It wasn't a question. "How far along?"

James flipped the rearview mirror on me for a second. He blinked his eyes rapidly. Kendall turned fully toward me, tugging her seatbelt around her neck, almost choking herself. The pupil of her eyes dilated. Her upper lip leaked beads of sweat. I half expected her to slap me. "Did Andy tell you? He's the only one who knows." Her crunched shoulders and angry tone overshadowed her words.

"Except for me. Your husband. Remember?" James snapped. "I'm one of those who know about it. Or do I not count?" He seemed intent on having me witness their marital discord.

All three of us stayed silent the rest of the way back. No one wanted to commit to the truth.

"I'll help you get your things up the stairs," James said as he stopped in front of my apartment. "Maybe we should meet for lunch, away from our spouses."

I took the beach bag from him. "I've got it." His eyes flashed in expectation. I gently touched the back of his freckled hand. "There's no need to meet." The tissue of lies about our marriages, I knew, were best left tucked safely within a locked box of emotional explosives. The truth could destroy us all. "We both know where our loyalties should be now."

He nodded. "You deserve better, Sue."

"So do you, James."

We hugged goodbye as old friends at a reunion might, grateful for a moment's kindness and shared understanding before parting forever.

In mid-October of 1986, after my seventh hour at Boston's Brigham and Women's Hospital, a young nurse emerged at the shift change, drenched in over-the-counter Tabu perfume. She entered with a gleeful cheer. "Well, hi there, mama. Looks like you're almost cooked." She glanced down. "Oh my. That baby's coming out." She began to chant in repetitive cycles to "push, push."

No longer able to function, much less judge my past choices in search of love and desire and my decided lack of control in lusty moments, my entire body collapsed.

"Don't stop now." The nurse raised her gloved hand to get my waning attention. "You're so close. I can almost see the baby. You're so brave to give birth without painkillers."

Brave or stupid, I thought, and in a moment, I simply gave up the shameful past to the painful truth of the present. The baby took over, and in the early morning hours, I gave birth to an eight-and-a-half-pound, almost *two-foot-long* baby girl.

"Congrats." The nurse held up the wet, squirmy baby. "You just gave birth to a toddler." She then looked at the doctor, her voice calmed to normal tones again, dismissive of the mother's existence, and added, "Geez, this baby is way too big for that mother."

"Now you tell me," I said.

Nurse and doctor glanced at me as if I'd been eavesdropping on their private conversation. They both chuckled together in one short spurt under their surgical masks, then turned back to their jobs. More pushing and massaging, and the doctor pulled out what he called a "perfectly intact placenta," all the while ignoring the newborn toddler laid across my chest.

The baby's head dangled off my right shoulder, while her slippery legs were flung over my neck. Instinctively, I lowered my infant daughter's body and encircled her in my arms. I stared in awe.

"I thought babies were supposed to be tiny cherubs." I

stroked her face. "This one looks like a long-distance sprinter."

The doctor and nurse shot each other knowing glances that medical personnel seemed to master when dealing with ignorant patients and a new mother's astonishment.

My husband, almost forgotten, stood behind me. He began to stroke the baby's wet arm, and I swelled with the possibility that the course of our partnership could be corrected. I embraced my newborn as we were rolled into the recovery room, alone together for the first time.

An unexpected maternal instinct kicked in within seconds. I refused to leave my daughter with anyone for the remainder of our time in the hospital. She slept soundly by my side with my arms firmly wound around her swaddled form. The hallway filled with doctors and nurses carrying out their duties in the factory-ordered delivery system.

In that moment, I realized that despite my obvious personal mistakes, this little girl and I could hit restart together. The possibility of forgiveness, the hope of redemption, blanketed us both.

What advice on surviving life's realities from girlhood to woman did I have to offer? Could I simply dream away the double standard, believe that it might evolve or disappear in her generation's lifetime? How would I teach her about the hazards and joys of being female with all the permutations of passion that the world sees as misguided and maligned?

Despite everything—from my deeply flawed humanity, past mistakes, and intensity of guilt at being both a lusty mistress and a lonely wife—the truth was I had no regrets. I had created another being from a simple act of intimacy.

I glanced out the frosted-glass door. White-coated ghosts roamed the noisy halls while the connection with my daughter grew to encircle my heart, empower my resolve, and change me forever. In a rush of maternal protectiveness, I held my tender charge and began to weep uncontrollably.

In that moment, I realized I had finally unbroken my own heart.

Epilogue

Even if I could suddenly take my hat and run, as my mother once advised, I knew I could never escape the need to love or to be loved. As new life emerged, I envisioned possibility without a sexual double standard. In the years that followed, no matter how many times I fell in and out of the affair or attempted to even the gender score with my husband or heal my marriage, it was only the love of children that mattered. I vowed, instead, to create a more equitable world where our daughters and sons could freely determine their own sexual fates.

Although it would take many years before I could render the courage to "take my hat," leave my marriage, and reconnect with my paramour, I continued to believe in love. For in the end, we all wear many hats in our search for love—spouse, lover, partner, parent, and friend. We redefine, like the Greeks, so many stages of love. Love for a newborn. Love for family. Love for a friend. And, with that understanding, I no longer held any need to run.

Acknowledgments

I would like to thank fellow memoirists from The Writers Center in Bethesda, Maryland. Most particularly, I appreciated the critiques and specific reviews from area authors Chris Palmer, Olaf Kula, and Kaldun Nossuli. I am indebted to beta readers Michael Thorpe, Laurie Morin, Jennifer Baugh, Regina Maier, and Kenneth T. Dean, whose honest and constructive input helped to shape the focus on the difficult stories while suggesting sharp revisions to the humorous ones. Much gratitude goes to developmental editor Diane MacEachern as well as to copyeditors Carly Catt and Virginia Magee.

Without the sharp wit of my mother and the emotional physicality of my dancing dad, I would never have learned the fine art of resilience. I thank my sisters, Sharon and Julie, for their support of what they kindly refer to as "Sue's free spirit." I also cherish the hilarious childhood tales my late brother, Mark, would reenact at every reunion.

Last but certainly not least, I am grateful to my lifelong lover and partner in passionate crime, Rodrigo Braña Segura. Despite the long days and many months he spent trapped with me during the COVID crisis, Rod's patience in dealing with my various mood swings while I reviewed old journals and revised memoir drafts to delve deeper into the more painful themes so many women endure allowed me the space to produce *The Practical Seductress*.

About the Author

Sue Camaione has spent her professional life working as an education reporter, publications' creative manager, proposal writer, and business development trainer focused on health research. Two of the chapters from *The Practical Seductress* were originally presented to Washington DC–area audiences at Storyfest Short Slam storytelling contests, in which she won second place. Sue is a member of The Writers Center in Bethesda, Maryland, where she resides. In addition to performing in area storytelling competitions, she is penning a dark comedy about domestic violence, while learning to play drums. She is also a literacy mentor to area students, hoping to foster a new generation of writers. Sue's sharp-tongued suffragette grandmother was her inspiration for writing *The Practical Seductress*. For more of Sue's writings, please visit her website at www.suecamaione.com.

SELECTED TITLES FROM SHE WRITES PRESS

She Writes Press is an independent publishing company founded to serve women writers everywhere. Visit us at www.shewritespress.com.

No Rules: A Memoir by Sharon Dukett. $16.95, 978-1-63152-856-9. At sixteen, Sharon leaves home to escape the limited life her Catholic parents have planned for her because she's a girl—and finds herself thrown into the 1970s counterculture, an adult world for which she is unprepared.

Anarchy in High Heels: A Memoir by Denise Larson. $16.95, 978-1-64742-136-6. The unabashed story of an all-female performance group unleashing their unique feminine satire in the early 1970s—a time when being a "funny feminist" was considered an oxymoron.

In Search of Pure Lust: A Memoir by Lise Weil. $16.95, 978-1-63152-385-4. Through the lens of her personal experiences as a lesbian coming of age in the '70s and '80s, Lise Weil documents an important chapter in lesbian history, her own long and difficult relationship history, and how her eventual dive into Zen practice became a turning point in her quest for love.

Times They Were A-Changing: Women Remember the '60s & '70s edited by Kate Farrell, Amber Lea Starfire, and Linda Joy Myers. $16.95, 978-1-938314-04-9. Forty-eight powerful stories and poems detailing the breakthrough moments experienced by women during the '60s and '70s.

Erotic Integrity: How to be True to Yourself Sexually by Claudia Six, PhD. $16.95, 978-1-63152-079-2. Dr. Claudia Six, a respected clinical sexologist and relationship coach, presents her unique method to uncovering your true sexual desires and attaining a more authentic and satisfying sexuality.

Fetish Girl: A Memoir of Sex, Domination, and Motherhood by Bella LaVey. $16.95, 978-1-63152-435-6. A kinky roller coaster ride through addiction, violence, motherhood, sex, and the creation of Evil Kitty, Bella LaVey's larger-than-life dominatrix persona, this singular memoir is the story of a woman attracted to extremes who is willing to go to great lengths to uncover and make peace with her true nature.